Yale Agrarian Studies Series

JAMES C. SCOTT, *Series Editor*

The Agrarian Studies Series at Yale University Press seeks to publish outstanding and original interdisciplinary work on agriculture and rural society—for any period, in any location. Works of daring that question existing paradigms and fill abstract categories with the lived experience of rural people are especially encouraged.

—James C. Scott, *Series Editor*

James C. Scott, *Seeing Like a State: How Certain Schemes to Improve the Human Condition Have Failed*

Steve Striffler, *Chicken: The Dangerous Transformation of America's Favorite Food*

James C. Scott, *The Art of Not Being Governed: An Anarchist History of Upland Southeast Asia*

Timothy Pachirat, *Every Twelve Seconds: Industrialized Slaughter and the Politics of Sight*

Edward Dallam Melillo, *Strangers on Familiar Soil: Rediscovering the Chile-California Connection*

Kathryn M. de Luna, *Collecting Food, Cultivating People: Subsistence and Society in Central Africa*

James C. Scott, *Against the Grain: A Deep History of the Earliest States*

Loka Ashwood, *For-Profit Democracy: Why the Government Is Losing the Trust of Rural America*

Jonah Steinberg, *A Garland of Bones: Child Runaways in India*

Hannah Holleman, *Dust Bowls of Empire: Imperialism, Environmental Politics, and the Injustice of "Green" Capitalism*

Johnhenry Gonzalez, *Maroon Nation: A History of Revolutionary Haiti*

Christian C. Lentz, *Contested Territory: Điện Biên Phủ and the Making of Northwest Vietnam*

Dan Allosso, *Peppermint Kings: A Rural American History*

Jamie Kreiner, *Legions of Pigs in the Early Medieval West*

Christian Lund, *Nine-Tenths of the Law: Enduring Dispossession in Indonesia*

Shaila Seshia Galvin, *Becoming Organic: Nature and Agriculture in the Indian Himalaya*

Michael Dove, *Bitter Shade: The Ecological Challenge of Human Consciousness*

Japhy Wilson, *Reality of Dreams: Post-Neoliberal Utopias in the Ecuadorian Amazon*

Aniket Aga, *Genetically Modified Democracy: Transgenic Crops in Contemporary India*

Ruth Mostern, *The Yellow River: A Natural and Unnatural History*

Brian Lander, *The King's Harvest: A Political Ecology of China from the First Farmers to the First Empire*

For a complete list of titles in the Yale Agrarian Studies Series, visit yalebooks.com/agrarian.

GENETICALLY MODIFIED DEMOCRACY

TRANSGENIC CROPS IN CONTEMPORARY INDIA

ANIKET AGA

Yale
UNIVERSITY PRESS
New Haven and London

Published with assistance from the foundation established in memory of Philip Hamilton McMillan of the Class of 1894, Yale College.

Set in Gotham and Adobe Garamond type by IDS Infotech Ltd., Chandigarh, India.
Printed in the United States of America.

Library of Congress Control Number: 2021933244
ISBN 978-0-300-24590-5 (hardcover : alk. paper)

A catalogue record for this book is available from the British Library.

This paper meets the requirements of ANSI/NISO Z39.48-1992 (Permanence of Paper).

10 9 8 7 6 5 4 3 2 1

Contents

CONTENTS

PART THREE

REMAKING AGRARIAN CAPITALISM

Abbreviations

APMC	Agricultural produce marketing committee
ASHA	Alliance for Sustainable and Holistic Agriculture
Biotechnology Department	Department of Biotechnology
BJP	Bharatiya Janata Party
Bt	*Bacillus thuringiensis*
CBA	Committee for Biosafety Assessment
CCMB	Centre for Cellular and Molecular Biology
CoS	Committee of Secretaries
CSDS	Centre for the Study of Developing Societies
CSIR	Council of Scientific and Industrial Research
DAC	Department of Agriculture and Cooperation
DGFT	Directorate General of Foreign Trade
DST	Department of Science and Technology
Environment Department	Department of Environment (1980–1985)
Environment Ministry	Ministry of Environment and Forests (Ministry of Environment, Forest and Climate Change after 2014)
EPA	Environment (Protection) Act, 1986
Food Safety Authority	Food Safety and Standards Authority of India

GEAC	Genetic Engineering Approval Committee (Genetic Engineering Appraisal Committee after February 2010)
GM	Genetically modified
GMO	Genetically modified organism
GRAIN	Genetic Resources Action International
GURTs	Gene Use Restriction Technologies
GVA	Gross value added
HT	Herbicide tolerant
IARI	Indian Agricultural Research Institute
IAS	Indian Administrative Service
ICAR	Indian Council of Agricultural Research
ICMR	Indian Council of Medical Research
IISc	Indian Institute of Science Bangalore
INR	Indian Rupee
Institutional Committee	Institutional Biosafety Committee
KRRS	Karnataka Rajya Raitha Sangha
MMBL	Monsanto Mahyco Biotechnology Limited
MRP	Maximum retail price
MRTP	Monopolies and Restrictive Trade Practices
NBTB	National Biotechnology Board
NOC	No Objection Certificate
NRCPB	National Research Centre for Plant Biotechnology
NSAI	National Seed Association of India
PIL	Public interest litigation
PL 480	Public Law 480
RCGM	Review Committee on Genetic Manipulation
rDNA	Recombinant DNA
RRF	Roundup Ready Flex

RRLH	Regional Research Laboratory Hyderabad
Rules 1989	Rules for the Manufacture, Use, Import, Export and Storage of Hazardous micro-organisms/ Genetically engineered organisms or cells, 1989
SACC	Scientific Advisory Committee to the Cabinet
UGC	University Grants Commission
UPA	United Progressive Alliance
WTO	World Trade Organization

Acknowledgments

This book has been long in the making and has accumulated many debts in the process. This is my attempt at acknowledging some of these. There are also several people who helped and guided my research, toward whom my gratitude runs deep, but who would prefer to remain unnamed.

I would like to start by thanking Jean Thomson Black at Yale University Press for her invaluable help and editorial inputs, and the series editor, James Scott, for his encouragement and support. I also thank Elizabeth Sylvia, Michael Deneen, and Margaret Otzel. Three anonymous reviewers provided insightful comments and criticisms. Ann Twombly sharpened the writing with her skilled and meticulous copy editing.

I thank the Wenner Gren Foundation for Anthropological Research (Grant number 8726), the National Science Foundation's Program in Science, Technology, and Society (Grant number 134382), the MacMillan Center for Area and International Studies at Yale, the South Asian Studies Council at Yale, and the Program in Agrarian Studies at Yale for their financial support. Portions of chapter 7 were published as "Merchants of Knowledge: Petty Retail and Differentiation without Consolidation among Farmers in Maharashtra, India" in the *Journal of Agrarian Change*.

For patiently explaining the case for recombinant DNA technology in India, I would like to thank C. Kameswara Rao, Deepak Pental,

B. Fakrudin, Arundhati Mukhopadhyay, P. H. Ramanjani Gowda, P. Ananda Kumar, and G. Padmanaban. For teaching me about the thrills and frustrations of agricultural and biotechnological research, I thank students and faculty at several universities, including the agricultural university where I conducted fieldwork, Delhi University, Jawaharlal Nehru University, the National Research Centre on Plant Biotechnology, the Indian Institute of Vegetable Research, Varanasi, and the Indian Agricultural Research Institute.

My understanding of the excitement surrounding transgenics was enhanced by interactions with entrepreneurs, managers, and scientists in India's seed companies. I am especially grateful to the management of a large seed company for allowing me to visit their R&D facilities and meet scientists and officers there over several days. Select staff at seed companies in Aurangabad and Jalna discussed their perspective on the seed business and GM crops at length, for which I am grateful.

Several institutions and people helped me piece together the history of India's state-led biotechnology program. I would like to thank senior officers and scientists at the Ministry of Environment, Forest and Climate Change for providing historical information to me, and for generously sharing their thoughts on regulatory frameworks for GM crops. Second, I would like to thank the late Pushpa M. Bhargava for allowing me to peruse his papers, for discussing the history of the Department of Biotechnology over several afternoons despite his ailing health, and for his admirable wit, passion, and zest. Third, I would like to thank serving and former scientists and officials of the Department of Biotechnology, and those with the Indian Council of Agricultural Research, for discussing the beginnings of biotechnology in India with enthusiasm. I am also grateful to the molecular biologists H. K. Das and the late Satish Maheshwari, the late policy maker Ashok Parthasarathi, and the late journalist and author Praful Bidwai for clarifying the context of science policy making in the 1980s.

A large number of libraries were critical for my research. I thank the staff of the Parliament Library, New Delhi, the Library of the Indian Agricultural Research Institute, New Delhi, and the Centre for Education and Documentation, Mumbai. I also thank Dinesh Abrol, who first referred me to the Parliament Library and gave me the requisite documents to access it. The staff of the Supreme Court lawyer Prashant Bhushan at Noida helpfully provided access to case files.

I would like to thank Madhav Gadgil, Anurag Chaurasia, officers of the Food Safety and Standards Authority of India, and scientists at the Centre for Cellular and Molecular Biology, Hyderabad, for their perspectives on regulation of GM crops. I am also grateful to the officers of the (unnamed) ministry where I did fieldwork to understand regulatory issues concerning GM crops better. For perspectives on GM crops as a matter of public policy, I am grateful to Jairam Ramesh and Basudeb Acharia.

This research would not have been what it is had several sharp commentators on GM crops in India (loosely called activists) not taught me how to evaluate critically the arguments put forth by the government and proponents of GM crops. Suman Sahai, founder of the Gene Campaign, met with me on several occasions to share her perspective on GM crops and provided access to her writings, documents from the public interest litigation (PIL) she filed before the Supreme Court, and data painstakingly collected by the Gene Campaign over the years. In terms of day-to-day access to documents in her office, Ranjan Mishra and Richa Srivastava were exceedingly helpful. Kavitha Kuruganti and Rajesh Krishnan (Coalition for a GM-Free India) were of immense help in locating government documents as well as scientific and news reports, and they patiently answered my many questions. I would also like to thank Aruna Rodrigues, Vandana Shiva, G. V. Ramanjeneyulu, Devinder Sharma, Sagari Ramdas,

Neha Saigal, Jai Krishna R., Soma Marla, Debal Deb, and Debdulal Bhattacharya for their perspectives and wisdom.

One of the most enriching, educative, and joyful phases of this research was my fieldwork with farmers, laborers, and entrepreneurs in Nashik district in western Maharashtra. I cannot thank them enough for the warmth with which they welcomed me into their lives and homes, spent hours with me, allowed me to accompany them on their trips for work and pleasure, and shared their experiences, perspectives, life stories, and, not the least, meals with me. Among many others, I would like to thank Mangal Mavshi, Nilesh, Keshav Bhau, Shivdas Appa, their parents, Nana and Akka, Shivaji Daji, Mangesh Bhau, Sudam Appa, the late Dhagu Nana and Akka, Raju Bhau, Bhausaheb, Balu, Dnyaneshwar, Nivrutti, Sandip, Ramesh, Rajaram, Keru, Somnath, Manik, Sunil, Deepak, Satish, Vasant, Bhausaheb Waghmare, Manda Mavshi, Rambhau, Aba Saheb, Ganpatrao, Dhananjay, Ravindra, Nilkanth, Jeetendra, Gopi Bhau, Tushar, Hiraman, Nana Achari, Ashok, Shriram and other residents of Palsi, Shinde, Makhmalabad, Dari, Matori, and "Khedgaon" and "Pimpalgaon" (real names of the two villages withheld). At the Krishi Vigyan Kendra in Nashik, Hemraj Rajput, Mangesh Vyavhare, Nitin Thoke, and Rajaram Patil graciously allowed me to sit through their workshops and helped me understand their extension efforts. P. D. Morankar kindly shared with me his ideas of making agriculture and our habits of consumption sustainable.

I owe an incalculable debt to Indian journalists who have steadily covered rural affairs, the environment, agricultural policies, and GM crops over the decades. Their work has been the first draft of history for countless researchers like me. In particular, I have relied on the writings of Latha Jishnu, Jyotika Sood, Priyanka Pulla, Gargi Parsai, Jaideep Hardikar, Priyanka Kakodkar, Sayantan Bera, P. Sainath, Nitin Sethi, and Harish Damodaran. It is catastrophic and sad how journalism is being decimated in India by hostile governments, indifferent proprietors and audiences, and editors unwilling to stand by the many committed reporters in India.

This research has also benefitted from conversations with Kanchi Kohli, Shalini Bhutani, Suhas Palshikar, Milind Murugkar, C. Niranjan Rao, A. R. Vasavi, Surinder Jodhka, Richa Kumar, Rajeswari Raina, P. S. Vijayshankar, Arupjyoti Saikia, Shiv Visvanathan, Jens Lerche, Milind Sohoni, N. C. Narayanan, Glenn Stone, Andrew Flachs, Esha Shah, Brian Wynne, Ajay Vir Jakhar, N. Seetharama, Felix Padel, Suryakant Waghmore, Kaveri Gill, and Ashis Nandy. The Network of Rural and Agrarian Studies remains a wonderful experiment in thinking collectively about agrarian and rural issues.

At the University of Southern California, where I began graduate studies, I would like to thank Peter Kim, Alexandra Michel, Sharon Hays, Lanita Jacobs, Norman Miller, and Nina Eliasoph. Vinay Lal generously guided me as I ventured into anthropology. At Yale University, I am immensely grateful to K. Sivaramakrishnan for training and mentoring me, and for his unfailing generosity and support over the years. I am also grateful to him for nudging me in directions whose importance I had not anticipated. James Scott, Sheila Jasanoff, Joanna Radin, Karuna Mantena, and Ian Shapiro provided invaluable help in framing this research and clarifying my arguments. Kasturi Gupta is the life of South Asian Studies at Yale, and her friendship, enthusiasm, and astuteness helped me resolve many a problem. In the Anthropology Department, Mary Smith, Frank D'Aria, Karen Phillips, Connie Buskey, and Marleen Cullen smooth the path for students to study and research without care. I would also like to thank Karen Hebert, Guntra Aistara, Mike McGovern, Doug Rogers, Helen Siu, Bill Kelley, Erik Harms, Narges Erami, Marcia Inhorn, David Watts, Inderpal Grewal, Priti Ramamurthy, Akhil Gupta, and Sudipta Kaviraj for their help at different stages of the doctoral program. The librarians at Yale and the Center for Science and Social Science Information provided valuable help and support while I was writing my dissertation. At the University of Michigan Ann Arbor, I am grateful to Omolade Adunbi, Ivette Perfecto, Mrinalini Sinha, Matthew Hull, John Vandermeer, Stuart Kirsch, Don Lopez, Will Glover, Farina Mir, Jeff Martin, Lee Schlesinger, Janelle Fosler, and Linda Turner. The libraries of the University of Michigan and conversations at the Center for South Asian Studies, the Michigan Society of Fellows, and the School for Environment and Sustainability enriched this research in multiple ways. At Ashoka University, I thank Malabika Sarkar, Upinder Singh, L. S. Shashidhara, Mahesh Rangarajan, Mukul Sharma, Amita Baviskar, Meghna Agarwala, Divya Karnad, Mitul Baruah, Ajmal Khan, Sonali Bawa, and Sweeta Sumant among many others. Students in my environmental studies and agriculture policy classes at both Ann Arbor and Ashoka kept me grounded.

I would also like to thank Yu Luo, Amy Zhang, Elizabeth Miles, Luisa Cortesi, Vikramaditya Thakur, Shaila Galvin, Radhika Govindrajan, Sarah Besky, Hosna Sheikoleslami, Adrienne Cohen, Mohsin Alam Bhat, Atreyee Majumder, Juned Shaikh, Madhavi Murty, Rohit De, Julie Stephens, Ashwini Deo, Sarover Zaidi, Manoj Gopalkrishnan, Harshada Sunthankar, and Varun Dabke. For inspiring me with real-life examples in research and action devoted to the causes of justice, sustainability, and democracy, I owe an enormous debt to A. R. Vasavi, the late Abhay Xaxa, Gladson Dungdung, Debal Deb, Debdulal Bhattacharya, Sharanya Nayak, and Chitrangada Choudhury. For their love and support over the years, I am also deeply indebted to my parents, Kaumudi and Pankaj Aga; my brother, Shamik; my grandparents Pyare Mohan and Kamal Khar; my relatives Nandini, Pradeep, Rajat, and Ragini Dasgupta; Sindhubala and Chandrahas Choudhury; Paroma and Noor; and above all, Chitrangada for help, direction, strength, wisdom, and support beyond what words can describe.

1
Introduction

Controversy dogs genetically modified (GM) crops all over the world. Are GM crops inevitable for "feeding the world"? Are they harmful to the environment and consumers? What do they mean for resource-poor farmers and farm laborers? Do they entail multinational corporations' control over local seeds and biodiversity? Do they threaten farmers' freedom to save and share seeds? There is little that unites opponents and advocates on these questions.

India leads the world as far as the intensity of *democratic* engagement with GM crops is concerned, that is, in terms of the diversity of concerns, groups involved, and the range of political, legal, and social institutions pulled into the debate—from consumers and farmers to doctors and scientists, and from political parties, state and national legislatures to regulatory bureaucracies and constitutional courts. Similar innovations in democratic politics are evident in other countries of the Global South such as Brazil, Mexico, Argentina, and Bangladesh.

Yet popular and scholarly commentaries on both the global GM debate and democratic politics in the South miss the significance thereof. The global GM debate remains firmly anchored in the West. This is the story of private companies taking the lead in developing GM crops, while the government restricts itself to assessments of health and environmental impacts. It speaks of developments elsewhere in terms of the global effect of multinational corporations like

Monsanto (acquired by Bayer in 2018) and Syngenta, and international NGOs such as Greenpeace. On the other hand, studies of Southern democracies are anchored in competing claims by different groups and movements, overlooking the question of how people construct and assess facts. By handing over scientific developments to Western corporations, and seeing the GM debate in the South only in terms of interests and movements, we do injustice to histories of technical innovation in the South and we miss the questions of deep democratic significance that GM crops pose there.

This book frames GM crops as a problem for science and democracy. How is democracy reconfigured in the course of controversies where conflicts of interest are intertwined with disputes over truth? I explore this question in the context of the ongoing controversy surrounding this policy question: Should India allow the commercial release of GM food crops? This dispute may well transform agriculture and food irreversibly in a country already witness to great agrarian distress, evidenced most starkly by the epidemic of suicides by farmers—over 300,000 suicides in the last two decades. Moreover, the debate on GM crops turns on, among other things, their impact on smallholder farmers. Given the country's very large population of smallholder farmers who may yet adopt GM food crops, the dispute in India assumes global significance and sheds light on the dynamics of technological change in populous, unequal democracies, and it offers lessons for Western polities, too. This book does not provide a definitive answer to this question, or whether GM crops are safe or unsafe, necessary or unnecessary, but it shows how such questions activate democratic contestations, rope in public and private institutions, and ultimately provide a fresh vantage point from which to explore the workings of science and politics in the context of agriculture.

This book traverses sanitized biotechnology laboratories, paper-strewn regulatory bureaucracies, bountiful farms laced with deadly pesticides, and vigorous protests on streets and online. It shows how the GM debate is decisively shaped by older histories of scientific development intersecting with political interventions. This is a story not just of farmers and private companies—but also of bureaucrats, political parties, state governments, scientists, policy makers, courts, and activists. Even farmers and private companies do not behave in ways that recall their counterparts in the West. They fight each other, but they also bristle among themselves. As these diverse constituencies encounter one another in different forums, sometimes in conflict, sometimes in collaboration, the GM controversy has modified the metaphorical genome—that is, the institutional structure and popular meanings of democracy—playing on the widespread, if somewhat misplaced, association of genome with architecture.[1] This is the ultimate argument of my book.

What Are GM Crops and Why Are They Controversial?

Agricultural biotechnology is a field of research and knowledge that goes beyond GM crops. It includes tissue culture techniques, bioinformatics, genome mapping, marker-assisted selection, and recombinant DNA (rDNA) technology. GM crops are those whose genomes have been modified by the insertion of usually foreign (for example, bacterial) genes through the rDNA technology. Such modification serves to incorporate traits into plants that are either absent or rare in their domesticated and wild varieties. For instance, Bt cotton is cotton modified with a set of genes (or a gene construct) that codes for the Bt toxin,[2] which acts as an insecticide against pink and American bollworms. This specific insecticidal trait is absent in wild and domesticated varieties of cotton. To take another instance, some scientists in India are working on a GM rice that can grow in salty water. This trait is found in a few rice varieties that used to be cultivated in the Sunderbans delta in eastern India (Deb 2017).

The starry-eyed assessments of rDNA technology contend that it will eventually render plant breeding obsolete, on account of its apparently greater speed and efficiency and the ability to move genes around across the barrier of species. Plant breeding is the older field of agricultural science involving the development of new crop varieties through targeted reproduction, hybridization techniques, and careful observation of inheritance of traits—in brief, Mendelian genetics. Take, for example, a wheat variety, A, that is otherwise suited to an ecology but grows too tall on the application of synthetic fertilizers, while another variety, B, responds well to synthetic fertilizers but is otherwise unsuited to the ecology. A plant breeder interested in growing more wheat with the application of fertilizers will cross A with B in a systematic fashion and then do further crossings until she has a new variety, C, which has all or most of the desirable traits of A, and which can withstand fertilizer doses like B. The Green Revolution was the achievement of conventional plant breeding.

Has plant breeding become obsolete with the coming of the rDNA technology? The answer is an emphatic no, as I discuss in chapter 2. For one, neither all crops nor all traits lend themselves to genetic modification—for instance, only a few varieties of cotton can be genetically modified, and these crops have to then be backcrossed into commercial cotton varieties to get market-viable GM cottonseeds. For another, to get a GM crop suitable for an agro-ecology, the GM trait has to be placed in a suitable variety or hybrid, which involves conventional breeding. As Simmonds (1983, 68) noted, the following steps are required to get a viable GM crop variety or hybrid:

> (a) the desired "foreign" gene must be identified and the DNA isolated; (b) the DNA must be multiplied in a suitable (probably bacterial) medium, a process called "cloning" . . . ; (c) the "cloned" DNA must be transmitted to recipient crop

> cells by a suitable "vector" which might be a plasmid, a virus, a liposome, a bacterial cell, or a micro-syringe; (d) the DNA must be incorporated into the recipient DNA . . . ; (e) the altered cells must be made to regenerate whole plants which must then; (f) be shown to express the new gene and transmit it sexually; (g) have the genetic potential to be "worked up" by conventional plant breeding methods to be in an agriculturally useful form.

This is itself an elaborate and intricate process with many variables and uncertainties, and whose final step involves conventional plant breeding.

Some scholars (such as Herring 2008), proponents (such as Federoff 2003), and developers of GM crops draw a straight line from domestication of crops and plant breeding to the rDNA technology. According to this view, plant reproduction is as much genetic modification as that accomplished through the rDNA technology, and therefore the term *GM* itself is a political construction. When people worry about the rDNA-triggered genomic alterations leading to plants expressing novel, potentially toxic, or allergenic proteins, or the altered genes spreading through the environment and "contaminating" biodiversity through pollination or gene flow, proponents argue that even conventional plant breeding involves genomic changes.[3] As a plant taxonomist, an advocate of GM crops, asked me in June 2011, "What is this GM label? Are you not a genetically modified version of your parents?"

I disagree. While the extent and mechanisms of regulation of GM crops in different countries are indeed tinged by politics, as they should be,[4] this does not mean that crops modified through rDNA technology can be lumped with crops bred through hybridization techniques. Plant breeding and rDNA technology involve vastly

GM from separate factor had plant breeding

different skills and techniques and belong to different streams of agricultural research, as subsequent chapters show (see also Kloppenburg 2004). Moreover, the uncertainties and unknowns of plant breeding are of a different nature than those of rDNA techniques (Bowring 2003, chap. 1). For instance, as the geneticist and critic of India's GM program, Dr. Suman Sahai told me, GM crops, unlike conventional crops, typically come with a viral promoter that ensures that the novel protein (say the Bt toxin) is expressed continuously. Whether this is benign or risky is less relevant than the fact that this is unlike conventionally bred crops, and consequently the risks are different. Thus, like Stone (2010), I use the term *GM crops* to designate crops produced, in part, through rDNA techniques. I also use the term *transgenics* interchangeably with *GM crops*. Even though the latter is a broader term, GM crops released and close to commercialization in India are all transgenics.

What is really at stake in lumping GM and conventionally bred crops together is the extent and nature of regulatory oversight of the research, development, and commercialization of the former. If the differences between rDNA technology and conventional plant breeding are minor, then GM crops should reach the market with as little scrutiny as conventionally bred crops—this is roughly the logic of substantial equivalence advocated by the U.S. government. The issue of regulatory oversight leads to larger questions of environmental sustainability, effects on health and environment, and whether GM crops will help in alleviating the global agrarian crisis or will further intensify it. Here it helps to take stock of which GM crops and traits are commercially grown around the world. The International Service for the Acquisition of Agri-biotech Applications (ISAAA),[5] the advocacy group for agricultural biotechnology including GM crops, estimates that in 2017 the cultivated area under GM crops was about 469 million acres across twenty-four countries. Of this, 53 percent of the land was spread over nineteen "developing" countries, while the rest was in five "industrialized" countries (ISAAA 2017).

The more revealing statistics, however, are those about crops and traits. Of the total acreage, 99% percent is under commodity crops: GM soy (50 percent), maize (31 percent), cotton (13 percent), and canola (5 percent). Maize and soy are at the heart of the global meat and processed-food industries. None of these are food crops that South Asians, whose food security needs are often presented as an argument in favor of GM crops, consume—barring crude and refined edible oil crushed from cottonseeds and soy. Two traits dominate commercialized GM crops—herbicide tolerance, or HT (47 percent of the acreage), and insect resistance, or Bt (12 percent). Another 41 percent is under stacked traits—that is, both HT and Bt. So 88 percent of the area is under HT and HT-Bt crops. Herbicide-tolerant crops obviate manual weeding—one can simply spray the corresponding herbicide (in the main, glyphosate, glufosinate, and dicamba) on the entire field, and everything other than the HT crop will perish. In theory, the Bt crop reduces the applications of external insecticides. Thus, most of the GM crops commercialized globally, in particular HT and stacked crops, are tailored for the routines of unsustainable, capital-intensive agriculture—that is, agriculture that relies on monoculture (rather than mixed and intercropping), purchased seeds, fossil fuels, and intensive applications of synthetic chemicals (Weis 2007). There are also some GM traits that enhance nutrition profile, of which Golden Rice, modified with the gene for beta-carotene, the precursor of vitamin A, has received considerable media attention. In 2016 over 150 Nobel laureates published a letter calling for the commercial release of Golden Rice and accusing Greenpeace of "crimes against humanity" for its activism against GM crops (Laureates Letter 2016). This was a breathtakingly ignorant and arrogant position to take, for serious doubts persist about Golden Rice (Aga

2016; Stone and Glover 2017). In any case, as nutritionists argue, dietary patterns that follow nutritional recommendations better correlate with health outcomes than eating or avoiding any particular food item (Nestle 2002, 355–56).

India formally released its first GM crop, Bt cotton, in 2002, developed by the Indian company Mahyco, in partnership with Monsanto. More accurately, India formally released Mahyco's cotton hybrids with the Bt gene from Monsanto crossed into them. This was partly a belated acknowledgment of other unauthorized Bt cotton hybrids already under cultivation and popular in western India for a few years (see Herring 2007a; E. Shah 2005). Monsanto also has held a 26 percent stake in Mahyco since 1998. After Bt cotton, Mahyco proposed to introduce Bt eggplant, or Bt brinjal, as it is called in India, marketed as resistant to the pest eggplant fruit and shoot borer. This got embroiled in controversy, as I discuss later, and was put under an indefinite moratorium by the federal Ministry of Environment and Forests in 2010. Developers of Bt eggplant had planned to release the seeds in the Philippines and Bangladesh after approval in India, as part of a partnership among Mahyco, Monsanto, Cornell University, the United States Agency for International Development, and public-sector institutes in India, the Philippines, and Bangladesh.[6] The moratorium in India consequently led to a slowdown of commercial releases of GM eggplant in the wider South Asian and Southeast Asian regions. In 2013, however, Bangladesh released Mahyco's Bt eggplant,[7] and 2015 saw Vietnam allowing the cultivation of GM maize, which raised hopes in the industry for a similar release in India, especially after another Bt eggplant, of unknown provenance, was recently discovered in Haryana, in northern India (Sushma 2019). There is also a public-sector GM mustard hybrid, featuring the HT trait, which is ready for release in India, though the government is yet to make a final call in the face of opposition from environmentalists, certain farm lobbies, and a few right-wing groups. Most of the development efforts under way in India rely on the HT and Bt traits.

Finally, why companies or state laboratories attempt genetic modification vis-à-vis other approaches to agricultural innovation has to do with their financial interests and political objectives, rather than with there being "no alternative" to GM crops, as biotechnologists sometimes claim. It's worth mentioning at this stage that agro-ecologists compellingly argue that neither food security nor agricultural sustainability depends on the development of GM crops, and, in fact, certain widespread GM crops erode sustainability (Altieri 1998).

The Agrarian Crisis and Food Security

It is impossible to grasp the hopes, fears, and concerns surrounding GM crops without contextualizing them in the deep crisis of agriculture plaguing India and, indeed, the entire world. India is a country of subsistence, marginal, and small farmers. According to the Agriculture Census 2015–16, there are 146.45 million farms in the country.[8] Sixty-eight percent of landholdings, classified as marginal, are smaller than 2.5 acres (1 hectare), while 18 percent of holdings are small (2.5–5 acres, or 1–2 hectares). Together they constitute nearly 47 percent of the total farm area. About 50 percent of the population depends on farming for its livelihood. The contribution of agriculture to the gross domestic product (GDP), however, is declining at a faster pace than the population depending on it (Reddy and Galab 2006). In 2014–15 the share of crop farming to India's gross value added (GVA) was 11.2 percent, and the GVA of agriculture and allied sectors declined by 0.2 percent (Ministry of Finance 2020, chap. 7).[9] At the same time, at least 52 percent of agricultural households are indebted, and for marginal farmers, agriculture is a losing proposition—they make less than they spend, on average, even taking off-farm income into account (NSSO 2014, 22).

These dismal statistics point to a deep agrarian crisis. The crisis was set in motion in the 1960s, when the Government of India initiated the Green Revolution program. Triggered by fears of food scarcity and the humiliation of importing shipments of wheat from the United States, this was a state-funded package for farmers comprising "high-yielding" wheat and rice varieties (that is, varieties that yielded more under conditions of fertilizer use and abundant water), subsidized chemical inputs, and guaranteed purchase prices. It was implemented in a few irrigated pockets of India, and its benefits accrued disproportionately to already well-off, landed farmers. The rice and wheat cultivars, and the requisite package of cultivation practices, were developed through transnational collaborative efforts supported by the Rockefeller and Ford foundations. While the Green Revolution did boost rice and wheat production in pockets, it also intensified synthetic chemical and water use in farming (Choudhury 2017), loss of biodiversity (Deb 2009), and inequality among classes of farmers, between landowners and landless laborers, and between regions (Frankel 1971; Shiva 1991; Subramanian 2015). Further, it led to a slowdown in public investment in infrastructure for broader agricultural development (Chand 2009). In brief, the Green Revolution addressed the problem of aggregate production of a few cereals at the expense, paradoxically, of ensuring access to food, land, and livelihood for all (see Kumar 2019).

In the past three decades, the opening up of India's markets to the world economy has been accompanied by further neglect of investment in agriculture and rural areas, erosion of subsidies and avenues for cheap credit, and a widening rural-urban disparity, which marginalizes issues afflicting farmers in the public policy agenda (Vaidyanathan 2006; Reddy and Mishra 2009; Vasavi 2012).[10] The crisis is particularly acute in the states of Andhra Pradesh, Karnataka, Kerala, Maharashtra, and Punjab. It is manifesting itself in the lives of farmers through the debilitating combination of lower yields, increasing cost of cultivation (as power and other inputs have become more expensive and effectively available only through the private sector—see chapter 7), and rising debts. So acute is the distress that an alarmingly large number of farmers are resorting to suicide.[11] Between 1995 and 2016, over 300,000 farmers have committed suicide, and lately the government has shown great zeal in massaging the data, refusing and delaying the release of figures (SenGupta 2019). In recent years, children, both boys and girls, of farming households have begun taking their lives because of stress or to ease the burden of marriage on their parents (Hardikar 2016). As the first report of the National Commission on Farmers (2004, 1), somberly titled *Serving Farmers and Saving Farming*, notes:

> The acute agricultural distress now witnessed in the country, occasionally taking the form of suicides by farmers, is the symptom of a deep seated malady arising from inadequate public investment and insufficient public action in recent years. The precise causes of the agrarian crisis are many and varied, but there are five basic factors which are central to the present crises. These are: unfinished agenda in land reform, quantity and quality of water, technology fatigue, access, adequacy and timeliness of institutional credit, and opportunities for assured and remunerative marketing. . . . The worst affected are small and marginal farmers, tenants, share croppers, landless agricultural labour and [indigenous] farmers, since their coping capacity is very limited. Women suffer more since they have little access to institutional credit or organised extension support.
>
> The ecological foundations of sustainable agriculture such as land, water, biodiversity, forests and the atmosphere

> are under varying degrees of anthropogenic pressures. Water tables are going down and land degradation and soil salinisation are on the rise. . . . Farmers' indebtedness is growing even in a State like the Punjab, which is the heartland of the green revolution.

Beyond the complex combination of factors, there are deeper changes sweeping through Indian society that are intensifying distress. The village as a social-cultural, hierarchical unit has collapsed (Jodhka 2012), individuation is on the rise, and, consequently, the boundaries of the farmer-self are narrowing (Mohanty 2005; Jodhka 2006). This translates to intensely personal experiences of risk exposure (Vasavi 2012)—one season of crop failure can mean the inability to provide for familial obligations like marriage, and humiliation within one's group and from dominant castes and patrons. Ultimately, what seems lost is the very possibility of imagining an alternative, dignified future in agriculture (Vasavi 2020a). Against this backdrop, the stakes in the GM debate have only heightened and taken on a moral force.[12] Advocates accuse critics of rabble-rousing while more and more farmers succumb to distress. They contend that biotechnology-backed technological advancement can usher in a second Green or Evergreen or Gene Revolution (Swaminathan 2010), to ramp up food production for a growing world population while addressing problems of water scarcity, pest management, and so on. This revolution will be evergreen in the sense that "smart" biotechnological interventions and advances in data mining and automation will alleviate the chemical intensity of agriculture along with the associated problems of pollution, soil salinity, and exposure to toxic agrochemicals. In framing GM crops and agricultural biotechnology in these terms, advocates try to draw on the positive sentiments of abundance and the end of hunger and scarcity that are popularly associated with the Green Revolution (see Scoones 2006).

Critics, on the other hand, accuse advocates of ignoring structural inequalities in terms of access to land, water, credit, and marketing infrastructure. This was more or less the charge against advocates of the Green Revolution, too. Further, critics contend that advocating for GM crops without addressing these inequalities amounts to pushing farmers further along the treadmill of capital intensity, debt, and crisis (Altieri and Rosset 1999), and that agro-ecological interventions offer a surer path to environmental sustainability and agrarian justice. They also sharply highlight how the second Green Revolution has powerful agribusinesses at the forefront (Thompson 2012; Bajpai 2015), unlike the first, which, for all its flaws, had states leading the charge and was thus to some extent subject to public oversight (see Patel 2013).

Advocates and critics frequently spar over consumers' interests, too. India has seen crippling inflation in food prices for many of the last ten years. A number of agricultural scientists and policy makers at the federal Department of Biotechnology hold that India needs GM crops to secure an adequate supply of food for a rapidly growing consumer base. This argument had particular force when the debate over Bt eggplant was at its peak, around 2010. On average, food products saw an inflation rate of 12.46 percent between March 2008 and November 2011 (Nair and Eapen 2012, 46).[13] Fruits and vegetables recorded an average inflation rate of 9.79 percent in the period from March 2008 to July 2010, while pulses saw an average rate of 15.24 percent. Proponents of GM crops point to this worrisome trend to make the case for the entry of transgenics in India. Different companies and public laboratories are working on transgenics in vegetables, fruits, pulses, and rice. As Dr. Usha Barwale Zehr, the chief technology officer of Mahyco, told me when I met her in August 2011: "Where is pigeon pea going to come from in the future? India imports more than 50 percent of its domestic demand. If we don't provide for our food, who will?"

Recent developments, however, have weakened this argument. In light of a range of factors from government interventions to a global recession in commodity prices, the problem has shifted to overproduction and surpluses in major crops such as wheat, pulses, and sugar (Damodaran 2018). In any case, opponents highlight that neither of the two principal GM traits directly improves yields. Nevertheless, there are other dimensions to food security, such as adaptation to climate change and tolerance to drought and other stresses, where the debate remains alive. It also remains far ahead of the actual development of well-performing GM crops with relevant traits.

The Global Struggle over GM Crops

The debate over GM crops has been vigorous and controversial for at least two decades, across countries and continents. To a large extent, the fierce debates turn on their risk-benefit analysis. This is typically framed through considerations of their agronomic performance vis-à-vis conventionally bred crops, their effect on the livelihood, income, and debt of farmers, especially small and marginal farmers in the Global South, and their capacity to freely save and exchange seeds (Herring 2007b; Paarlberg 2008; Qaim 2009). Other contentious issues include the impact of GM crops for biodiversity, ecology, and consumers' health and choice; the role of GM crops in food security—that is, the ability of societies to meet their food requirements domestically, at least for a few key staple crops; and what GM crops portend for food sovereignty, specifically, the capacity of communities to shape the way culturally appropriate and healthy food is produced, distributed, and consumed. In brief, a spectrum of concerns—from those related to ecology, sustainability, and health to those about agrarian distress and the subordinate position of both farmers and consumers vis-à-vis agribusinesses—surround GM crops.

Some of the most sustained scholarly reflections on GM crops have occurred in the arena of political economy (Stone 2010). There is a broad agreement that GM crops have to be considered in the history of commodification in and corporate control over agriculture (Lewontin 1998) and the ongoing agrarian transformation in different parts of the world. The retooling of nitrate production facilities in the West, serving wartime demand for munitions, to manufacture urea after World War II; the production of synthetic pesticides derived from fossil fuels; the breeding of new crop varieties to suit the needs of mechanization and chemical applications; and the turn to hybrid seeds, which forced farmers to purchase fresh seeds every season: all are critical milestones of this process (Kloppenburg 2004). In the West, where contracts with farmers and patents are more easily enforced than elsewhere, GM crops prevent legally what hybrid seeds preempt through Mendelian genetics—the reuse and free exchange of seeds by farmers. Also decisive have been more recent developments in the United States such as the extension of patents to life forms in 1980 (Kevles 1994) and the passage of the Bayh-Dole Act in the same year. This reconfigured the relationship between publicly funded research and private applications (Kenney 1986; Robbins-Roth 2000), allowing private industry to dominate the space of agricultural innovation in inputs, including seeds.

This has occurred in tandem with transformations in the discipline of biology owing to the molecular turn in biochemistry (Cohen 1984; Morange 1998) in the United States and Europe. The rich literature on the history of twentieth-century biology in the West has mapped the contingent factors that remade it into a field amenable to capture by informational sciences with a view toward intellectual property and profits (Heller 2001; Sunder Rajan 2006). The outcomes of these contingencies, in particular the extension of property regimes over genes, seeds, and plant varieties,[14] as well as the dominance of transnational agribusiness corporations and their expanding reach over ever-larger parts of the world through international trade regimes such as the WTO, constitute the background of most scholarly and activist accounts of the struggle over GM crops in different parts of the world (Otero 2008; Schurman and Munro 2010; Fitting 2011; Pechlaner 2012). Indeed, transnational corporations have played a preeminent role in framing GM crops as a pro-poor and an environmentally sustainable technology (Glover 2010), implicitly making some questionable presumptions about poverty and those afflicted by it (Jansen and Gupta 2009). Advocates have adopted more or less the same frame to push GM crops in various agro-ecologically and sociologically dissimilar parts of the world (for example, Koundal and Lawrence 2000; Paarlberg 2008). A famous study published in the prestigious journal *Proceedings of the National Academy of Sciences* is so blind to these dissimilarities that it claims Bt cotton a success in India for "smallholder" farmers on the basis of a sample of households owning over 10 acres (4 hectares) of land (Kathage and Qaim 2012)—that is, the top 6 percent or so of landowning farmer households.

Advocates do not deny the need for regulation; they insist only that the regulation be based on "sound science" (for example, Heap 2013). The idea that scientists and experts can settle all political disputes through their recourse to value-free facts is a critical political maneuver by advocates of GM crops (Kinchy, Kleinman and Autry 2008; Newell 2009).

The scholarship on opposition and challenges to GM crops contrasts the emphasis on "sound science" with people's understandings of risk that encompass issues of livelihood and cultural and ecological degradation and inequality (Jasanoff 2005; Purkayastha and Rath 2010; Macnaghten and Carro-Ripalda 2015).[15] For instance, Kinchy (2012) demonstrates the political and economic stakes associated with the movement of GM traits to unintended crops and geographies and the challenges this fomented in Mexico (see also Fitting 2011) and Canada. Similarly, the opposition to GM crops in Costa Rica and France is linked to the defense of place-based sovereignty (Pearson 2012; Heller 2013). Similar issues are at play in the Global South, where there is a greater emphasis on livelihood concerns for subsistence and smallholder farmers (Sahai 1997; Kuruganti 2006; Otero 2008; Pelaez and da Silva 2008; Scoones 2008; see also Lapegna 2016).

Thus, the literature on the struggles over GM crops predominantly frames them as a contest between transnational corporations, wedded to narrow regulatory science on the one hand, and transnational networks of place-based activists and (smallholder) farmers on the other. In this way, the struggle over GM crops is global, in the sense that transnational agribusinesses and networks of activists are clashing over them in different parts of the world.

The Absence of Domestic and Regional Institutions

This may seem unremarkable until one notices the absence of regional institutions, national states, and regional histories of science and politics in accounts of the GM debate outside the United States and Europe. Even as many accounts conclude that opponents and challengers of GM crops are breaking down boundaries between experts and lay publics (Heller 2002), or between facts and values (Levidow 2001), neither do we have a sense about the sites where these contests are taking place, nor do we grasp the historical constitution of these struggles. The GM debates, especially in the Global South, seem to be occurring in the air, without a historical or institutional anchor.

To be sure, specific offices and agencies making decisions about GM crops, such as the Department of Biotechnology in India and the Interministerial Commission for Biosafety and Genetically Modified

Organisms in Mexico, find a place in writings about those countries (for example, Scoones 2006; Newell 2008; Fitting 2011; Kinchy 2012). But how did these institutions arise, and how were their mandates fixed? The neglect of these questions is striking considering that the very definition of biotechnology and its relationship with other areas of science and policy in any given country owes more to such national institutions, and the regional histories of science they embody, than to global agribusinesses or activism. Further, demands that different groups place before political institutions have a great deal to do with what those institutions can do and have done in the past. Such demands, the idioms in which they are couched, and the symbols they mobilize are not isolated from the successes and failures of other such groups in earlier times and at other places.

The lack of a focus on regional histories of politics and science in which regulatory institutions are embedded is symptomatic of a translation of historical contingencies of the Global North to the Global South. The implicit assumption is that contingencies of history of biotechnology in the West have become fundamental structures influencing GM debates even outside the West, rendering regional histories of science, politics, and agribusiness capital outside the West relatively unimportant, if not irrelevant.[16] At times, this translation is implicit; that is, scholars argue that developments in the North dominate and structure those in the South, and therefore it is the location of a specific country vis-à-vis the North that is analytically significant. For instance, Kinchy (2012, 21) notes: "National policies themselves are influenced by international trade relations, treaties, and laws. Far from being isolated instances, bounded by national borders, the politics of genes out of place in each situation are markedly influenced by the policies and regulations of dominant global actors. The character of the debate in each case is significantly affected by the location of each group of agricultural producers in relation to global food commodity chains. Understanding these global systems is essential to making sense of the extremely heated and contentious responses to genetic engineering that have emerged around the world."

This view also finds support among a section of anti-GM activists. Vandana Shiva—who finds mention in a large number of commentaries on GM debates globally—often draws a straight line from the Monsanto headquarters in St. Louis, Missouri, to farmers in India, while treating mediating institutions, such as the Indian state and domestic seed companies, as corrupted by and beholden to transnational corporations (Shiva 2013). Other scholars frame opposition to GM crops in the Global South in terms of "diffusion." For example, according to Herring (2010), it was the European Union's construction of GMOs, rendered global through the Cartagena Protocol on Biosafety, that was picked up through transnational advocacy networks by anti-GM activists in different countries. Similarly, Buttel (2003) suggests that the resistance to GMOs originated in northern and northwestern Europe, from where it extended elsewhere.

Certainly, these accounts are valuable for highlighting how campaigns on GM crops get constituted through the transnational circulation of ideas, frames, and people. In another sense, however, they deepen the mystery. Transnational agribusinesses are undoubtedly powerful actors; they nevertheless need channels of access and allies in different societies to influence domestic policy making. Similarly, even if local and domestic activists are supported by international NGOs, they still have to rely on culturally meaningful frames and tropes, and these tropes, once deployed, observe a logic of their own. In fact, in a very different context, Sudipta Kaviraj (1988, 2431) had noted that the state is best seen as a terrain and an actor, rather than a mere expression of class (or power) relations (see also Shapiro 2003). This suggests that campaigns can hardly target only transnational actors like the WTO or Monsanto. Rather, in any society, transnational corporations, international NGOs, domestic activists, and institutions contend with one another with different, unequal resources and capacities, and in these contests, state institutions are as much actors as they are acted on. Thus, neglecting the role of domestic institutions in channeling the GM debate makes little theoretical or empirical sense. Theoretically, ignoring regional specificities allows scholars to construct an abstract unity to "global struggles" over GM crops, essentially folding the diversity of experiences with GM crops into narratives of small farmers globally battling transnational agribusinesses (for example, Patel 2007; Fitting 2011; Heller 2013), or of elite activists allied with international NGOs like Greenpeace keeping GM crops from farmers who might benefit from them (Herring 2010; Paarlberg 2008).

This abstract unity begins to unravel the moment we attend to the specificities and particularities of the GM debates in any part of the world. Sheila Jasanoff (2005) has demonstrated the institutional histories and epistemology underlying the different trajectories of the GM debate in the United States, the United Kingdom, and the European Union, and there is no reason to think that a story outside the West can be written without similar, careful attention to regulatory and policy-making institutions in the regions concerned. Empirically, too, the abstract unity collapses under scrutiny. India has had a relatively small but significant domestic seed industry since the 1960s. Unlike that in the United States, it grew in collaboration with, and not in opposition to, public breeding efforts. Its relationship with the state and with farmers bears the impress of this history of collaboration, and it is this, rather than Monsanto directly, that has introduced GM cottonseeds to Indian farmers. It is quite untenable that this sector has become subservient to Monsanto and thus can be written off in any discussion of GM crops in India—indeed, chapter 6 shows that the stakes for domestic seed companies are quite different from those of transnational agribusinesses. To provide another example, Vandana Shiva mounted the first legal challenge in India to GM crops by filing a public interest litigation (akin to a class-action suit) in the Supreme Court as early as 1999. Since this was before India signed the Cartagena Protocol (in 2001), and four years before the protocol came into force (in 2003), it makes no sense to credit European developments for Shiva's legal maneuvers in India. Politics over GM crops anywhere needs to be contextualized in regional histories of state formation, popular politics, and histories of (agricultural) science and agrarian capitalism. Otherwise, the challenge they pose to our conceptions of science and democracy are lost to sight, along with the innovations that activists, bureaucrats, courts, and political parties attempt, as they reckon with domestic imperatives and transnational forces. This is the mantle for my book.

The GM debate has triggered intense ferment and galvanized wide-ranging concerns in India. It has generated friction among sciences, raised the question of which sciences can speak for agriculture, and, most important, demolished the notion that science is a priori in the public interest. It has cleaved familiar constituencies, such as farmers, scientists, and seed companies, and mobilized new ones. In tracking these dynamics, this book reassembles "science," "state," and "agrarian capitalism" and shows how they come together in new ways across spaces where science in action meets democracy at work, and how they push the GM dispute into globally uncharted terrain.

Science

Advocates hold that GM crops herald the onset of the second Green Revolution in agriculture to renew the "miracle" of bumper harvests of the 1960s Green Revolution for a future world of 10 billion humans. In contrast, I argue that the seeds of agricultural biotechnology were sown in India alongside, and not after, the Green Revolution. Through research in multiple public and private archives, I have uncovered a previously untold account of the establishment of biotechnology as a state-funded science in India in the 1960s and 1970s, and I explore its tensions with older fields of agricultural sciences. This story is vastly different from the Western history of biotechnology. But, more important, it highlights conflicts among different fields of plant sciences, which resonate still today. Agricultural biotechnology in much of the world is not an updated, sophisticated version of the agricultural sciences of the Green Revolution (see Kloppenburg 2004). Rather, it is quite a different field of science, and the struggle surrounding GM crops partly concerns the issue of which body of science can serve farmers' welfare and agricultural development. Many commentators believe that the science of GM crops is relatively settled, and that controversy surrounds only the legal and pricing arrangements through which they are introduced in different societies (Schurman and Munro 2010). I argue that in India, as elsewhere, scientists themselves are deeply divided on the GM issue. For instance, influential ecologists have critiqued GM crops on the grounds of environmental impacts, whereas a group of medical doctors calling itself Doctors for Food & Bio-Safety has vigorously attacked Bt eggplant on the grounds of food safety (see chapter 5).

Such protests throw open the question of which fields of science can legitimately speak for GM crops and their effects, a question that is profoundly difficult to settle through mass politics.

They highlight a problem that has received less attention from scholars of science and technology studies (see Jasanoff 2012), namely: How does science contend with vastly different cultural-historical practices of knowing, such as those of law, bureaucratic regulation, popular politics, and livelihood engagement in farms, forests, and so on? Activists and sociologists of science in former colonial countries like India had first drawn attention to this question (Shiva 1991; Nandy 1988; Alvares 1992). Concerned about the role science has often played in marginalizing knowledge systems of groups like farmers and indigenous communities, however, they tend to oppose science with "indigenous knowledge" at a high plane of abstraction, downplaying the fact that these dichotomies can break down in practice (for example, Gupta 1998; Sekhsaria 2019),[17] and that at any rate it cannot be presumed that indigenous knowledge is unsullied by domination and violence (Nanda 2004). Instead of counterposing technical claims about GM crops with the broader knowledge of farmers and activists, I examine how different ways of constructing truth claims collide with one another in different sites such as the Supreme Court, the Parliament, regulatory bureaucracies of the Government of India, and new sites like social media platforms. This broadens the theater of politics of knowledge.

The State

In 1986 India became the first country in the world to establish a federal Department of Biotechnology. Reporting directly to the prime minister, the department had the express mandate of promoting biotechnological products, including GM crops. The Indian case thus directly contradicts the notion of the neoliberal state restricting itself to safety assessments. More important, the department's efforts to promote agricultural biotechnology brought it into conflict with other arms of the government. Few know that in the early 1990s, before Monsanto could release GM cotton in the United States, the company tried to partner with the Indian government to release the transgenic crop through public institutions. The Biotechnology Department strongly backed the proposal and negotiated favorable terms with the company. Nevertheless, the proposal failed in the face of unyielding opposition—not from activists, but from senior scientists in the federal Ministry of Agriculture, incredible though it may sound today (see chapter 3). The state as a disaggregated, internally divided structure is especially important to understand the twists and turns of the GM debate, especially in the South.

With the aim of studying democracy in the open-ended terms of how it actually works (Paley 2002), anthropological studies have uncovered the diverse meanings associated with democracy (Banerjee 2007) and observed the limited capacity of democratic processes to resist co-option by dominant interests in society (for example, Albert 2016). Studies of Indian democracy show that it functions through politics of patronage and redistribution along entrenched divisions of caste and religion (Kothari 1970; Michelutti 2008; Witsoe 2013). Compelling as these accounts are, they take for granted what must be empirically explored—the process through which interests are discovered, organized, and articulated. Controversies regarding technical innovations bring this process to the fore because they trade in uncertainty (Jasanoff 2004; Callon, Lascoumes, and Barthe 2011). The uncertainty stems both from democratic structures—turnover in governments and fragmentation of power—and from disputes over science. This does not mean that organized interests of class or caste become irrelevant, only that how they get activated—at times along and at other times crossing sociological divisions—has to be empirically explored.

Thus, this book considers the different ways proponents and opponents of GM food crops pivot around the state. It underscores that the state is marked by ceaseless friction among federal government departments (Gupta 2012), and between states and the federal government. Poor coordination in the bureaucracy (Hull 2012; Mathur 2015) and a somewhat independent judiciary add to the flux.[18] For instance, since the late 1980s, even before private companies and activists arrived on the scene, the Biotechnology Department clashed with the Ministry of Agriculture and the federal Ministry of Environment and Forests over the priorities of agricultural biotechnology. The logic of checks and balances forced the government to hammer out a compromise administrative structure to regulate biotechnology. This did not resolve the underlying issue as much as postpone conflict.

The nub of the matter is that democratic regimes generally offer multiple axes of power and rifts. These, along with electoral politics, bureaucratic delays and wrangling, the federal structure of government, and judicial oversight, open up opportunities for different constituencies to intervene in controversies. For this reason, the esoteric intricacies of biotechnology have posed less of a barrier to participation in the GM debate than is commonly thought. Activists in recent years have successfully mobilized right-wing Hindu groups, some state governments, and the Parliament against GM food crops, making their release by the federal government more difficult. Such moves have altered the working of the government and invited a rethinking of its limits. To show these processes at work, this book engages in an ethnography of the state from federal bureaucracies in New Delhi to the field agents who work most closely with farmers.

Agrarian Capitalism

Finally, this book locates the GM debate in far-reaching transformations of agriculture and agrarian capitalism that have occurred since the Green Revolution. Whereas anti-GM voices raise the specter of "foreign takeover" of "our agriculture," advocates point to the near-universal adoption of GM cotton as undeniable proof of the technology's success. The adoption story of Bt cotton hides more than it reveals, as far as the working of agrarian capitalism is concerned. For one, it masks the fact that it was the agriculture ministry that steadfastly opposed a public-sector Bt cotton, in partnership with Monsanto, in the early 1990s. For another, Mahyco received government approval to commercialize Bt cotton in 2002, only after it came to light that Navbharat, a Gujarat-based company, illegally commercialized smuggled "stealth" Bt cottonseeds in western India (Shah 2005; Herring 2007a). The illegal release was to the chagrin of both the Ministry of Environment and Forests and the Mahyco-Monsanto partnership, and it sparked multiple interministerial and federal-state government disputes, in addition to constitutional challenges before the Supreme Court.

There is no denying that farmers are already beholden to the seeds and chemicals supplied by domestic and multinational agribusinesses. The increasing consumption of chemical inputs, however, has also allowed a small section of young, rural men to foray into retailing for agribusinesses in their bid to escape spiraling agrarian distress. As this book demonstrates, such retailers exercise considerable influence over what farmers purchase. This makes it quite challenging to isolate farmers' choices from retailers' incentives to sell certain products and corporate marketing efforts to promote new technologies (see Aga 2019; Choudhury and Aga 2019).

This book also highlights the role of home-grown Indian seed companies, usually ignored in accounts of the GM debate. Studying the founding figures of Indian seed companies reveals that the latter grew in alliance with the state and in response to the lack of adequate state capacity to service the agenda of agricultural development after independence. This orients them in particular ways toward the state, farmers, and newer entrants like transnational companies. In recent years, deploying nativist (*swadeshi*) appeals, Indian companies have successfully lobbied the government against multinational firms in order to corner a greater share of profits from GM cottonseed sales. In April 2018, on a complaint by Nuziveedu, one of India's largest seed companies, the Delhi High Court invalidated Monsanto's patent over GM cotton. This decision was set aside by the Supreme Court in January 2019 and sent back to a lower court for consideration. Though the April 2018 ruling has a loose parallel in Brazil (Peschard 2019),[19] such overturning and challenging of intellectual property rights is without precedent in the West. As much as activists love to hate Monsanto, it is not the only company in town. And its grip on the Indian government is less firm than critics acknowledge.

Genetically Modified Democracy

Democracy is best understood as interconnected theaters of action that span multiple realms, such as political parties, bureaucratic administration, law, science, and institutionalized and emergent collectives and mobilizations. Some of these theaters are self-evidently concerned with power and politics, such as intergroup alliances and competition expressed through social movements, protests, and legislative and electoral politics. Others operate through registers different from those of power and politics, such as law, science, and bureaucratic norms; what unfolds in these theaters is not overwhelmed by politics and yet has political implications. Scientific controversies like that over GM crops highlight the problems with limiting an inquiry into democratic functioning to only one or a few theaters of action. To illustrate, the response of political parties to GM crops is shaped by proceedings in the Supreme Court, which in turn are shaped by conflicts within the sciences.

By design, democracy multiplies arenas available to individuals and groups for participation—for instance, through elections, a federal structure of government, and separation among legislative, executive, and judicial functions—while, at the same time, making these structures vulnerable to pressures for greater or lesser inclusion. This was especially evident in the years of the second Congress-led United Progressive Alliance (UPA) government (2009–14), when I conducted much of this research. However, even in the far more centralized, authoritarian National Democratic Alliance (NDA) governments (2014–19; 2019–present), led by Prime Minister Modi, the ferocity with which the regime has gone after journalists, activists, and even mildly independent institutions indicates the tendency of democratic polities to multiply arenas of contestation. Individuals and groups with different and differing capacities mobilize these structures and circulate plural and antagonistic perspectives, driving the motor of politics. In the process, democracy is reconstituted through these interlinked theaters of action. These theaters function sometimes in tandem, at other times at cross-purposes, without any necessary coordination or coherence. In conceptual terms, democracy is the sum total of processes feeding off and into multiple, heterogeneous theaters of action.

To track the GM debate in India, it is necessary to keep sight of all these theaters. Consequently, I examine how multiple processes such as state and private capital investing resources in biotechnology, bureaucrats crafting rules and regulations, activists making claims, and farmers purchasing seeds and other inputs enable and transform the logic of democracy, while also unsettling the authority of biotechnology. Given that processes are fundamentally historical, this is the most productive way to situate the controversy over GM crops at the intersection of the anthropology of democracy and science and technology studies, against the backdrop of agrarian change in India.

As different groups clash over GM crops, they not only pit corporate and regulatory science against dissident science (Delborne 2008) and other kinds of truth claims, but also call into question who may and who may not participate in decision making over GM crops, agriculture, and food. By taking the battle over GM crops to different forums, such as the Supreme Court, political parties, street protests, and social media, they certainly expand the range of actors who can participate in the GM debates, but, more fundamentally, they alter the architecture of democratic decision making, whose influence extends far beyond the realm of agricultural biotechnology.

Following GM Crops

This book is based on close to thirty-six months of archival and multisited field research between May 2011 and August 2017, of which I spent twenty-four continuous months, from January 2013 to December 2014, in my field sites. I conducted research at the principal sites where facts about GM crops were constructed and advanced, and I followed them as they confronted one another at forums such as courts, regulatory offices, legacy and social media, and industry and government-organized symposia. My principal field sites were small farms in western India, agricultural biotechnology laboratories in the public and private sector, an NGO in northern India critical of GM crops, and, finally, a federal ministry involved with regulation of GM crops, which has to respond to claims and counterclaims produced by different groups and make decisions with far-reaching consequences. Along with participant-observation in these sites, I conducted interviews with about forty biotechnologists and agricultural scientists in the public and private sectors, over fifteen policy makers and bureaucrats, about ten environmental and sustainable agriculture activists, the founding members and senior managers of three private seed companies, and senior journalists covering science, environment, and agriculture. While conducting ethnographic research in western India, I also interviewed close to ten village-level retailers for seeds and agrochemical inputs and field marketing personnel of agribusinesses such as Syngenta, Bayer, and Dow, and farmers around Nashik city, in the state of Maharashtra.

I supplemented ethnographic inquiry with research in several archives, notably the Parliament Library and the library of the Indian Agricultural Research Institute, and accessed official documents from different federal ministries and state governments by filing multiple Right to Information requests. I also consulted official documents archived by the late Pushpa M. Bhargava in Hyderabad. Bhargava was one of India's foremost biotechnologists, a science policy maker, and the founder-director of the Centre for Cellular and Molecular Biology. I supplemented and contextualized the (sometimes sparing) information I gleaned from these sources with accounts published in different newspapers and magazines, most valuably the *Hindu*, the *Indian Express*, and *Down to Earth*, the last published by the Centre for Science and Environment in New Delhi, and also those archived at the Centre for Education and Documentation in Mumbai. Finally, I followed GM crops–related campaigns and battles on social media like Facebook and Twitter.

The GM debates are unfolding across India, in state capitals, in cities, on social media, in newspapers, in farmers' fields and people's homes, and this mix of methods at multiple sites was necessary to keep pace with the controversy. This is not simply a matter of tracking an expanded set of actors. Of course, different constituencies bring different perspectives to bear on GM crops. The point is to account for the production of the different standpoints in the GM debate, as well as to show how the dynamic of the controversy impels actors beyond, and even in directions contrary to, their articulated positions.

This book is an ethnography as much of science as of democracy. It insists that power and knowledge available to different actors have to be ethnographically calibrated in the rough-and-tumble of democratic politics, rather than presumed from without. If multinational corporations find it easier to lobby the federal government, they struggle to hold their own in the vernacular sphere of state-level politics. Activists, spurned as "anti-national" by the government science establishment, manage to get a sympathetic ear at the Supreme Court. This book thus excavates how truth claims and political platforms are painstakingly cobbled together out of resources such as bureaucratic routines, legal precedents, scientific studies, field trials, the rich store of symbols and rhetoric from anticolonial struggles, and state support to science. In sum, this book demonstrates how the debate has expanded the forums for staging conflicts over GM crops and multiplied the groups involved.

The book is organized into three parts, which reassemble sciences, the state, and agrarian capitalism, respectively. The first part, "Institutionalizing Biotechnology," traces the beginning of biotechnology in India as fundamentally a state project, in marked contrast to its incubation by means of venture capital in the United States. In the 1960s and 1970s, botany and plant breeding were the two main disciplines for the study of plants in India. Biotechnology, or new biology, as it was called then, was grafted onto this base. Chapter 2 chronicles the conflicts among plant sciences surrounding the emergence of biotechnology in India, in the same period as the Green Revolution. It underscores that biotechnology stayed aloof from agriculture, for all the talk of revolutionary applications on farms—claims that foreshadowed those of the Evergreen Revolution today.

Within barely twenty years of the birth of the field, India established the federal Department of Biotechnology in 1986. Chapter 3 recounts how and why the government came to accord such a high priority to biotechnology, in a country where there were no biotechnology start-ups and hardly any universities working in the area. It highlights how the establishment of the Biotechnology Department accelerated the process by which the Ministry of Agriculture lost control of agriculture policy in India. Crucially, biotechnologists, with little practical knowledge of farming, began to mold farm policy.

The second part, "The Government of Biotechnology" turns attention to the escalating controversy over policy making and state regulation of GM crops. Chapter 4 describes the genesis and design of the regulatory structure for GM crops in India and demonstrates that not only interests, but also divergent epistemologies, are at stake in disputes over regulation. These disputes became further vexed as Bt eggplant, India's potentially first GM food, inched closer to commercial release in the late 2000s. Chapter 5 looks at the different campaigns against GM crops and their institutional anchors. Building on the work of Dr. Vandana Shiva and others, young activists deployed protests, petitions, and social media campaigns to broaden and deepen the battle over GM food. They deftly jockeyed states against the federal government, the opposition against the ruling party, and department against department in their bid to block Bt eggplant.

The third part, "Remaking Agrarian Capitalism," turns attention to emerging alliances and conflicts in the agrarian political economy. Chapter 6 demonstrates that there is no singular "corporate interest" in GM crops by looking at India's domestic seed companies, often neglected in the GM debate. I show that these companies grew in the shadow of the state, unlike the situation in the United States, where a domestic seed industry grew in opposition to public breeding and seed-distribution programs. As a consequence, GM crops represent different opportunities and constraints for domestic vis-à-vis transnational firms, which generates friction. Further, the two main GM traits—pest resistance and herbicide tolerance—cleave corporate interests in agriculture differently, and these interests themselves are an outcome of historical pathways to agricultural innovation and development.

Chapter 7 traces the competitive dynamic among seed companies down the supply chain to the farm; it studies how farmers access new technologies in the form of seeds, pesticides, and other chemical inputs. In the vegetable-cultivating tracts of western India, young male farmers of the dominant landed Maratha caste have taken to retailing corporate seeds, pesticides, and other inputs in their quest to secure their life outside farming. Their transactions with farmers trouble the widespread notion that farmers' preferences for corporate seeds and chemicals can be inferred from sales figures. The chapter also indicates that even without GM crops, private agribusinesses already enjoy a tenacious hold over agriculture. Ultimately, interlocking investments and aspirations within heterogeneous blocs of capital and farmers allow for surprising cross-sectoral alliances, and these drive the contentious politics of GM crops.

The book ends with reflections on the possibilities and difficulties of addressing questions of food security and sovereignty through the narrower issue of GM crops and, more broadly, the conundrum of addressing questions of justice and aspirations by means of a politics of technology.

Finally, I am often asked whether I am pro- or anti-GM. I am neither. I am, however, skeptical of the notion that the deep-rooted problems of agriculture and food can be addressed in any significant and lasting manner by tweaking crop DNA—these problems lie in the realm of policies and politics, and in those realms lie their resolutions. In my view, if one has to take a position from the perspective of ecological sustainability and agrarian justice, then the emerging and innovative field of agro-ecology is conceptually sounder and empirically more promising than rDNA technology (Vandermeer et al. 2018). Certainly, on ecological grounds and on grounds of safety, there are strong reasons to be wary of herbicides and HT crops—reasons also echoed by a majority of experts advising the Supreme Court, which I discuss in chapter 5. More generally, though, if one has to take a position on a specific GM crop, one should consider the trait being introduced, the crop being modified, the specific legal and regulatory arrangements through which GM crops are introduced, and the political economy, ecology, and sociology of the region where they are introduced. Once again, this book is a study of the debate over GM food as it has emerged and transformed democratic functioning in India. As such, it does not try to say whether GM crops ought to be introduced in India, though it does provide certain crucial considerations that bear on that question.

PART ONE

Institutionalizing Biotechnology

2

Revolution of the Chemists: "New Biology" and the Beginning of Biotechnology in India

On July 29, 2014, Prime Minister Narendra Modi addressed India's top public-sector agricultural scientists of the Indian Council of Agricultural Research (ICAR)—the government body under the Ministry of Agriculture for steering and funding agricultural research across the country.[1] After applauding "the Indian farmer," Modi exhorted the ICAR to find low-cost solutions to improve farmers' incomes and to raise productivity while lowering irrigation requirements. The director general of the ICAR at the time, Dr. S. Ayyapan, responded, "We think GM crops are the way forward in this country under your leadership" (Bera 2014). Globally, GM crops overwhelmingly incorporate only two traits, both of which are more suited to the needs of capital-intensive farmers, rather than resource-poor, smallholder farmers, and in any case, the ICAR has no GM crop to offer Indian farmers despite over two decades of expensive R&D efforts. Yet Ayyapan pinned the hopes of India's distress-ridden agriculture on genetic modification.

How has the Indian national agricultural research system reached a juncture where GM crops are presented as the solution to what its own National Commission on Farmers (2004) argued are multiple, complex problems? This and the next chapter trace the puzzle of how limited tools of agricultural biotechnology, such as recombinant DNA (rDNA) technology, have come to eclipse older, broader fields of agricultural sciences like plant breeding. How did biotechnology take root in India and what effect did it have on public breeding efforts?

In scientific as well as policy circles, agricultural biotechnological interventions are frequently referred to as constitutive of the Gene or second Green or the Evergreen Revolution, to build on the positive associations of the Green Revolution (see, for example, Swaminathan 2010). Popularly, the Green Revolution connotes food self-sufficiency, an end to scarcity, and improvements in the conditions of farmers. Over the last four decades, however, it has attracted critical attention on ecological grounds and on the grounds of exacerbating inequality within and between regions of India (see Frankel 1971; Dhanagare 1987; Shiva 1991; Subramanian 2015), and for not actually solving the problem of hunger (see Patel 2013; Siegel 2018). Even favorable accounts concede that the program provisioned consumers with cheap cereals at the expense of the vast majority of farmers (Evenson and Gollin 2003). Several scholars have investigated the degrees of continuities and shifts between the two revolutions (Visvanathan and Parmar 2002; Scoones 2006). I follow a different strategy by sidestepping the framing of "revolution" and focusing on changing configurations of state-led interventions in agriculture (Gupta 1998; Saha 2013). Through what pathways of research and policy did the "Evergreen Revolution" enter the space of implementation as part of national food security efforts?

A Place for Biotechnology among Sciences in Independent India

Biotechnology is a deceptive field of knowledge. Its first deception lies in the claim to constitute a unified field of knowledge, when actually it is at best an umbrella term for particular nooks and corners of fields that otherwise have little to do with one another, such as tissue culture, fermentation, vaccine production, and immunology. Another deception lies in the suggestion, implied in the name itself, that biotechnology is an advance on biology at large. If biotechnology bears some continuity with biology and appears as a sleeker and technologically gifted extension of biology, it is only because biology has undergone a sea change since the 1960s. It has effectively become colonized by shifts in other disciplines—notably chemistry, which saw the rise of molecular studies (Cohen 1984; Bud 1993). Of equal importance is the fact that, in the process, biology has entered into a new relationship with capital (Busch et al. 1991; Etzkowitz 2002).

The origin of biotechnology, like the origin of nuclear sciences, lies in the expanded scope that physics and chemistry got in the West in the early twentieth century, especially during the Second World War (Kendrew 1970). The potent mix of vast funding through the Rockefeller Foundation and a lingering fascination with eugenics came together in the emergence of new biology, especially on the campus of the California Institute of Technology, or Caltech, around the 1930s (Kay 1993). By the 1970s and 1980s, the field became better known as molecular biology or biotechnology. New biology defined life in terms of physical and chemical mechanisms at the cellular and subcellular levels and focused principally on macromolecules like proteins and later nucleic acids such as DNA. The research program set into motion through these contingencies had an influence far beyond Caltech, as students and scientists from many parts of the world studied new biology in the United States and then attempted to build the field in their respective countries.

The early practitioners of new biology in India were typically trained in the United States and United Kingdom, at the doctoral or postdoctoral level. They began in disciplines other than biology, often (applied) chemistry. After returning to India, they tried to replicate and graft laboratory facilities from abroad onto the existing base for plant sciences in India, which at the time were largely concerned with field research. Unlike their American counterparts (Kohler 1991), however, new biologists in India could not rely on private foundations for funding their research. They perforce had to find a niche within the ecology of state-funded science. The hitch was that biology in India was marginal to state science in the years after independence.

Organized scientific activity began sporadically in the colonial period in fields important for the imperial political economy. During the Second World War, calls for promoting scientific and industrial research intensified in the country, leading to the establishment of organizations like the Council of Scientific and Industrial Research (CSIR) in 1942 (Krishna 2011). With independence in 1947, Prime Minister Jawaharlal Nehru accorded high priority to science and technology, and he cultivated leading scientists such as Meghnad Saha, Shanti Swaroop Bhatnagar, and Homi J. Bhabha. Nehru was concerned not just with technological development, but with supporting the basic sciences in order to promote the cultivation of "scientific temper" (Nehru 1946, 512; see Arnold 2013), essentially the spirit of rational inquiry, free from dogma and revelation. He strongly felt that the cultivation of scientific modes of thought was the surest way of alleviating conflict in a "traditional" society marked by sectarian strife.

These twin prongs—industrial development through technology, and cultivation of scientific temper through science education—assumed the institutional form of national research laboratories and universities, respectively (Visvanathan 1985). Universities were the principal sites for training students, with some research on the side, while fundamental and applied research was the preserve of national laboratories such as the National Physical Laboratory, the National Chemical Laboratory under the CSIR umbrella, institutions of the federal Department of Space and Department of Atomic Energy, and institutions under the ICAR (Bhargava and Chakrabarti 2003; Anderson 2010). Scientists pursuing plant sciences were either based in botany departments in universities or involved in agricultural and plant-breeding research under the ICAR.[2] It says something about the culture of biology that there were no biologists advising Nehru or bustling in and out of the Planning Commission.[3] As a corollary, there was no National Biological Laboratory to mirror those for physics and chemistry.[4] This picture was to change by the 1980s.

New biology in India began in universities in Calcutta and Delhi, in biochemistry departments (Sopory and Maheshwari 2001). At Calcutta University, B. C. Guha, who had worked with Sir F. G. Hopkins at the University of Cambridge, initiated the biochemistry program under the Applied Chemistry Division (Chatterjee and Burma 2004). A second group in Calcutta coalesced around S. M. Sircar and his students, notably S. P. Sen and B. B. Biswas, at the Bose Institute. A third group emerged at Delhi University. I profile three scientists below who belonged to the first generation of new biologists in India. These were individuals who lived through and wrought the shifts taking place in biology. Their lives illustrate the birth pangs of biotechnology in India.

Satish Chandra Maheshwari, Professor and Founding Head, Center for Plant Molecular Biology, Delhi University (1933–2019)

Satish Chandra Maheshwari not only belonged to India's first generation of new biologists, but was also one particularly attentive to the changes wrought in botany by new biology, because of the fact that his father, Panchanan Maheshwari, was one of India's finest botanists (or embryologists, to be precise) in the 1940s and 1950s. Describing what biology was like in his student days, Maheshwari told me:

> [It was] largely anatomy, taxonomy, structure, embryology. Embryology means the structure of plant reproductive plants

> and how they grow. . . . My father was a specialist in plant reproduction, in that classical sense. In those days there wasn't molecular biology, so they sectioned the material under the microscope. . . . Many times [there are] little variations in embryology—one family may have certain variations and another family may show some other variations. You can use these characters . . . to know taxonomy, which groups are which. In fact, my PhD thesis was in embryology; in those days there was little else in biology. . . . I worked on one of the world's smallest flowering plants [duckweed]. And it's just a little pistil. In one [millimeter], there is one stamen and one pistil. The flower is so reduced it has no petals, no sepals. . . . By embryological structures you can get some idea of which are the closest relatives. . . . So in my [father's] day it was all descriptive. . . . When we were students, we were drawing mostly in our lab books, drawing first the plants, the structures we saw under a microscope. We never understood any molecular basis. Then after the DNA revolution came, thinking changed.[5]

In the period Maheshwari describes, the concept of interdisciplinary work was absent. He laughingly told me that the idea that botanists should also understand chemistry had little support in his student days. Physics, too, was not considered important for botanists.

When the double-helix structure of DNA was discovered, Maheshwari was in his final days of the master's of science program. He found embryology limiting and wanted to get into new biology, for which he needed a good background in biochemistry. An opportunity to go abroad presented itself, however, only after he had finished his PhD. In 1959 Maheshwari went first to Yale University on a postdoctoral fellowship, and he then went to Caltech. At Caltech, Maheshwari worked in James Bonner's lab on RNA polymerase. He was part of the team that discovered the enzyme in plants.

Things took an adverse turn when he returned to Delhi University around 1961. The microscope ruled in Indian botany departments, and there was neither any interest in nor the facilities for new biology. When I asked him how biologists in India responded to the new paradigm, he told me: "Usually, in botany departments, this led to wars. . . . When I came back, I said [the science happening here] should change. . . . My colleagues said Satish Maheshwari is not a person who should be here. And we faced difficulties in buying equipment because people wanted microscopes, we wanted centrifuges." The "wars" were not just over departmental infrastructure, but also over research funds and recruiting students.

In the 1960s India was importing wheat from the United States and paying for it in Indian rupees under the Public Law (PL) 480 "Food for Peace" program. This was the program that triggered the Green Revolution. The American government decided to deploy the Indian rupees it collected to fund research projects in India. This was the first time scientists were able to propose projects with budgets running into millions of rupees. Many people benefited from the PL 480 funds, including at least two laboratories for new biology—one set up by Satish Maheshwari and the other by B. B. Biswas, at the Bose Institute, Calcutta.[6] Maheshwari accessed PL 480 funds and started building his lab for molecular biological work.

Along with his student Sipra Guha, Maheshwari researched the effect of hormones and other parameters on anther culture of *Datura innoxia*. They made the discovery of haploid plants growing through anther cultures. Haploid plants were of interest because of their utility for sustaining true breeding lines for agriculture—if you could generate haploid plants, there would be no need of fertilization and hence no way for lines to mix. This could in theory drastically accelerate plant breeding. This was the first time that haploid embryos had been obtained in culture—something that many others, including Maheshwari's father, had attempted to achieve (Maheshwari 1990). This original work got them two articles in the journal *Nature* (Guha and Maheshwari 1964, 1966), and was cited when Maheshwari was conferred the prestigious Shanti Swarup Bhatnagar Prize for Science and Technology in 1972.

Maheshwari's work on haploid embryos attracted the keen interest of M. S. Swaminathan, the scientist who had headed ICAR and had become one of the key architects of the Green Revolution, and who was close to Prime Minister Indira Gandhi. From 1980 until 1982, Swaminathan was a member of the Planning Commission, and, seeing Maheshwari's embattled position at Delhi University, he offered Maheshwari a position in one of the agricultural research institutions. Maheshwari declined the offer, however. He explained: "I prefer working on fundamental problems rather than applied. Let other people who are more interested in agriculture [work on applied problems]. I couldn't tell one wheat variety from another. So I am not the kind of person to work on improving yields. I told Dr. Swaminathan, 'I don't want any center on haploid research, you give me a center on plant molecular biology, [to undertake] basic studies.' Fortunately, he agreed."

Had Maheshwari moved to an agricultural research institution, he would have had to work on actualizing haploid-based research as a tool for accelerated breeding. Moreover, he would have been encouraged to work on important cultivable crops that ICAR institutions were focusing on, such as rice and wheat, and not *Datura*. But Maheshwari was not interested in agriculture. He considered such work "applied," whereas his interests were in "fundamental problems," even though developing breeding programs from rice and wheat haploid embryos is a scientific problem in its own right, and not a straightforward application of techniques from *Datura*.[7]

Given Maheshwari's background and training, neither his preference for laboratory-based "fundamental" experimental work, nor his lack of interest in field-based plant breeding work, what he called "improving yields," is surprising (see Knorr Cetina 1992). There had been a long-standing debate in Indian science policy framed by the basic-applied distinction (Ghosh 1943; Blackett 1963; Bhatnagar 1950).[8] This debate saw multiple experiments in designing research laboratories, chiefly on the question of whether basic and applied scientific research needed to be housed together or as separate institutions (Visvanathan 1985). There was no satisfactory resolution and, by the 1970s and 1980s, the basic architecture involving universities essentially conducting teaching, and independent research institutions conducting applied and industrial research, was challenged in multiple ways, as basic and applied research agendas began to crisscross universities and industrial research institutions. This was the context in which Maheshwari sought an independent center for basic research inside the teaching-focused Delhi University. Swaminathan, as a member of the Planning Commission and chairman of the powerful Scientific Advisory Committee to the Cabinet, got the necessary approvals for this request. Thus was born the Centre for Plant Molecular Biology, which became a separate department in 1988. Swaminathan also secured for this center independent funding from the Department of Science and Technology (DST), which was established in 1971 with a broad mandate, but which typically did not fund university departments in that period. The basic-applied dichotomy, in the specific context of Indian science policy, served to create one of the first centers for molecular biology in India, distant from both botany and agricultural research, giving a fillip to research that had begun with PL 480 funds from the U.S. government.

Pushpa Mittra Bhargava, Founder-Director, Centre for Cellular and Molecular Biology, Hyderabad (1928–2017)

In the last twenty-odd years of his life, Pushpa Bhargava made news primarily as an unrelenting critic of the federal Department of Biotechnology and India's regulatory regime for GM crops. But, in fact, he was one of the earliest proponents of genetic engineering and one of the key architects of new biology in India.

Bhargava's doctoral research was in synthetic organic chemistry at Lucknow University, for which the distinguished organic chemist, Nobel laureate, and former president of the Royal Society, Sir Robert Robinson, served as the external examiner. After finishing his PhD at the age of twenty-one, Bhargava joined the institution that would later become the Regional Research Laboratory Hyderabad (RRLH), and finally the Indian Institute of Chemical Technology, under the CSIR. He had a productive career in chemistry, publishing many papers, including a paper in *Nature* when he was about twenty-five (Bhargava and Zaheer 1953).

At this point he decided to turn to biology.[9] He went first to McArdle Laboratory for Cancer Research at Madison, Wisconsin, in 1953, and then to the National Institute for Medical Research in London, "two of the best places in the world." Around 1958, when he was thirty, he returned to the RRLH and became the head of the Biochemistry Department. At that point in India, there were only a handful of groups venturing into new biology.[10]

Bhargava and other biochemists decided to hold periodic, informal meetings of Indian biochemists and new biologists, which culminated in the Guha Research Conference, named after B. C. Guha. This was a young group, secure in its conviction of the importance of new biology to plant sciences, biology, and science in general. The members of the conference were among the first Indians to be conducting research in new biology in Western laboratories, and, perhaps by virtue of this fact, many of them were already acquainted with one another. At this point in India, as I have noted, there was no national institute for biology, as there were for physics and chemistry. New biologists were keenly aware of this slight. Bhargava took the lead in mooting a proposal for an equivalent of the National Physical and Chemical Laboratories for the "modern" biological sciences. His colleague and the director of RRLH, S. Husain Zaheer, became the director general of CSIR in 1962, and he asked Bhargava to prepare a formal proposal.

The proposal, however, ran afoul of the larger body of botanists and biologists in the country. At issue was the demarcation between "modern biology" that Bhargava favored and the "traditional" biology that was the mainstay in India then. Bhargava's proposal emphasized biochemistry to the exclusion of older divisions of biology such as botany, zoology, and fisheries. This did not go down well with biologists. As Bhargava recounted, "Consequently, the committees [Zaheer] set up—and I was a member of one of them—one after another opposed setting up of a laboratory which would be devoted to sciences such as biochemistry, which was thought by the traditional chemists and biologists as being neither biology nor chemistry and, therefore, no science!" (Bhargava 2002, xiv).

Bhargava even got Melvin Cohn, who became one of the founders of the Salk Institute in California, to advocate the promise of new biology to Indian biologists, but even that gambit did not succeed against their determined opposition. Bhargava's opponents were not objecting to a national laboratory for biology per se. They wanted the laboratory to reflect the divisions of biology that they were familiar with, such as botany and fisheries. At issue was not the scientific promise of new biology, but its contention, implied in the distinction between traditional and modern, of being the future of all biology.

Bhargava explained the traditional-modern difference to me:

> Biology before 1950s was entirely descriptive. You described an animal. An animal has four legs, it has such and such structure, this is what its habitat is, what its habits are. You can look at a plant through a microscope and say this is what its structure is. It was descriptive, not experimental. . . . And you did not ask the question "How?" and "Why?" You answered the question "What?" What is it? What does it look like? And modern biology asks: What is it made of? What is its chemistry? How are all chemical constituents made in the system? What does it look like at all levels of resolution? . . . What is the mechanism of functions? To explain them in terms of chemistry, biochemistry, and structure.

Bhargava caricatures the biology of his opponents here. He reproduces the prejudice that laboratory scientists have long harbored for their colleagues in field-oriented biology.[11] While the latter's work had a descriptive thrust, they were not restricting themselves to "What is it?" questions. They were asking other and perhaps equally interesting questions, such as those from within the paradigm of population genetics. The work of J. B. S. Haldane in India in the same decades in which Bhargava was lobbying for the national biological laboratory (Dronamraju 2010), and that of the botanist B. M. Johri at Delhi University (Mohan Ram 2003) serve as useful examples. It was Bhargava's attempt to project new biology as the future of all biology that derailed his proposal. Bhargava lost the battle, and, instead of a national laboratory for the biological sciences, the CSIR established the Institute of Himalayan Bioresource Technology, reflecting the older divisions of biology.

Difficulties with institutionalizing new biology were not unique to India. For instance, in the United States, by the mid-1960s, as biochemists sought more and more federal government funding, they were challenged by other fields of science (Yi 2015). Bhargava continued to champion the cause of new biology and succeeded about a decade later, in 1977. To understand why this success came when it did, it is important to understand the shifts taking place within the state science complex in India.

The CSIR was geared to promote industrial and applied research, and its failures to break away from research-for-the-sake-of-research had led to many experiments in institutional redesign. One solution to invigorate application-oriented research, proposed by its director general, P. K. Kitchlu, in the 1960s, involved organizing the CSIR around mission-oriented laboratories pursuing "objective basic research" (Visvanathan 1985, 254). This odd category involved basic research motivated by practical problems of production; it was research in service of well-defined objectives or missions.[12] This orientation got a further boost as production-based approaches to problems shadowed redistributive approaches. The most significant emblem of this shift was the Green Revolution in agriculture in the 1960s (Raina 2011), but even Nehru's encouragement of import-substitution industrialization reflects the same orientation. The CSIR mandate emphasized research that could service the problems of industrial production, such as research in material sciences, minerals, petroleum, and in physics and chemistry (Krishna 1987). The RRLH, where Bhargava headed the Biochemistry Unit, was a CSIR laboratory. In his continuing efforts to establish an institution dedicated to new biology, he began to emphasize unprecedented applications with revolutionary potential. Genetic engineering—introducing foreign genes into organisms to make them do new things—was high on the list of potentially revolutionary applications.

When one juxtaposes Bhargava's scientific writings with his more general public-oriented accounts of that time, one notices a certain slippage that points to the political work of aligning new biology with government priorities of the day. Such work was vital for securing support in the form of tangible and intangible benefits for the field from the national Congress government, committed as it was to public programs of poverty alleviation and agricultural modernization. Consider, for example, Bhargava's narration of his sentiments in the 1960s with respect to the promises of new biology. "Gradually between 1960 and 1972, it had become clear to thinking biologists around the world . . . that modern biology was poised for a technological revolution and that the emergence of the new biotechnology was around the corner. In 1971 we had a long, invited review published in *Progress in Nucleic Acid Research and Molecular Biology* on uptake of non-viral nucleic acids by animal and plant cells. While writing this review, it was clear to me that even though an enormous amount of bad work had been done in this area, there was no question that technologies would be developed for putting in foreign genetic information in higher organisms such as animals and plants" (Bhargava 2002, xv).

The review article he quotes actually voiced many doubts about such technologies. Bhargava and Shanmugam (1971) end the article on a skeptical note, saying, "We are strongly of the opinion that more experiments are required to establish . . . (ii) DNA-induced transformation e.g., with respect to drug resistance, morphological trait, or a defined biochemical property." Of course, one is comparing two different registers of writing; yet it is exactly this gap between the promises that animate policy-oriented persuasion and the qualified claims of peer-reviewed science, wherein lies much of the politics of science (Jasanoff 1995).

Bhargava's efforts found sympathy with the distinguished leather scientist Y. Nayudamma, who took over as the director general of the CSIR in 1971. It helped that in the West, new biology was growing more confident and publicly raising hopes of a major revolution through genetic engineering. In 1975 the prestigious *British Medical Journal* published an editorial in which it delineated how genetic engineering could be of worldwide significance to agriculture by engineering cereals and other non-leguminous crops to fix their own nitrogen (*British Medical Journal* 1975). Bhargava wrote a strongly worded letter to Nayudamma with a copy of the editorial. As he recounted: "Knowing that Dr. Nayudamma was already favourably inclined towards the development of modern biology in the CSIR, I wrote to him a personal letter in which I said that I merely wanted to put on record, lest posterity may ask as to what *our* scientists were doing when the biological revolution was occurring elsewhere, that our scientists had been talking about it even before most of the world had started thinking in that direction. And that the fault did not lie with them, but with those who administered science" (Bhargava 2002, xvi, emphasis in original).

In the shadow of the Green Revolution, witnessing the increasing dependence of agriculture on urea, Bhargava offered the promise that through genetic engineering, scientists could introduce the nitrogen fixation trait in non-leguminous plants, so that the need for urea could be reduced, if not eliminated. Given that fertilizers alone accounted for 60 percent of the energy costs of wheat production in the country (Jain 1985, 335), and that India was incurring a sizable expenditure importing fertilizers, this must have sounded very attractive to the political class of the day. Nayudamma appointed a committee comprising new biologists such as Obaid Siddiqi, Pran Talwar, and Bhargava himself to look into a new center for new biology. Bhargava drafted the charter, which the committee approved, and, thus, the biochemistry division of RRLH was spun off in 1977 to become the Centre for Cellular and Molecular Biology (CCMB) under the CSIR. Bhargava was its founder-director.

Jatin Sen, DST Unit on Genetic Engineering at a Premier Public University in North India (1933–)

Jatin Sen (real name disguised) was born to an elite, politically powerful family in colonial Dhaka (present day Bangladesh) in 1933.[13] Sen moved to Calcutta in 1948 during the turmoil of independence and partition. In Calcutta, Sen did his undergraduate studies in chemistry at Presidency College. He then moved on to what may well have been the finest such department in the Global South at that time—the Applied Chemistry Division at the University College of Science, Calcutta University, where B. C. Guha made his career. Sen finished his master's of science in applied chemistry in 1955 and took up doctoral work in biochemistry on amino acid metabolism.

In 1964 Sen traveled to Stanford University on a Fulbright Fellowship, where he worked with Avram Goldstein on *E. coli*, the bacterium workhorse and model working system. Those three years were crucial for Sen's career because it was there that he learnt to "work with *E. coli* . . . protein synthesis in *E. coli*, RNA synthesis in *E. coli*, coupling of RNA synthesis and protein synthesis."[14] In 1969 he moved to the premier Indian Agricultural Research Institute (IARI) under the ICAR in New Delhi, headed then by M. S. Swaminathan. Sen's research, based as it was on *E. coli,* was not easy to relate to agricultural sciences and applications. Recognizing that stresses—such as heat, cold, and drought—of various kinds were an important topic in agricultural research, however, Sen decided to model stresses on bacteria. So he started work on cold stress and starvation stress. "I was able to get good publications, but they were not directly related to agriculture," he recounted.

Pursuing this line of research was not easy, however. For one, there was a general problem of infrastructure, machine tools, instrumentation, and consumables or reagents that are vital for research at the cellular and subcellular level. As Maheshwari's case also illustrated, new biologists in India in the 1960s and 1970s faced tremendous difficulties setting up their laboratories and keeping them running—because the instrumentation, machines, and reagents were not manufactured in India, and foreign exchange for imports was hard to come by.

At that time, the IARI had one of the finest genetics divisions in India. So why did Sen find it difficult to organize a bacterial genetics laboratory? This is the conflation that one has to guard against. Whereas an uncritical projection backward of current trends of genetics research might suggest a (wet) laboratory setting, the genetics departments of those times, and to a large extent of current times as well, specialized in field research. The research on genetics at the IARI then, as now, was primarily oriented toward breeding (through crossing and selecting) improved rice, wheat, and other crop varieties and hybrids for farmers. Breeding work is difficult, cumbersome, time-consuming, and labor-intensive, but it is not critically dependent on expensive instrumentation and foreign currency, and this was all the more true in the 1970s.

Even the "gene" for breeders was not a fragment of DNA, but a metaphor for units of heredity. As Sen put it, "Whatever you know about hereditary crosses was basically the concept of gene—Mendel's law, [its applications in terms of trying] to get a better breed of wheat, of rice, by crossing and by looking at characters, phenotypes. [You did not look at] actual DNA . . . The genetics people at IARI were very strong *but that's the way they did genetics*" (emphasis added). Here Sen, like Maheshwari, reaches for the basic-applied distinction. It is no surprise, then, that plant breeders were not invitees to the Guha Research Conference, the forum being the preserve of "basic" scientists working at the cellular levels rather than with the whole plant.

Following Rheinberger (1997), we can conceive of the differences between genetics research of that time and what Sen and other new biologists were trying to do in terms of experimental systems. Experimental systems are the social, technical, and instrumental units that organize the material culture of research while structuring the paradigms one thinks within. They are "vehicles for materializing questions" (Rheinberger 1997, 28). Sen's research, involving unfamiliar (to breeders) material artifacts like centrifuges, magnetic stirrers, and expensive reagents, belonged to a different experimental system. He asked questions of bacteria suitably transformed or selected for laboratory research (Knorr Cetina 1992; Creager 2002), rather than study bacterial problems in Indian farms. Thus, at the IARI of that time, Sen's requirements may have been peculiar for a scientist. New biology, then and now, goes hand in hand with huge budgets (Kevles 1997).

One day, Sen was presenting his research on bacteria at a divisional meeting where the new director of IARI and the wheat breeder, A. B. Joshi, was invited. Sen recalled, "After [Joshi] heard my talk, he put his hand on my back and said, 'It's all fine, but what does it have to do with agriculture?' I tried to explain that 'I work with temperature stresses, nutrition stress.' He was a hard-core agricultural geneticist; he didn't accept that." Thus, Sen decided to move to more hospitable grounds and joined the Life Sciences Department at a premier public university in northern India, as a professor. There he was unlikely to be asked questions about agricultural applications.

In 1978 Sen left for San Diego on a University Grants Commission (UGC) fellowship to learn rDNA technology with Donald Helinsky. "Those were the days when, in Helinsky's lab, they would construct new plasmids, take this portion from here, that portion from here . . . trying to get the property they want." Sen went on from San Diego to William Rutter's lab at the University of California's School of Medicine in San Francisco. William Rutter had just succeeded in inserting the insulin gene into *E. coli.* Herbert Boyer of

Genentech fame was conducting experiments to coax bacteria into producing novel proteins.[15] Sen explained: "That was one reason for going to San Francisco. I made friends with Herb Boyer and got all the strains from him. Herb Boyer used to make all the enzymes in his lab. There were no commercial companies then who'd give those restriction enzymes [and] ligases. I got all the strains and we started making those . . . in the lab ourselves. That's how we started. . . . We would make T4 DNA ligase, *EcoRI, BamHI, . . . HindIII, PstI, SalI*. . . . I learnt how to do it from Herb Boyer."

When Sen returned to India around 1981, he brought with him all the necessary strains, along with the know-how to make enzymes and to conduct research using rDNA technology. He effectively imported the experimental system from San Francisco to India. In this way, his university became one of the first centers in India to initiate rDNA research.[16] At that time, the DST decided to fund three units for genetic engineering—at Sen's university, under his headship, at the Bose Institute in Calcutta, and at the Indian Institute of Science (IISc) Bangalore. Sen was then getting interested in *Azotobacter vinelandii*, a bacterium isolated from Wisconsin that fixes nitrogen in the soil, and he wrote a proposal to work on this bacterium. For this work, he requested and received nitrogen fixation, or *nif*, genes from England. He reasoned that this work might prove useful for agriculture.

The promise of genetic engineering for nitrogen fixation had played a crucial role in the establishment of the Centre for Cellular and Molecular Biology under Bharagava's leadership. Bhargava was also involved with steering research efforts funded by the DST. As he had mentioned to me, when I met him in New Delhi in May 2013, "[In the 1970s and 1980s,] we of course talked about what genetic engineering can do, and I said something at that time, which does not make any sense today. I said that if we can transfer nitrogen fixation genes into non-leguminous plants, it'll save us money on fertilizer.

Fertilizer is an energy-intensive industry. . . . As it turns out, nitrogen fixation is controlled by seventeen or eighteen genes, and so it is a virtual impossibility to transfer all these genes into non-leguminous plants as a package, but at that time, we did not know [this]."[17]

Recalling what Bhargava had told me, I asked Sen if they had tried to transform plants with the *nif* genes. He denied this. Whereas designing plants that can fix their own nitrogen was the "dream," the project itself was more modest and concerned the study of molecular genetics of nitrogen fixation in *Azotobacter*.

Yet the Annual Report of the DST for 1984–85 describes one of the two main objectives of Sen's project as "development of eukaryotic system for use as host to bacterial nitrogen fixing genes." The last paragraph of this section also documents an attempt to transform a wheat germ system with nitrogen-fixation genes. As we saw with Bhargava, this points to the gap between the claims that animate policy and funding proposals and the actual research undertaken. Sen's work on *Azotobacter vinelandii*, however, did give India its first paper on rDNA technology, published in *Gene*, a major international journal. Sen continued to work on *nif* genes until he retired in the late 1990s.

The Birth of Biotechnology

Young scientists, typically trained in (applied) chemistry at Western universities, returned to India in the 1960s and 1970s, and they imported laboratory-based paradigms and infrastructure for studying life that were new in Indian plant sciences. New biologists worked with plant tissues and plant and bacterial cells in tissue culture media. They manipulated these in vitro, and they studied physical and chemical mechanisms rather than whole plants or organisms as they were found on farms. In other words, they worked in laboratory settings with plant parts and cells domesticated from nature to suit the experiment. They measured their success in terms of publications in journals like *Nature* and *Science*.

Plant breeders and botanists worked largely with plants as they grew in the fields. Breeders in particular conducted experiments to cross, select, and multiply crop varieties and hybrids with improved traits such as disease resistance and high yield with the application of fertlizers. They measured their success in terms of varieties and hybrids released for farmers. Nearly all senior plant breeders I interviewed proudly recounted the number of varieties they had released. Some of them also sardonically remarked that their contribution to agricultural science should not be measured in terms of peer-reviewed publications, obliquely referring to long curricula vitae of biotechnologists. No wonder that Sen found the Indian Agricultural Research Institute inhospitable for his research, and Maheshwari declined Swaminathan's offer to join an agricultural research institute. The gulf between new biology and established fields of plant sciences in India can thus be understood in terms of the broader tension and the hierarchical relationship between laboratory and field science, which lies at the heart of modern science. Since the mid-nineteenth century, laboratory sciences have tended to claim priority and privilege over field-based disciplines (Kohler 2002), and it is scarcely an accident that the three scientists profiled here demarcated and elevated new biology vis-à-vis botany and plant breeding in terms of basic or fundamental versus applied, modern versus traditional, and cellular versus organismic. At the same time, new biologists were an embattled minority in India. How did they manage to attract the attention of India's science policy-making elites and garner scarce resources for their work? This is where their institutional locations proved to be decisive.

The problem of scarce funding and inadequate infrastructure was not unique to new biology. As a newly independent nation with low foreign exchange reserves and international trade relations marked by an adverse balance of payments, all scientific endeavors encountered these problems to some extent (see, for example, Phalkey 2013 for nuclear research). What made these problems especially serious for new biology was that there was virtually no base for this field in India, unlike agricultural sciences, chemical technology, physics, and chemistry. Stalwart scientists in other fields, such as Harbhajan Singh (plant breeding), Asima Chatterjee (chemistry), Satish Maheshwari's father, P. Maheshwari (embryology), and K. S. Krishnan (physics), were trained largely in India. In fact, P. Maheshwari felt that there was no need for scientists to go abroad for their PhD research (Mohan Ram 2004, 1761). In contrast, the first generation of new biologists was trained largely in the West. On their way back, they brought with them not only this embodied training of body and mind, but also the physical and chemical infrastructure to graft a new ontological order for plant knowledge in India. The contrast with plant breeding and botany is striking. Plant breeding requires land, agro-biodiversity, and labor. Botany of that time required microscopes, which were manufactured in India. Thus, new biology, reliant on instruments and reagents not produced in India, needed an unprecedented amount of funding and foreign exchange. Lacking other sources of funds, new biologists had to turn to the state.

The Indian state, under the Congress, saw science as central to modernizing the Indian economy and society. Thus, appeals for state funding had to align with this vision. This placed a dual burden on new biologists. Dependent entirely on state support, new biologists needed to make their work relevant to nation building. At the same time, to compete with already established fields of agricultural research and botanical sciences, they needed to differentiate themselves. The three profiles in the chapter illustrate the risks, uncertainties, and contradictions of boundary work (Jasanoff 1995)—that is, the work of demarcating scientific fields through which new biologists promised revolutionary applications in a variety of fields, from agriculture to medicine, while remaining firmly ensconced within laboratories and without dirtying their hands with actual field research and development.

In fact, there is an interesting contrast between the creation of CCMB and the way Maheshwari got his center at Delhi University. Maheshwari anticipated that haploid plants can accelerate breeding, but he himself refused to join an agricultural research institute and actualize the promise for India's major food crops. He lobbied Swaminathan for an independent center inside a university with DST funds on the grounds of pursuing basic research. In the same period, Bhargava lobbied the CSIR, the lead council for coordinating industrial research, for an institution for the same "basic" research by promising revolutionary applications. His efforts to promote "modern" biology ended up muddling the basic-applied dichotomy that framed Maheshwari's efforts. In part, this has to do with the fact that these categories did not easily map onto empirical differences in research practices; basic versus applied was not the most useful distinction to be made between botany and plant breeding on the one hand, and new biology on the other, as I mentioned earlier. More important, the successful launch of new biology was a product of the contradictions and schisms in the organization of state science, and it signaled a key aspect of the relationship between science and democracy in India.

New Biology and the Green Revolution

The period after the Second World War has typically been studied in terms of the rise of newly independent nations and postcolonial nation building (see, for example, Gupta 1998; Guha 2007). Yet this was also the period of intensive transnational exchanges and connections in the realm of ideas, social movements, and the sciences. In particular, "technology transfer" in the domains of space research, atomic energy research, defense research, public health, heavy industry, manufacturing, higher education, and agriculture went hand in hand with international cooperation and agreements, under the auspices of either Cold War alliances or organizations like the United Nations and the Consultative Group for International Agricultural Research (CGIAR)[18] (Abraham 1998; Amrith 2006; Krige and Rausch 2012).

In the 1950s, through efforts underwritten by the Indian state and promoted by the Rockefeller and Ford foundations along with the U.S. government, the seeds were sown for transnational rice- and wheat-breeding efforts and trials with synthetic chemical inputs to launch the Green Revolution in India. The program made production and yield the reigning paradigm for the ICAR and agricultural research (Raina 2011), brought prominence and public appreciation to plant breeding, and justified state investment in agricultural research and education on the planks of national self-sufficiency (or food security, in today's parlance) and eradication of hunger (Kumar 2019; Siegel 2018). In the same period, transnational circulation of scientists and scientific knowledge led to the birth of new biology in India. Different groups were assembling national biotechnology and genetic engineering programs globally—in India, in the United States (Yi 2015), and elsewhere—from chemical bits and pieces (genes, plasmids, tissues, and so on) that were standardized or validated with plant, bacterial, and other organismic life from different national origins.[19]

Analyses that place the biotechnology-led Gene Revolution in a relationship of continuity and change with the Green Revolution (see, for example, Scoones 2006; Visvanathan and Parmar 2002) miss several crucial aspects of the history of both these programs. The two emerged in parallel with one another in terms of time period, from similar technical cooperation modalities between India and the West, but the locus of research implicated in them was quite different. Scientists involved in the two interventions differed vastly in terms of training. Consequently, the experimental systems they worked with and their institutional locations also diverged.

The science of plant breeding involves working with whole plants in fields. Given the challenges of research without controlled conditions, many breeders say it is an art. More important, compared to biotechnology, breeding is much closer to farming. I was alerted to this when I contacted Dr. P. S. Sirohi, former head of the Division of Vegetable Science at IARI, who worked on breeding from the 1960s until the early 2000s. When I asked him about public-sector experiments on GM vegetables, he said he did not have much to say because he was not familiar with them. He did, however, speak in very respectful tones about the politician Sompal Shastri, former federal minister of state for agriculture (1998–99) and former member of the Planning Commission (1999–2004). As Sirohi told me, Shastri was himself involved in farming and knew a thing or two about breeding, which is why he could grill breeders with tough questions, for which breeders respected him and listened to him. Similarly, while conducting ethnographic research with farmers, I met a few who challenged me to get expert scientists from universities to compete with them on producing a good crop. Breeders and extension officers, too, sometimes spoke of farmers who devised impressive agronomic practices of their own and conducted experiments in breeding.

The back-and-forth, the mutual intelligibility and dialogue that are possible between breeders and farmers or breeders and politicians close to farming are hard to imagine in the case of new biology. This is in part because the Green Revolution was a concerted effort directed by the national government involving senior politicians collaborating with and closely reviewing the work of plant breeders and agricultural scientists. In contrast, new biology arose in a more uncoordinated, diffuse manner. With articulate spokespersons like Bhargava and a degree of organization through forums like the Guha Research Conference, new biologists were able to take advantage of the tensions and overlaps in the organization of state science. Structures parallel to the ICAR, such as the CSIR and the DST, supported the establishment of dedicated centers for new biology. While these parallel councils and departments also enjoyed access to and support from the Congress national leadership, their mandate was the broader program of scientific and technological development, rather than the more tractable goal of national food grain self-sufficiency. So while new biologists promised a revolution, they were relatively insulated from the pressure of demonstrating actual results in terms of applications.

Moreover, new biology, with its relatively exorbitant demands for instrumentation and foreign exchange, was unlikely to find a sympathetic ear among the breeders who ran the ICAR. Their views were closer to those of the notable botanist Frederick C. Steward, fellow of the Royal Society, who wrote the biographical piece for the society upon P. Maheshwari's death:

> While Maheshwari may have, and did, deplore India's economic inability to furnish his, or other, Indian laboratories with instrumentation and facilities on the western scale, nevertheless and despite these limitations he preserved and developed other values. He encouraged the powers of observation, the manipulative skills born of an understanding of, and respect for, botanical organization; and he thus helped to bridge the gap between the classical descriptive period in morphology and the modern experimental and biochemical one in ways which do justice to both without violence to either.

> In these days when "molecular biology" is in the ascendancy, and when we are often more adept in tearing the living system apart than in interpreting how it grows, develops and works as an integrated whole, Maheshwari's balanced biological view is one that should be, and perhaps in India will be, preserved. (Steward 1967, 261)

Plant breeders have to preserve this "balanced" view because of the very nature of their work, which requires the powers of observation and manipulative skills that rely on a knowledge and discernment of botanical organization, but all this was dismissed as "applied" work by new biologists.

Puzzling though it may sound today, the fact of the matter is that new biology did not have much to do with plant breeding. Beyond promises, the Gene Revolution bore only a tenuous connection with ideas and applications for agricultural research, as they were being debated within the ICAR in the 1960s and 1970s (see Saha 2013). And new biology was much more removed from the working knowledge of farmers and was harder for farmers and their representatives to participate in or shape the direction of. Yet it is in new biology that the promise for genetic engineering was first articulated, and from where it slowly moved into the space of agricultural research, with profound consequences for democratic struggles over GM crops.

3

The Bureaucratic Consolidation of Biotechnology

By the late 1970s, new biologists in India had been able to carve out institutional niches like the Centre for Cellular and Molecular Biology (CCMB). In the 1980s, their quest to establish new biology in the country went from strength to strength and culminated in the form of a powerful *federal bureaucracy*. The Department of Biotechnology, established in 1986 and reporting directly to the prime minister, marked a major victory for the fledgling science. The victory also brought consequences that new biologists had not bargained for, however—but I am getting ahead of myself.

Roughly three decades into independence, the division in Indian science policy making between "applied" industrial development through technology and cultivation of scientific temper through ("basic") science education became increasingly undermined as research glossed as "basic" began to be taken up by industrial research institutions like the CCMB. These experiments in institutional redesign and coining of new, increasingly vague terminology in science policy such as "objective basic research" (Visvanathan 1985, 254) had to do with the deeper frustrations of launching indigenous programs for technology development in India. Even by the late 1960s, there was a widespread notion among top science administrators and senior politicians of the ruling Indian National Congress that state investment in science was not bearing adequate returns in terms of economic, human, and technological development. As Prime Minister Indira Gandhi noted in 1970, barring agriculture, transportation and communication, and certain areas of manufacturing, "the nation has not secured sufficient returns from the quantitative expansion of scientific research and education" (quoted by Nayudamma and Singh 1976, 48–49). Although there were persistent attempts at institutional redesign for correcting this (see Visvanathan 1985; Anderson 2010), the problem had deeper roots in India's policy of economic development through import substitution industrialization—that is, through reducing imports of finished goods and replacing them with domestic production often based on imported technologies.

Import substitution industrialization, combined with the regulation of industrial and commercial activity through permits and quotas, effectively offered no incentives for technological innovation, as India's domestic industry was shielded from competition from within and without. Different elements of the policy, such as import duties, state investment in capital-intensive, heavy industries, and licensing of industries in the consumer goods section, allowed a few business houses to dominate the private sector by purchasing off-the-shelf machinery and technologies from abroad, without any significant investment in research and development (Chibber 2003). Consequently, industrial research undertaken by public institutions had few takers. As Y. Nayudamma, then the director general of the CSIR and one of India's most perspicacious science policy makers, observed, in an essay co-authored with Baldev Singh (1976, 47):

> While the Scientific Policy Resolution resulted in a positive and dynamic approach by the Government towards promotion of science education, training of scientific and technical manpower in India and abroad, [and] setting up of sophisticated R&D infrastructure and facilities, their role in promotion of industrial

> development . . . remained largely undefined, and in practice uncommitted. In the absence of any rapport or effective communication with R&D set up, the industrial and technical development became oriented to looking towards, and dependent upon, readily available sources of production technologies abroad. A paradoxical situation emerged that . . . massive investments in science and technology remained non-productive in terms of their non-conversion into visible industrial production [even as] massive industrial growth took place reflecting . . . patterns and technological characteristics of the advanced countries and interlinked with sources of its origin overseas.

As a remedy, the Indira Gandhi government established the Department of Science and Technology (DST) in 1971. Reducing India's "foreign dependence" for technology and achieving self-reliance was one of the key mandates of the DST, as outlined in the Science and Technology Plan of the Fifth Five Year Plan, 1974–79. Also important was the desire to create enabling conditions for Indian scientists to participate in national development efforts and to stem their migration to foreign countries.

Divergent Designs for State-Led Biotechnology

In this context, the DST, in its meeting of January 13, 1979, decided to identify focus areas for funding and promotion, on the basis of their capacity to make breakthroughs in science and their relevance to national development.[1] To identify thrust areas for the life sciences, M. G. K. Menon called for a meeting of about forty-five practicing biologists at Baroda on September 9, 1980. As the secretary of the Department of Environment and the DST and the director general of the CSIR simultaneously, Menon was at that point one of India's most powerful and influential science administrators. Jatin Sen told me that he made a passionate case for genetic engineering at this meeting, to which Menon responded favorably.

To take the recommendations of this meeting forward, Pushpa Bhargava drafted a base paper, titled "Objective of the Proposed Meeting on Working Out the Modus Operandi for Development of Modern Biotechnology in the Country," and forwarded it to Menon. The paper identified "six technologies with immediate prospects." These were "(a) genetic engineering (including interferon technology); (b) immunotechnology; (c) enzyme technology; (d) tissue culture; (e) photosynthesis; and (f) alcohol production." The base paper saw a technological revolution coming:

> It is now widely recognized in the country that modern biology represents an extremely important area on the frontiers of modern science. Recent advances in modern biology have led to the possibility of development of technologies which could play a vital role in transforming our economy and life styles and may, indeed, become a prime determinant for such transformation. . . .
>
> It is also realized that successful development of these technologies in a country like India . . . is also likely to lead to tangible social-economic benefits. Moreover, . . . such a development may aid the change in life styles of our people along directions largely considered as desirable, on a massive scale—for example, by reducing the pollution by making modern factories obsolete, by providing cheap and new kinds of fuel, and by developing new plant species and (say, insect and pest resistant) breeds. Development of expertise in these technologies will also provide an insurance against undesirable impositions in the country.

After making the case for the six technologies, the base paper states that new institutional frameworks are needed to develop the technologies at a substantial scale, and it proposes a few options—namely, a body under the DST, a separate department headed by a person of the rank of secretary to the Government of India, and a public-sector company like the Steel Authority of India Limited.

Competing Proposals

The follow-up meeting was held at the DST on July 28, 1981. It was a high-powered meeting of several new biologists and science administrators. Pushpa M. Bhargava, B. B. Biswas of the Bose Institute, G. P. Talwar of the All India Institute of Medical Sciences, Maharani Chakravorty from the Banaras Hindu University, and Jatin Sen were among those invited. Among science administrators, the deputy director general (crop science) of the ICAR, M. V. Rao, the director general of the Indian Council of Medical Research (ICMR),[2] V. Ramalingaswamy, and G. S. Sidhu of the CSIR were invited, along with M. S. Swaminathan, member (science), Planning Commission, and chairman, Scientific Advisory Committee to the Cabinet (SACC). M. G. K. Menon chaired the meeting.

The precise form to be taken by state investment in biotechnology was at stake in the meeting. Menon was in favor of rapid promotion of biotechnology, but his preferred model was that of a high-level commission on the lines of the Atomic Energy Commission. The commission-based organizational structure was an innovation of Menon's mentor, Homi J. Bhabha (see Anderson 2010) and had been implemented in India's space, atomic energy, and electronics programs. The most forceful case for heavy organizational and financial commitment came from Bhargava. Whatever the organizational model, he thought that it was important to integrate support to individual scientists for R&D along with major investment in infrastructure for industrial production, particularly in the areas of agriculture (for designing new varieties of plants and food crops), medicine (for vaccine development), chemicals, metallurgy, and environment. He envisaged a corporation with about five thousand people working under ten top-level scientists, and an investment of about 400–500 million rupees for the first four to five years.

Others, however, had a more modest vision. For instance, before any discussion of corporations took place, Sen wanted simplified procedures for customs duty exemption on basic chemicals, reagents, and other perishable items necessary for new biological research. He emphasized the need for strengthening programs for training and manpower building in biotechnology through university programs under the University Grants Commission (UGC). S. Ramachandran of Bengal Immunities felt that it was necessary to identify specific products and estimate the return on investment before going ahead with corporations. And M. V. Rao of the ICAR, a wheat breeder involved with the Green Revolution, called for a bank for microbial (type) cultures and for strengthening of training programs and existing centers, and he cautioned against corporations diverting funds away from existing centers.

New biologists sought state investment for a range of motivations. They were keen to achieve self-reliance and to make a name for India and Indians in the emerging field. There were also more practical considerations. New biologists across the country were facing problems of paucity of foreign exchange, reagents, and consumables, which could not be resolved laboratory by laboratory. These problems required a state-coordinated response. To justify state investment, new biologists had to show wide and significant applications aligned with the goals of government policy making, namely, societal transformation and technology-based development. There was much vagueness about how new biology might actualize its potential, however. This was partly because new biologists had preferred not to dirty their hands with practical issues of product development, and partly because the people who called the shots in the meeting were science administrators rather than practicing new biologists.

Both the commission structure and Bhargava's proposal for an R&D-cum-production unit implied a top-down centralized approach to launching biotechnology-based industries. The problem was that there were no clear products or industrial applications to organize production around, as S. Ramachandran pointed out. Sen's proposal was modest in that it required government intervention only to the extent of facilitating imports of chemicals and launching education programs in universities, while the ICAR's M. V. Rao's proposal was even more tepid.

The decisive vote in the meeting was cast by Swaminathan, the most senior attendee. Swaminathan called for strengthening support to individual scientists and a major intervention in the education sector to train teachers and to introduce biotechnology in university curricula. In terms of organization, he proposed an interagency body with representation from the Finance Ministry for raising funds and coordinating efforts. He suggested that this body be headed by the chairman of the SACC,[3] Swaminathan himself, and offered to take this idea up for approval with the Cabinet of Ministers. Perhaps because Swaminathan was the most powerful government functionary at the meeting, the consensus veered toward his less-than-ambitious proposal. This came as a deep disappointment to Bhargava. In July 2014, when I met Bhargava in Hyderabad, he told me that he had taken up this matter separately with Swaminathan after the meeting. Swaminathan had at that point told him that since he was leaving for Manila in 1982 as the director of the International Rice Research Institute, this was the best he could do. Thus, at the Indian Science Congress of 1982 in Mysore, Prime Minister Indira Gandhi announced the establishment of the National Biotechnology Board (NBTB) within the DST.

The NBTB and the Formation of the Department of Biotechnology

The NBTB was a body mandated "to coordinate, identify and oversee priority areas of development and planning and build up required manpower and infrastructure development and large scale use of high technology products and processes in the multidisciplinary areas of biotechnology."[4] Organizationally, it was set up as an inter-agency body, exactly as Swaminathan had proposed. The directors general of the CSIR, ICAR, and ICMR, secretary of the Department of Atomic Energy, and chairman of the UGC were members of the board. For quick execution of the board's decisions, the secretary (expenditure) of the Ministry of Finance was also made a member. The board was headed by the chairman of the SACC, and the secretary of the DST was appointed the vice chairman. S. Ramachandran, mentioned earlier, was made the member-secretary, with the rank of additional secretary to the government. Each agency represented on the board was requested to commit 5 to 10 million rupees to the board annually, and in the first year of its establishment, NBTB had a budget of about 50 million rupees, with the promise of 250 million rupees over the subsequent three years.

While a detailed account of the NBTB's activities is beyond the scope of the chapter,[5] efforts were initiated in infrastructure development, including centralized import of restriction enzymes and biochemicals, as well as in setting up indigenous production facilities for the same. Second, training workshops for scientists were organized in existing research centers. For instance, B. B. Biswas's laboratory received 200,000 rupees to conduct a course on organization and cloning of plant genes. Graduate and postdoctoral programs in biotechnology were instituted in several universities, including the Jawaharlal Nehru University, Madurai Kamraj University, University of Poona, some of the Indian Institutes of Technology, and Jatin Sen's university. The NBTB also initiated junior and senior fellowships for scientists in India to pursue training at Indian and foreign institutions. Through such fellowships, many junior and senior scientists got to travel to leading centers of new biology in India and the West to learn techniques such as plant tissue culture, rDNA technology, and animal embryo transfer technology. Third, the NBTB also successfully lobbied the United Nations Industrial Development Organization (UNIDO) to establish a component of the International Centre for Genetic Engineering and Biotechnology in India. Fourth, the NBTB provided funding for research projects. By reappropriating some of the funds pledged to the NBTB, the ICAR established its first institutions for biotechnology.[6] The Indian Agricultural Research Institute (IARI) got the Biotechnology Centre in 1985, which became the National Research Centre for Plant Biotechnology (NRCPB), administratively separate from the IARI, in 1996. The ICAR set up two other centers at the Indian Veterinary Research Institute in Izatnagar and the National Dairy Research Institute in Karnal. V. L. Chopra, then a professor of genetics and plant breeding at the IARI, became the first head of the Biotechnology Centre, and under his leadership the center targeted improvements in crops like chickpeas and mustard through approaches such as mutagenesis, somaclonal variation, and rDNA techniques.[7] Finally, the NBTB also initiated work on safety guidelines for rDNA research.[8]

The spending pattern of the NBTB in 1984–85, reported in Table 1, indicates the relative priorities of some of these areas. This is from a total budget of 86 million rupees. The biggest outlays were for initiating graduate programs in a few universities and importing and domestically manufacturing enzymes, reagents, and radio-labeled nucleotides

Table 1. Allocation of Funds by the NBTB, 1984-85

Funding Head	*Expenditure in Indian rupees (millions)*[a]
Training programs and courses in universities[b]	37.5
Synthesis and application of oligonucleotides and biochemicals[c]	7.9
Infrastructure[d]	3.0
Research[e]	0.084
Total	48.484

a. The figures are compiled from the annual report of the DST, 1984–85.

b. Includes funds to universities for strengthening multidisciplinary teaching and training for biotechnology.

c. Funds were disbursed to the Centre for Biochemicals, IISc Bangalore, and Delhi University.

d. For the Regional Experimental Animal House at the National Institute of Nutrition Hyderabad.

e. For projects at Delhi University on tissue culture of bamboo and Madurai Kamaraj University on bacterial pesticides.

for biotechnological research. Effectively, the NBTB formalized and bureaucratically organized the import and grafting of the experimental system of new biology, which scientists like Jatin Sen had done on an individual basis earlier. Crucially, the NBTB concerned itself basically with funding research and teaching, without any coordinated attempt to translate the research into practical innovations. This is not a statement of intent. Rather, the interagency board, staffed by administrators and bureaucrats removed from the world of practicing scientists, was structurally limited to disbursing funds.

This led Bhargava, among others, to complain that the NBTB was inadequate to the task of launching biotechnology in a big way in India.[9] For one thing, agencies and departments committing money to the board were then reappropriating the same to fund biotechnology in their own institutions, which resulted in a piecemeal, uncoordinated approach. For another, Bhargava felt that the structure of the NBTB—staffed by secretaries and directors general—excluded the very people and organizations at the front line of biotechnological research, and in any case the board was subservient to the authority of the secretary of the DST. Partly because of these considerations, in February 1986 Prime Minister Rajiv Gandhi elevated the NBTB to a full-fledged Department of Biotechnology, the first of its kind in the world.

The Constitution of Biotechnology as a Bureaucratic Field of Administration

Unlike statutory boards (such as the Central Board of Direct Taxes and the Central Pollution Control Board), the NBTB was a transient fix proposed by Swaminathan to launch a new technological initiative without the heavy lifting involved in establishing a full-fledged federal department or a public-sector corporation.[10] Once established, however, the limits of this model quickly became apparent, which led to its elevation to the more familiar federal department.

With the establishment of the Biotechnology Department, there were a series of administrative changes. The member-secretary of the board was promoted to the rank of secretary to the Government of India—this post was assumed by S. Ramachandran after it was offered to Bhargava. As a department, it was able to make its own budget, deal directly with the Planning Commission and the Finance Ministry for getting it approved, and enjoy a direct line to the prime minister and the Cabinet. It was also able to join the Committee of Secretaries as an equal and exercise a direct channel to the Cabinet secretary.[11] The Biotechnology Department's budget increased from about 180 million rupees in 1986–87 to about 330 million rupees in 1987–88. This was, by way of comparison, about 21 percent of the entire budget of the DST in the same year (about 1.55 billion rupees).

Following the creation of a new department, the government had to amend the Allocation of Business Rules, which define and demarcate the mandate and jurisdiction of federal ministries and departments. Department officers were quite keen to take charge of the entire field of biotechnology within the Government of India. P. K. Ghosh, who had been with the department since the 1980s and retired as a very senior officer in 2002, told me: "We decided that, first of all, we should become the administrative [department] in the government for biotechnology, for all activities; otherwise no one will listen to us."[12]

This was done through an amendment to the Government of India (Allocation of Business) Rules 1961.[13] According to the amended rules, the Biotechnology Department was charged with, among other things:

- Identifying, setting up, and supporting centers of excellence for research and development in biotechnology
- Acting as a screening, advising, and approving agent for the government with regard to importing and transferring of new technologies for the manufacture of biological and biotechnological products and their intermediaries
- Acting as the central agency for the import of genetically manipulated materials, cultures, cells, specimens, tissues, and biotech products, including DNA and RNA of any type or size and for promoting their production in the country

In terms of programs and initiatives, the department continued the work of the NBTB but with more resources and greater authority. For instance, it took over the Centres for Genetic Engineering at Sen's university, the Bose Institute, and the Indian Institute of Science from the DST, as well as the National Institute of Immunology. Along with the fellowships and research programs it was already supporting as a board, the department initiated some new technology missions, such as one on oilseeds.

What was more momentous was the constitution of biotechnology as an arena of bureaucratic administration. Not only did the shift from an interagency board to a department allow biotechnology administrators greater play in policy making, but it also restrained them in ways that they did not anticipate. I explore two cases to illustrate the point.

New Industrial Policy of 1991

In 1991, as the P. V. Narasimha Rao government was contemplating liberalization of the economy, the Biotechnology Department issued a proposal to classify seed production as an industrial activity. Ghosh discussed this with me:

P. K. GHOSH: Agriculture was not considered an industrial activity, and we were thinking that it should be. Otherwise, agricultural activities will not be eligible for loans. . . . We thought agriculture will not progress like this.

ANIKET AGA: By agriculture what do you mean?

P. K. GHOSH: Seed production, [a] very important activity. I'd written a paper [in which] we had said that . . . all said and done, the genome of the plant contributes to 50 percent of [yield]. All factors remaining the same, the genetic trait is actually the basic backbone for increasing production. Then you give fertilizer, pesticides, water, etc. . . . Therefore, if hereditary material is available in a highly productive form, then that will make agriculture very highly productive. So . . . we thought that [developing] hybrid seeds, highly productive varieties must be treated as [an] indus-

> trial activity. . . . Besides producing hybrid seeds and varieties by sexual reproduction, we can also produce plants by plant tissue culture in a lab. So therefore plant tissue culture activity . . . should also be considered as [an] industrial activity. So this industry will grow very fast, and . . . hence agriculture will be benefited.
>
> So we made a proposal. Dr. Ramachandran . . . liked this idea. We floated a paper [saying] that [producing] hybrid [and] high-yielding seeds and plant-tissue culture activities should be [classified] as an industrial activity. This was accepted by the government. . . . This was a big success for us."[14]

Curiously, in the paper he mentioned, Ghosh (1997) did not offer any evidence for the claim that the plant genome was responsible for 50 percent of the yield. He presented the claim as a hypothesis backed by experience.

In any case, the seed sector was already being liberalized in small steps, through first the Industrial Licensing Policy of 1987, then the New Policy on Seed Development 1988, and then the Plants, Fruits and Seeds Order 1989 (Rao 2004; Kolady, Spielman, and Cavalieri 2010). This was happening against the backdrop of the Uruguay round of multilateral trade negotiations. To expand and consolidate the General Agreement on Tariffs and Trade, the precursor of the World Trade Organization, Northern countries were pressuring India and other Southern countries to open up agriculture and other sectors to foreign investment, intellectual property regimes, and global trade. The policy changes in the seed sector in India sparked misgivings within the ICAR (Sharma 1994, 60), but they sailed through with the backing of the Commerce and Industry ministries and, as Ghosh recounted, the Biotechnology Department. The "big success" for the department led those industries concerned with "high-yielding hybrid seeds," "synthetic seeds," and "certified high-yielding plantlets developed through plant tissue culture" to receive automatic approvals for foreign technology agreements and for 51 percent foreign equity partnerships (Ministry of Industry 1991, Annex III). These interventions proved crucial for reshaping the terrain of agricultural research in India. They allowed India's domestic seed industry, which was rather small at that point, to partner with transnational agribusinesses like Monsanto for technology sharing and financial investment, shoring up their market position.

The Entry of Monsanto's Bt Cotton into India

Genetically modified cotton is the third-most cultivated transgenic crop in the world, in terms of acreage, after soybeans and maize (ISAAA 2017). In India, the private company Mahyco partnered with Monsanto to release insect-resistant Bt cotton in 2002, and within a few years Bt cotton occupied over 90 percent of cotton farms. Indeed, India leads the world as far as land area planted with GM cotton goes (ISAAA 2017). For a variety of reasons, including the fact that India has one of the largest numbers of small landholders growing Bt cotton, the performance of Bt cotton has attracted considerable controversy and popular and scholarly scrutiny, which is of global interest (Herring and Rao 2012; Stone 2012; Kranthi and Stone 2020). That said, this is not the place to delve into the multiple facets of the controversy.[15]

What concerns this chapter is a brief episode when Monsanto tried to partner with the Indian government to release Bt cotton before it struck an alliance with Mahyco. Around 1991, before Bt cotton received approval for commercial release in the United States, Monsanto reached out to the federal Ministry of Agriculture. At that time Monsanto was in a position of weakness and hence willing to bargain. A retired senior officer of the Biotechnology Department who was closely involved with the negotiations told me that the Biotechnology

Department was very keen on the proposal, as was the minister for science and technology, P. Rangarajan Kumaramangalam.[16] The minister for agriculture, Balram Jakhar, a politician representing large-holder farmers in Punjab, was also eager to push the deal through. The debilitating opposition came, however, from the unlikeliest of quarters. V. L. Chopra, the first head of IARI's Biotechnology Centre, had by then become the director general of the ICAR. At that point Monsanto was asking for U.S. $16 million along with about 7.5 percent royalty for approximately eight years, which Chopra found too steep. After multiple rounds of negotiation with Monsanto, the Biotechnology Department went back to Chopra with a final request for U.S. $2 million and the additional guarantee that Monsanto would train Indian scientists in the development of transgenic crops after a few years. In 1991 U.S. $2 million would have translated to about 50 million rupees. Chopra dismissed the offer and instead asked the Biotechnology Department for a much smaller sum, with which, he claimed, the ICAR would develop the same transgenic product. The deal fell through.

M. S. Swaminathan introduced Mahyco's founder, B. R. Barwale, to Monsanto around 1993 (Damodaran 2017). Mahyco sought to capitalize on the deal ICAR had refused. Around 1994–95 it negotiated an agreement with Monsanto to introduce the latter's Bt gene in its proprietary cotton hybrids. For this, Mahyco needed to import 3.5 ounces (100 grams) of Monsanto's Coker-312 transgenic variety of cotton. Under the New Policy on Seed Development 1988, mentioned earlier, any import of seeds required clearance by the office of the Plant Protection Adviser under the recommendation of the Department of Agriculture and Cooperation (DAC) of the Ministry of Agriculture. This is where Mahyco got stuck. The New Policy on Seed Development is silent on transgenic seeds, and so none of the import rules applied to Coker-312. The DAC stalled the matter by refusing to give permission. At this point, Mahyco approached the Biotechnology Department, and a very high-ranking officer (who wishes to remain unnamed) along with the secretary decided on their own to issue the permission for import.[17] They did not consult the federal Ministry of Environment and Forests either, whose rules governed imports of genetically modified organisms (GMOs). Mahyco thus used this permission granted in 1995, beginning the process by which transgenic Bt cotton was officially released in India in 2002, through private companies, rather than through the public research system. By 1998 Monsanto had acquired a 26 percent stake in Mahyco. In multiple ways, the bureaucratic consolidation of biotechnology as a federal department had ramifications far beyond the preoccupations of new biologists.

The Transformation of Scientific Authority into Bureaucratic Administration

The base paper that Bhargava had prepared for the meeting in July 1981 defined biotechnology in terms of six techniques and processes, such as genetic transformation. As Ramachandran had observed in the meeting, essentially these were cell-culture techniques with applications in a wide variety of areas—from agriculture and pharmaceuticals to environment. The decision to govern biotechnology through a federal department was an outcome of many contingencies. But once the decision was made, the conditions in which the Biotechnology Department began decisively inflected the course of biotechnology. The elevation to a federal department certainly granted biotechnology administrators greater power, prestige, and autonomy, but it also hemmed them in ways that they had not bargained for.

Once the NBTB became a department, it was subject to a very different order of scrutiny and procedural propriety. Its budget proposals were reviewed and vetted by the Parliament, and it had to work with the Finance and other ministries as an equal to push its proposals through; this is where it was caught on unfamiliar terrain. In amending the Allocation of Business Rules, the government handed over "biotechnology" to the Biotechnology Department. But agriculture, medicine, and environment belonged to other ministries—the Ministry of Agriculture, the Ministry of Health and Family Welfare, and the Ministry of Environment and Forests. In effect, biotechnologists gained a department on a par with others but in the bargain lost the interagency structure that could have more easily resolved conflicts.

In the case of a deal with Monsanto for Bt cotton, its proposal was blocked outright by Chopra, the director general of ICAR. Even decades after the incident, the former officer of the Biotechnology Department I spoke to exuded frustration and sadness at Chopra's unrelenting opposition. Nevertheless, what is analytically significant is how the transformation from an interagency board to a line department fostered and circumscribed its capacity to influence policy decisions. As a line department, the Biotechnology Department could no longer make decisions in the same manner as it could when it was an interagency board run by a small group of elite scientists and science administrators. The transformation into a department embedded biotechnology in a structure that mediated relations with other arms of the government (federal, state, and local departments and agencies) and industry bureaucratically, through a legal-administrative separation of powers and mandates. The relatively unfettered authority and room for discretion available to the NBTB owing to its direct line to the prime minister (through the SACC) and the Planning Commission (through the member for science) was considerably hemmed in with its elevation to a federal department. Had Monsanto's proposal come before the board, both Chopra and the officer would have had to make their cases before a peer group of scientists. More crucially, the member for science and the chairman of the SACC, who were senior to the director general of ICAR, would be in a position to resist Chopra's opposition and persuade him to come around to a different point of view.

The back-and-forth between Monsanto and the Biotechnology Department on the one hand, and the department and the Ministry of Agriculture on the other, was very different. The Biotechnology Department held sway over matters of biotechnology, but not over agricultural science, over which the ICAR's authority was supreme. This distinction may not make much sense when one thinks of GM crops, but they were administratively two separate realms and, thus, neither the secretary of the Biotechnology Department nor the ministers concerned could force Chopra to budge. Whereas earlier decisions could be made by consensus within a close-knit group of scientists, now every decision was mediated through a bureaucratic structure involving formal proposals, interdepartmental memos, interministerial committees to iron out differences, firm limits to the administrative mandate of any particular department, and overall coordination provided not by a group of peer scientists, but by nonexperts in the Union Cabinet.

Around 1995, when Mahyco's proposal to import Bt cottonseeds from Monsanto was stalled by the Ministry of Agriculture, the Biotechnology Department came to its rescue by issuing the permit. The high-ranking officer told me that he had taken a huge risk in granting the permission, sidestepping the Ministry of Agriculture and without consulting the Ministry of Environment and Forests. He had the secretary's support, but this was very much a decision made by the two officers without consulting the minister or anyone else. In 1999, when the activist Vandana Shiva filed India's first public interest litigation (PIL) before the Supreme Court on GM crops, questioning the legality of the entire process by which Mahyco's Bt cotton was approved, the officer recalled feeling worried that he might go to jail for issuing the permission letter.

That the department issued the permission without having framed rules or formally designated officers to approve imports suggests that senior officers continued to exercise discretion and authority as if they were still running an interagency board. Well into a decade of its existence, the department betrayed discomfort and unfamiliarity with working bureaucratic channels and levers—such as formally allocating responsibilities, recording decisions on paper with appropriate justifications, placing ("putting up" in bureaucratic parlance) matters before senior officers of the department, and then pursuing them with parallel departments.

Because the Allocation of Business Rules made the Biotechnology Department the agency for approving imports of "biotechnological products," his fears did not come true. The distinction, in this case specious, between seeds (overseen by the Ministry of Agriculture) and "biotechnological products" (overseen by the Biotechnology Department) allowed the latter to bypass the former, and Bt cotton was finally brought to India. By 1996, however, Monsanto had received approval for the commercial release of Bt cotton in the United States. When it struck a deal with Mahyco to transfer the Bt gene into Mahyco's proprietary cotton hybrids, Monsanto was in a considerably stronger position and demanded stiff payment terms, which Indian farmers and companies have had to pay.

Carving Out Biotechnology from Agriculture

In the seeds sector, the Biotechnology Department's push for liberalization, aided by other line ministries, enabled technology collaborations, mergers and acquisitions, and equity arrangements between the domestic seed industry and transnational corporations such as

Monsanto. The Biotechnology Department pushed for liberalization in response more to its own perception of a technology and innovation deficit in the seeds sector than to demands from private agribusiness capital. The resulting changes helped galvanize India's fledgling domestic seed industry, which grew from nine to forty companies in the period 1985–95.

Additionally, the department's efforts in the arena of education led to the emergence of a class of biotechnologists in the country—students in regular universities and agricultural universities who had taken their undergraduate or graduate (including doctoral) training in biotechnology. The creation of a class of biotechnologists generated its own pressure on the state science complex and the government to create employment opportunities for them and to showcase their talent and achievements.

The Biotechnology Department tried to get private industry to absorb the burgeoning number of biotechnologists. Still, when it took stock of its manpower program in 1994, it found that of the 878 students admitted to its graduate and postdoctoral programs between 1986 and 1992, 283 (32 percent) were working as research fellows in universities and government agencies and 79 (9 percent) had gone abroad for further education. Indian industry employed 99 (11 percent), 52 (6 percent) were employed by the government, and 21 (2 percent) were working abroad. In essence, the department's programs at various institutes and the government itself were absorbing a large chunk of the manpower.[18]

In parallel, through visiting fellowships and training programs, the department had also created a class of scientists trained in molecular biological techniques. Since there was no corresponding investment in upstream research, these scientists were equipped with tissue culture or rDNA techniques but had no background in the upstream work of gene discovery or the downstream work of varietal release.

They were trained in transforming plants, but they lacked the genes and constructs to do so, on the one hand, and the breeding skills to develop varieties and hybrids, on the other.

As far as agricultural research is concerned, the Biotechnology Department, over time, effectively became a parallel structure to the ICAR, involved in training scientists and setting research priorities divorced from the latter. Given the excitement about biotechnology and its messianic promises, research priorities even within the ICAR shifted as a consequence of this parallel structure—both because biotechnologists were being recruited by the ICAR and because of funding available from the department. As P. K. Ghosh (1997, 25) wrote in an article:

> During 1989–97, nearly Rs. 270 million or nearly 4% of its total budget was spent by [the Biotechnology Department] alone on plant molecular biology research, where the projects primarily focused on developing transgenic plants of higher economic value. There had also been marginal support from the Indian Council of Agricultural Research, Department of Science & Technology, Council of Scientific and Industrial Research and certain other agencies. The combined expenditure of all these agencies would not exceed Rs. 70 million. The private sector units have started allocating some funds during the last three years and their investment could be estimated to be of the order of Rs. 100 million.

Thus, 61 percent of the total funding for transgenics research came from the Biotechnology Department. In essence, India's GM agriculture program was being built by the department, not private seed companies and certainly not the ICAR, and it was the department that facilitated private-sector initiative in GM cottonseeds.

This marked a striking contrast to the United States, where, in roughly the same period, university-industry relationships took the lead in biotechnology. These were spurred by a conducive policy environment, which allowed university faculty to commercialize some of their federally funded research through startups and public universities to set up for-profit corporations, among other arrangements to commercialize biotechnology (Busch et al. 1991; Thackray 1998). The *Diamond v. Chakrabarty* ruling by the U.S. Supreme Court in 1981, which allowed genetically modified microorganisms to be patented, gave a further fillip to private investments in biotechnology (Kevles 1994; Berman 2008). In a perceptive study, Kaushik Sunder Rajan (2006) explains the divergence between United States and India in terms of a cultural difference between messianic and nationalist biotechnology programs, respectively. To my mind, historical contingencies underlie the difference in cultural emphasis. New biology in the United States emerged with private philanthropic funds, bearing the promise to fundamentally transform society and human relations (Kay 1993), and it was consolidated through industry-university partnerships. In most other countries, there was no agency other than the state to launch biotechnology programs. Specifically in the case of India, the NBTB, which was itself a contingent outcome, and the Biotechnology Department channeled the transnational excitement about biotechnology into the Indian research system, aligning it with the state's commitment to national development. In the process, the department ended up reordering research priorities in agriculture.

The Foundation of the Biotechnology-Backed Revolution

The rise of the Biotechnology Department thus furthered a trend that had been in motion since the 1970s—the slow disinvestment in agriculture (Frankel 2005; Jha and Acharya 2011) and the centralization and ossification of public agricultural research (Rajeswari 1995; Raina 2011). The underlying factors are too complex for an adequate treatment here. Briefly, the success of the Green Revolution spawned a class of commercial farmers in a few pockets of India who were able to launch movements on the basis of their interests and skew public agricultural budgets toward subsidies and procurement prices rather than capital formation (Mishra and Chand 1995). Agricultural research, consequently, became concerned with narrow problems of aggregate food production and supply, rice, wheat, and a few other crops being the dominant focus. Further, state governments progressively lost the capacity to direct agricultural research to their specific agro-ecological and sociopolitical circumstances, as the federal ICAR began to set the tone and content of research programs nationally. The issues of poverty; hunger; unequal, caste-based access to land, water, credit, and other inputs; and unemployment—the tenacious difficulties experienced by the vast majority of Indian farmers—disappeared from the horizon of agricultural research (Raina 2011).

Instead, these became issues to be tackled by programs of rural development, which were initially housed within the Agriculture Ministry but shifted to an independent ministry after 1979.[19] The separation of the rural development bureaucracy effectively deflected concerns of equity and redistribution from programs of agricultural development. Equally significant was the establishment of the federal Ministry of Food Processing in 1988, to cater to the output of commercially oriented farmers in Punjab and other Green Revolution areas, and to create employment opportunities in rural areas. Conversely, concerns about agricultural research became marginal to and dissociated from programs of community welfare, rural infrastructure, and employment. Thus, the prongs of the critiques of the Green Revolution, such as the increasing regional inequality and the worsening of the lot of agricultural laborers and tenant farmers

(Agarwal and Narain 1985), became issues for building constituencies through rural development programs, rather than agenda points for reorienting agricultural research.

More broadly, the intensified political ferment in India after the 1970s galvanized new constituencies and brought new problems to the fore for political resolution. The rising profiles of the Rural Development and Food Processing ministries were responses to the growing power of agrarian populism, mobilized by the beneficiaries of the Green Revolution (Balagopal 1985; Brass 1995). This was, in part, the economic crisis of the 1980s, which paved the way for liberalization (Balagopal 1992). Similarly, and with profound consequences for the GM debate, as later chapters highlight, the growing clout of elite conservationists during Indira Gandhi's later years as prime minister (Rangarajan 2009) was reflected in the sweeping regulatory powers available to the federal Ministry of Environment and Forests, established in 1985. In parallel, science administrators exercised considerable influence through Prime Minister Indira Gandhi, which led to the establishment of new scientific departments such as the Department of Electronics, the DST, and the Biotechnology Department. The subsequent Rajeev Gandhi government launched National Technology Missions in telecommunications, among others (Mukherji 2014).

In effect, nothing less than a refashioning of the idea of the public good and development was at stake, as new ministries like those for biotechnology, environment and forests, food processing, and rural development rose to prominence and older ministries, such as that for agriculture, lost ground. Though contingencies like Prime Minister Indira Gandhi's support of scientists such as Swaminathan and Menon did play a role, ultimately, the very working of democracy led to the emergence of new constituencies and the political necessity to accommodate their demands (Balagopal 1992). The humdrum details of bureaucratic governance detailed in this chapter, in fact, over time reconfigured the state in far-reaching ways and, in the agricultural realm, laid the foundation for the biotechnology-backed Evergreen Revolution. These bureaucratic shifts constituted the conditions of possibility for biotechnology in India, and they continue to shape and limit its agenda.

On separate occasions, three retired high-ranking officers of the Biotechnology Department told me that they considered Bt cotton their greatest professional success. The Bt cotton they referred to is not the public-sector Bt cotton, but Bt cotton developed by private companies like Mahyco in partnership with Monsanto. And they are not wrong. Barring Mahyco, most seed companies in India in the 1990s were not particularly interested in GM crops, and, until the advent of Bt cotton in India, many of them had not invested in rDNA research. The Biotechnology Department then can rightfully claim credit for creating the conditions for the advent of GM crops into the seed business in India. This suggests that the nature of capital employed in agricultural biotechnology is very much of the staple bureaucrat capital variety (Balagopal 1986) rather than BioCapital (Sunder Rajan 2006). Without suggesting that the entry of Bt cotton into India was inevitable, one can still appreciate how different the trajectory of the GM crop in India would have been had Chopra agreed to partner with Monsanto to release Bt cotton through public institutions, in inexpensive varieties and hybrids.

Whither Democratic Oversight?

In the 1960s a number of chemists undertook higher studies in the West and returned to India with the zeal to establish new biology. In a few decades, they won a high-powered federal department. The Biotechnology Department created a specialized class of "biotechnologists" in India, began to set the priorities of agricultural research in parallel to the ICAR, contributed to the decline of the Agriculture Ministry, played a role in the liberalization of the seeds sector, and, more specifically, helped launch corporate Bt cottonseeds in India. Did policy makers and people outside the government appreciate the long-term significance of the developments shepherded by the department? Did the Biotechnology Department have an overt mandate from the public or lawmakers for the changes it wrought?

There was not much media attention to these policy changes. Praful Bidwai, the left-leaning science reporter, was one of the few writing about biotechnology in the 1980s. His articles written in 1983 recognized the potential of biotechnology to revamp agriculture and industry, even as he worried about the potential for corporate takeover of agriculture and food (Bidwai 1983a, 1983b). They also offer sharp criticisms of the biotechnology program for diverting funds into research areas that had no base in India, for aping trends in the West, and for seeing biotechnology as a "socially, no-side-effects panacea for the ills of underdevelopment, especially in agriculture" (Bidwai 1983c).

Within the circle of agricultural scientists, there were anxieties about biotechnology overshadowing broader agricultural research.[20] For instance, at a symposium on agricultural applications of biotechnology organized at Madras in 1986, the plant breeder M. H. Arnold[21] (1987, 4, 8–9) observed: "Caution must be exercised to ensure that resources devoted to molecular biology are not permitted to distort the overall balance of a breeding programme. . . . Indeed, most plant breeders, who have been exposed to recent research in recombinant DNA, would argue that it would be a mistake to attempt to incorporate these new technologies into a breeding programme until the resource requirements of current approaches have been fully met. The new techniques should be seen as additional, but expensive, tools for the plant breeder, not as a substitute for established methodology."

At the same time, Y. Nayudamma devoted what ended up being the last years of his life thinking about biomass-based industrialization as a platform for addressing unemployment, poverty, and ecological degradation, on the one hand, and enlarging the circle of technical innovation and knowledge production beyond scientists and technical experts to include the working masses, on the other. Because these cautionary notes and imaginative ideas were articulated from outside the Biotechnology Department, they failed to influence its orientation; precisely because of the way biotechnology and agriculture were administratively structured and their mandates demarcated, these concerns ended up falling outside their focus.

But what about political leaders—the Cabinet, the Parliament—who were, in different ways, responsible for ensuring coordination between departments, harmonizing their goals and steering them? The evidence suggests that politicians' grasp of what was being pushed in the name of biotechnology was quite limited. In fact, ironically, there was a persistent confusion between biotechnology and the work done by agricultural scientists and plant breeders. At the inauguration of the Fifteenth International Congress of Genetics at New Delhi in 1983, Prime Minister Indira Gandhi described the possibilities of genetic engineering as both "fascinating and frightening," and then went on to talk about new varieties of wheat, cotton, and sugarcane (*Times of India* 1983). In effect, she credited biotechnology with the achievements of plant breeders.

The few times questions were asked about biotechnology in the Parliament, Cabinet ministers in their replies committed the same folly of talking about improved varieties and hybrids—precisely the things that new biologists wanted to distance themselves from. The starkest illustration of the promise as well as confusion surrounding biotechnology occurred in the Rajya Sabha (the upper house of the Parliament) in the Monsoon Session of 1987, in the exchange between

K. Vasudeva Panicker (a member of Parliament) and Shivraj Patil, minister of state for Defence Production and Supplies in the Defence Ministry. Panicker had asked if the government proposed to set up what he called "biotechnology information" in the country and, if so, what might be its main functions and objectives. The question was directed toward Prime Minister Rajiv Gandhi, who held the science and technology portfolio, but Shivraj Patil answered on Gandhi's behalf and quickly landed on unfamiliar turf. On the question of priority areas for biotechnology, Patil answered:

> Biotechnology is one of the very important technologies in the world today. It is going to be helpful to us in agriculture in the areas of health, in industry and in many other areas. Initially, we are emphasizing on biotechnology which is relevant to the health. We want to emphasize on the study of biotechnology which will be useful to agriculture but at the same time, we are trying to study biotechnology which is pertinent to the industry also. Emphasis, however, is going to be on health and agriculture and there would be some study in the field of industry also.[22]

Unfortunately, despite the repetition of health, industry, and agriculture thrice in different formulations, the House was still not satisfied. Patil's answer piqued the curiosity of another member of Parliament, Vishwa Bandhu Gupta, who perhaps felt that Patil had not been specific enough. So Gupta interjected, asking whether there were plans for the "future development in [outer] space" of biotechnology. Patil answered, "Biotechnology is relevant for the space also because when the human beings go into the space, what effect the conditions available in the space have on the human body is also studied." Patil is to be thanked for phrasing this last sentence in the passive voice. Evidently, senior politicians and the Parliament had much less of a handle on science policy, and larger forces being set into motion through it, than they perhaps had had in Prime Minister Nehru's time (see Phalkey 2013).

In the 1960s India's Ministry of Agriculture undertook the Green Revolution. About two decades later, as the forces unleashed by the Green Revolution brought about a churn in politics in different parts of the country, older ministries went into decline and new ministries rose to prominence. The Biotechnology Department thus confronted and contributed to a rapidly changing political economy, a political order unable to reconcile the demands of different sections of society,[23] and a state unable to frame policies for the long term (Kaviraj 1986; Mishra and Chand 1995; Chibber 2003). The limited mandate of biotechnology, its administrative separation from environment, agriculture, and health, the disarticulation from broader questions concerning the future of agriculture, and its struggle to defend its scientific authority in the face of challenges, the foundation of all of which was laid in the 1980s, became the ingredients of the GM debate that was ignited in the 1990s.

PART TWO

The Government of Biotechnology

4
Regulating GM Crops

The launch of state-funded biotechnology programs was accompanied by concerns among policy makers regarding managing the safety of biotechnological interventions. Regulating biotechnological research and development proved to be much more vexed an issue than promoting the same, for questions of regulatory design in general highlight the broader problem of knowledge in democracy. By *knowledge* I mean the schemes (Scott 1998), practices (Latour 1999), and modes of reasoning (Jasanoff 1995) through which facts—authoritative statements about reality—are produced and defended against rival statements. The process of knowledge production invariably involves valorizing and validating certain claims and methods while discounting others (Sivaramakrishnan 1999). This process, however, does not occur in a historical, social, or ecological vacuum (Uberoi 2002). It has to perforce contend with the subjects and objects of knowledge (Pickering 1995; Knorr Cetina 1999). Thus, the production of knowledge is inherently a fraught enterprise.

In democratic settings, the enterprise acquires added complexity because the process of knowledge production must satisfy not only rigorous standards of proof (however constructed, validated, and accepted), but also equally rigorous standards of public acceptance and trust (Wynne 2007). I use *public* in the way John Dewey (1927, 35) defines the term: the group formed by "those indirectly and seriously affected for good or for evil" by the transactions and activities of two or more actors (human, corporate, or institutional). The concept of *public* is thus more differentiated than *citizens*, and it is flexible enough to accommodate coalitions of actors who may otherwise not share any ascribed identity or social location. Further, the public is by definition a knowledgeable public, insofar as it can discern and anticipate consequences of actions. Building on the idea of folkways, Sheila Jasanoff (2005) conceives of civic epistemology as the shared (knowledge-)ways through which publics produce, evaluate, contest, and accept truth claims. Civic epistemology highlights the culturally embedded, historically shaped modes of reasoning through which people, whether scientists, farmers, activists, or bureaucrats, come to judgments about what and whom to believe—and on what grounds.

In this light, not only divergent interests and positions, but also (and more fundamentally) different civic epistemologies are at stake in scientific controversies in democracies. Indeed, this chapter demonstrates that India's regulatory regime for GM crops, which arose in the late 1980s, fused two civic epistemologies in its working. They interlock and underpin the way government bureaucracies respond to claims and counterclaims made by different groups in the GM debate. Since bureaucracies principally function through paper documents, I locate these epistemologies in modes of documentation: the making of claims through and in written texts. The two kinds of documents are scientific and legal-administrative.

Legal-Administrative versus Scientific Mode of Documentation

We can make an analytic distinction between two kinds of claims that bureaucratic documents make—scientific and legal-administrative. These are idealized poles of a spectrum along which lie most documents. By scientific mode of documentation, I mean the capacity of documents to claim correspondence to matters in the world or, in brief, reality.[1] This enables scientific documents to construct facts while disputing rival facts (Latour 1999, 2004). This is not to suggest some heroic model of science uncovering truths. Rather, it is to recognize the kernel of truth in such oversimplified descriptions: appeals to the world and enrolling agencies therein are critical components of scientific activity, even as it unfolds in a community of peers through power-laden conventions and norms. This is one reason scientific claims do not preclude findings that may contradict them, or findings that may be provisional.

On the other hand, something other than claiming correspondence to matters in the world is at stake in documents such as the official records of the Emergency in Delhi (Tarlo 2001), or the 1975 World Bank report on Lesotho (Ferguson 1990), to take two examples. These documents, which I call legal-administrative, bear a different burden—that of representing claims arising from political or legal considerations irrespective sometimes of their fidelity to corresponding social realities (Mitchell 2002; Mosse 2005). When these documents are generated by the government—when the government is making a claim—often the overriding concern is with representing the view of the state, which is not always coherent or internally consistent. In the best of times, which these are not, a democratic state has multiple objectives, such as promoting the welfare of the people, securing justice, and enabling economic growth, not all of which are mutually compatible. For this reason, appeals to reality are not always critical to, and do not constrain, the production of legal-administrative documents. Nor are legal-administrative disputes settled one way or another through appeals to external truth, even in theory. Rather, the burden of precedent, "pressure" from those in power, due process, borrowing procedures from courtrooms (such as conducting a hearing), and evaluating claims on the basis of other, secondary documents

(Hull 2012; Mathur 2015; Aga and Choudhury 2018) propel the course of such disputes. This is why I call this mode legal-administrative. At the extreme, external reality becomes irrelevant, and it is the file that dictates what is true in the world; for instance, in cases of disputes over mining, government documents commonly falsify or mute the opposition of local peoples (Choudhury 2019; Choudhury and Aga 2020b), and Gupta (2012, 146) reports an officer telling him, "If it is not in the file, it does not exist."

Scientific and legal-administrative modes of documentation both trade in facts, constitute forms of logic and reasoning, and are open to revision and appeal. Nevertheless, the role of historical contingency in constructing truths is a key difference between the two. Legal-administrative claims are deeply beholden to precedent and the burden of evidence existing on a file (Hull 2012). In deciding how to respond to a matter at hand, bureaucrats invariably refer to how their predecessors dealt with similar matters. The decisions made and reasoning adopted by their predecessors constrain how bureaucrats function in the present. Officers are deeply aware that their actions and decisions will become part of a permanent record that will be accessible to other officers, citizens (through the Right to Information Act, 2005), and commissions of inquiry. This awareness casts a long shadow on how officers work and constrains the extent to which they will depart from how their predecessors have thought about an issue. This is also why officers often make notes in the passive voice (see, for example, Raghunandan 2013).

Scientific documents, too, work within epistemic cultures (Knorr Cetina 1999), but they seek to qualify earlier understandings or bring to light previously unknown facts (see Latour 2004), rather than perpetuate those earlier understandings. This tendency is an aspect not only of research publications but, equally, of policy-oriented writings. Pushpa Bhargava's base paper for organizing state-funded biotechnology illustrates this. The base paper is less concerned with the way scientific activity has been organized in the past; it seizes on a new field of knowledge and asks for novel organizational forms. Consequently, the identity of the author of a particular scientific document does not have the same salience as that of a legal-administrative document, as authors expect their writings to be superseded by newer findings, analyses, and facts over time. Legal-administrative and scientific documents thus not only construct and evaluate claims differently, they also differ in the ways they construct bureaucratic memory and the importance they accord to it. The dynamic between scientific and legal-administrative claims animates both the design of the regulatory regime for GMOs in India and some of the most significant challenges to it.

The Split Structure of India's Regulatory Regime for GMOs

The regulatory regime for GMOs in India arose as part of the broader story of the environment becoming an object of law. This happened most intensely from 1972, the year of the United Nations Conference on the Human Environment at Stockholm, to 1986, when India enacted the Environment (Protection) Act (EPA) (Sivaramakrishnan 2011). This was the period in which the federal Department of Environment was instituted within the Government of India (in November 1980), and a series of pollution control statutes, such as the Water and Air Acts,[2] were enacted, culminating in the EPA 1986 (Vyas and Ratna Reddy 1998). Concerns regarding hazardous substances and toxic chemicals, more than statutes for air and water pollution control, shaped the way the Indian government sought to regulate GMOs.

The Scientific Advisory Committee to the Cabinet (SACC) had been instituted on March 12, 1981, under the chairmanship of M. S.

Swaminathan, then the member for science in the Planning Commission. It was a group of elite scientists and science administrators reporting to the federal Cabinet of ministers, and it enjoyed privileged access to the prime minister, especially during Indira Gandhi's tenure. The SACC was keen to evolve a "policy framework relating to import, licensing, usage and distribution of hazardous chemical substances, micro-organisms, etc."[3] By 1982 the SACC had designated the Environment Department as the nodal authority for framing legislation on hazardous chemicals and microorganisms, since the latter was already working on legislation for regulating pollutants. By this time, of course, the National Biotechnology Board had also been established within the federal Department of Science and Technology.

In its first year, the National Biotechnology Board set up the Recombinant DNA Advisory Committee to frame safeguards for rDNA work, which were based on those framed by the National Institutes of Health in the United States. Pushpa Bhargava, Jatin Sen, V. L. Chopra, Joseph Padayatty were members of the committee. As in the American model, guidelines devised by the Advisory Committee asked research institutions to create Institutional Biosafety Committees, comprising in-house and external members, to oversee rDNA research.[4] By 1986 such committees had been created in over forty research institutions.

In 1985 the Department of Environment, along with the Department of Forests, part of the Ministry of Agriculture and Rural Development, was reconstituted as a separate Ministry of Environment and Forests, and the National Biotechnology Board became the Department of Biotechnology in 1986. Consequently, the design of the regulatory regime had to respect the separation of power and responsibilities between the Environment Ministry and the Biotechnology Department. Further, responsibility for regulation also had to be divided across the federal structure of government. Let us consider the split between the Biotechnology Department and the Environment Ministry first.

The Allocation of Business Rules for the Government of India, amended with the establishment of the Biotechnology Department, made the department the nodal agency for biotechnology products and programs and for safety guidelines. At the same time, environmental protection was the mandate of the Environment Ministry, which is the nodal authority for the EPA, 1986—the key federal legislation governing environmental protection in India. After the passage of the EPA, there were protracted deliberations between the Biotechnology Department and the Environment Ministry on regulatory design. Both brought to bear their own preoccupations on this matter. On the one hand, the department was framing safety guidelines through its advisory committees for laboratory best practices. On the other, the ministry was putting together large-scale administrative infrastructure of pollution control boards at the state and federal levels and framing rules for the safe use of toxic chemicals. Further, the character of the Environment Department changed once it became a Ministry. It had been a body staffed and headed largely by scientists and science policy makers. Once it became a separate ministry, however, officers of the elite Indian Administrative Service (IAS), who were generalists rather than specialists, claimed its top positions, arguing with some justification that regulation was both a technical and legal-administrative matter, and it therefore could not be left to scientists alone. Scientific staff continued to serve in the ministry but occupied middle and lower rungs in the hierarchy.

The Environment Ministry and the Biotechnology Department proposed a two-committee model of regulation—the Review Committee on Genetic Manipulation (RCGM), hosted by the department, and the Genetic Engineering Approval Committee (GEAC), hosted by the ministry. The RCGM was tasked with monitoring the safety-related aspects of ongoing research projects and with bringing out manuals and guidelines for regulatory oversight. Its membership comprised representatives from the Biotechnology Department, the ICAR, the Indian Council of Medical Research, and the Council of Scientific and Industrial Research. Further, it could co-opt other experts in their individual capacity. The GEAC, on the other hand, was charged with addressing broader concerns of risk assessment and management. It had the administrative responsibility for authorizing field trials (that is, the cultivation in open fields for research and evaluation purposes) of GM crops, commercial release, and permitting requests to import or export GMOs. It was chaired by an additional secretary of the Environment Ministry, usually an IAS officer. One rung below secretaries, additional secretaries are the second-highest tier of bureaucrats in a federal ministry. A representative of the Biotechnology Department serves as co-chairperson, to ensure coordination between the two bodies and to represent the point of view of the RCGM at the GEAC. In addition, the GEAC includes the directors general of the three councils mentioned above, the chairman of the Central Pollution Control Board, as well as representatives from different ministries and departments, such as Atomic Energy, Industrial Development, and so on. For some years, the directors general and chairpersons have been appointing their nominees to participate in the GEAC. The member-secretary of the GEAC is a member of the RCGM, and vice versa, to ensure coordination.

The other split in the regulatory structure concerned the distribution of responsibilities to the federal, state, and district governments. Officers of the Environment Ministry keenly realized that state and district governments were much closer to the theater of rDNA action than federal officers in New Delhi. Consequently, making sure laboratories complied with safety guidelines and rules required the active cooperation and vigilance of state and district governments.

In broad terms, the ministry was in favor of delegating inspectional and regulatory functions to the state and district governments. Whereas the Constitution (Forty-second Amendment) Act, 1976, which incorporated environmental protection into the Indian Constitution for the first time, and the federal Environment Department, created in 1980, had a centralizing thrust, by the time the Environment Ministry began framing rules under the EPA in the late 1980s, it had begun to see virtue in working with state and district governments. In contrast, the Biotechnology Department had little need to work with district and state governments, and thus it restricted its involvement to the RCGM and the GEAC at the federal level. Its only task at the institutional level was appointing a nominee to Institutional Committees. For the design of rDNA regulatory mechanisms, officers of the Environment Ministry most directly drew on the structure for controlling pollution and regulating hazardous chemicals, the rules for which were framed in 1989.[5] This comprised the offices listed in Table 2. Similarly, the Environment Ministry planned a Biotechnology Safety Inspection Directorate at the state level and a District Level Committee in the districts to regulate rDNA work.

On July 26, 1989, the Committee of Secretaries (CoS)—the high-powered committee of all secretaries to the federal government, chaired by the Cabinet secretary—met to discuss the rDNA safety guidelines. The CoS felt that the guidelines unnecessarily multiplied the bureaucracy of Inspection Directorates while being vague about their actual enforcement.[6] In his response to Cabinet Secretary T. N. Seshan, Environment Secretary Mahesh Prasad clarified that they were not creating a parallel bureaucratic infrastructure, but rather constituting committees at the state and district levels, as provided in the rules for hazardous chemicals. The Environment Ministry renamed the Biotechnology Safety Inspection Directorate, giving it the title of State Biotechnology Coordination Committee, to be chaired by the chief

Table 2. Structure for Hazardous Chemicals Management[a]

Federal government	Central Crisis Group under the secretary of the Environment Ministry, and supported by the Hazardous Substances Management Division of the Environment Ministry
State government	State-level crisis group under the chief secretary. The Department of Environment/Labour as the nodal department. Pollution Control Board/inspector of factories at the field level
District government	District emergency authority under the district collector. Pollution Control Board/Regional/District Office/ inspector of factories at the field level

a. This structure was conceived in the late 1980s. The Environment Ministry established it with some changes as part of the Chemical Accidents (Emergency Planning, Preparedness, and Response) Rules 1996, under the EPA.

secretary, and its membership coming from the state departments of health, environment, and so on. The chief secretary, an IAS officer, is the most senior civil servant serving the state government. She is the counterpart of the Cabinet secretary at the state level. The District Level Committee was convened by the collector and comprised a factory inspector, a representative from the Pollution Control Board, the district health officer, the district agricultural officer, and the commissioner of the Municipal Corporation or Board, among others. The collector is the foremost officer, usually from the IAS, in charge of revenue collection and administration of a district. In light of these revisions, on September 19, 1989, the Cabinet secretary approved the rules, and on December 5, 1989, the rules were published with the title "Rules for the Manufacture, Use, Import, Export and Storage of Hazardous Micro-organisms/Genetically Engineered Organisms or Cells."

The Episteme of Regulation, 1989–Present

The membership and strength of these proposed bodies, along with the reporting relationships at the district, state, and federal levels, were debated for several years within the Environment Ministry before the enactment of Rules 1989. The record of deliberations from the period betrays considerable anxiety about the adequacy of these structures to the daunting task of regulating interventions at the microorganismic and genetic scales. The Environment Ministry, troubled by the question of whether a bureaucratic structure was agile and sensitive enough to detect and respond to hazards of genetic modification, sought a solution in tinkering further with the bureaucratic design.

Effectively, officers of the Environment Ministry were trying to devise ways of codifying, controlling, and representing "hazardous micro-organisms" and "genetically engineered organisms or cells." Their uncertainty harks back to the struggle to epistemologically order and administer an unfamiliar terrain, which is a general problem for all regimes (Scott 1998). Indeed, Prasad confessed in his clarifications to the Cabinet secretary, "This is an emerging area for the State Government and the Pollution Control Boards. In a way, this is an emerging area for the [Environment Ministry] also."[7]

Whereas the safety guidelines issued by the Biotechnology Department were adapted from those developed in the United States and concern precautions such as containment measures, Rules 1989 sketch a bureaucratic architecture for regulation, without specifying a substantive regulatory framework or how regulation will work. First, they define terms such as *biotechnology* and *genetic engineering*. Second, they define various regulatory committees and their membership and demarcate their jurisdiction, reporting relationships, and appeals mechanism. Schedules accompanying the rules classify animal and human pathogens (bacteria, fungi, viruses) by risk group, which has a bearing on which committees will oversee work involving them. Essentially, the rules extend state making into the terrain of microbes and genes by extending the "ideological and organizational power of the . . . government to penetrate society, exact compliance, and invoke commitment" (Sivaramakrishnan 1999, 5). They "classify, categorize, and bound" (Cohn 1996, 5) this hitherto unregulated space and proclaim the sovereignty of the state therein. They describe which bodies exercise oversight over rDNA technology, but they say very little else (see Table 3).

Table 3. Structure of Regulation of GM Crops under Rules 1989

Federal government	RCGM (hosted by the Biotechnology Department). Members include: Representatives of the Biotechnology Department Representatives of the ICAR, ICMR, CSIR Experts—generally from public institutions in their individual capacities Member-secretary, an officer of the Biotechnology Department	GEAC (hosted by the Environment Ministry). Members include: Additional secretary, Environment Ministry (chairperson) Representative of the Biotechnology Department (co-chairperson) Representatives of the Ministry of Industrial Development, Departments of Biotechnology and Atomic Energy Directors general of ICAR, ICMR, CSIR, Health Services Plant protection adviser, Directorate of Plant Protection, Quarantine and Storage Chairperson, Central Pollution Control Board Three experts, generally from public institutions in their individual capacities Member-secretary, an officer of the Environment Ministry

State government	State Biotechnology Coordination Committee. Members include: Chief secretary (chairperson) Secretary, State Department of Environment (member-secretary). Secretaries of Departments of Health, Agriculture, Industries and Commerce, Forests State pathologists and microbiologists Chairperson, State Pollution Control Board
District government	District-level committee. Members include: Collector (chairperson) Factory inspector Representative of Pollution Control Board District agricultural officer District health officer or chief medical officer District microbiologists and pathologists
Research institution	Institutional Biosafety Committee. Members include: Head of the institution Scientists engaged in DNA work Medical expert Nominee of the Biotechnology Department

The Environment Ministry was under pressure not to institute a structure parallel to the bureaucracy of pollution control boards and factory inspectors. So the regulatory regime relied on a committee of officers who had other full-time responsibilities. Also, in tasking the state-level and district-level committees to regulate by visiting and seeing laboratories, we can discern a reliance on survey modality, whose roots go deep in the way Indian society and landscapes were formatted for administration in colonial India (Cohn 1996). Officers of the Environment Ministry can scarcely be faulted for delegating much of the actual field-level inspectional and regulatory work to the states and districts. They wanted states and districts to take these tasks seriously, and, hence, as an internal memo of the ministry explained, the district- and state-level committees were made statutory and their membership fixed.

Yet this very reliance on a committee headed by the chief secretary at the state level and the collector at the district level already portended problems—in fact, it virtually guaranteed failure of execution. The chief secretary, as the most senior civil servant in states, was then, and now, a member of several committees in addition to shouldering many other responsibilities. Similarly, the collector is single-handedly responsible for implementing the schemes and plans of all state and federal government departments at the district level and heads multiple committees as well.[8] Consequently, under pressure to attend to more politically salient tasks, neither of the two offices was likely to have the time and resources for overseeing rDNA work. This structural weakness implied that there was effectively a vacuum in the link between the federal committees (the RCGM and the GEAC) and the Institutional Committee at the research facility. Despite several regular missives from the Environment Ministry to the states, this weakness remains to this day, as many collectors are unaware that they must regulate rDNA work, and many state-level committees barely meet because the chief secretary is tied up with other, more pressing responsibilities.[9] Effectively, the very structure put into place to ensure the serious involvement of and committed oversight by state and district governments had the consequence of producing self-policing through the Institutional Committee, overseen by the distant RCGM and the GEAC. (Let us note that this structural weakness makes it easier for illegal GM seeds to circulate among farmers, beyond the gaze of the committees in New Delhi.)

Formally, the structure remains unchanged to date, though almost immediately after enactment, the Environment Ministry began the work of amending the rules. As early as November 1990, K. M. Chadha, joint secretary (joint secretaries head divisions within the ministry and are two rungs below the secretary) in the ministry, wrote to the states, observing:

> The implementation of these rules has since been discussed with the concerned Central Ministries, State Governments and other experts. Through these consultations, the consensus has emerged that the rules essentially provide procedural requirements for regulating the hazardous microorganisms and genetically engineered products. The substantive aspects need to be incorporated in the rules so as to provide adequate safeguards while dealing with these substances. The techniques pose new risks and, therefore, the research as well as the manufactured products should be regulated by very specific and transparent provisions of the law. Moreover, the deliberate release of such substances into the environment requires careful consideration of potential risk and regulations are required to be more strict than those of chemicals.[10]

Several major amendments were proposed regarding definitions, type of tests to be conducted for determining health and environmental safety, and a step-by-step review process, among other issues. In addition, feedback from the states, and requests to relieve the collector and chief secretary from chairpersonship of the district-level committee and the State Biotechnology Coordination Committee, respectively, were also to an extent addressed in draft amendments.[11] Nevertheless, the amendments were never enacted, except once, in 2005, to make minor changes in terms of designations of the bureaucrats servicing the GEAC. In 1999 the Environment Ministry came close to enacting amendments, but it then backtracked because by then the activist Vandana Shiva had filed a PIL against the Government of India on regulatory matters, and the Ministry of Law felt that amending Rules 1989 at that point might jeopardize the government's stand before the Supreme Court.

Given the wide scope available to the RCGM and GEAC to conduct "case-by-case evaluation" as they deemed fit, however, many new practices were introduced over the years without formally amending the rules. The triggers for this elaboration were both internally perceived need and pressure from courts and activists. So a step-by-step review process, standardized forms and checklists for field evaluations of GM crops and data reporting, among other things, were instituted through guidelines issued by the Biotechnology Department from time to time. The fact that these tweaks were executed through guidelines, rather than through formal amendments to the rules, came back to haunt the government, as I will describe later.

Over the years, the language of "hazards" was slowly abandoned, as regulation was reoriented toward "biosafety" as an organizing concept. One important factor for this shift was the realization among officers of the Environment Ministry and the Biotechnology Department that the states and districts were structurally, and in terms of training, ill-equipped to oversee rDNA research. As the member-secretary of the GEAC at that time, an officer of the Environment Ministry, told me in April 2013, they found that the logic of pollution control, hazardous substances, installations, and factory inspection just did not work for biotechnology, where there was often little to *see* through the naked eye. Another contributing factor was the shift taking place internationally. In 1994 India ratified the Convention on Biological Diversity, and in 2003 it ratified the Cartagena Protocol on Biosafety, which emphasizes the language of biosafety. At some time in that period, the Environment Ministry was administratively reorganized, and the GEAC was moved out of the Hazardous Substances Management Division into the Conservation and Survey Division. For all these reasons, biosafety slowly overshadowed hazard management as an organizing framework.

Biosafety is a much more abstract and diffuse framework than the regimented one of factory inspections; it has a different emphasis in terms of underlying epistemology. If the emphasis earlier was on site visits and emergency plans, biosafety emphasizes following good laboratory practices and procedures, preparing regulatory dossiers to be assessed by the RCGM and the GEAC, and documenting compliance. Biosafety signals an "audit culture" (Strathern 2000) of accountability rather than a culture of inspection and penal action. Even from the beginning, having delegated much of the work of inspection and monitoring to the states and districts, the RCGM and GEAC concerned themselves primarily with paper evaluations: evaluations through documentary representations.[12] The reliance on documentation further increased as the emphasis on biosafety overshadowed the concern with hazardous-substances management. Tellingly, none of the committees got involved with the nitty-gritty of the reliability and accuracy of the data generated about the performance of GM crops. They saw their role as merely evaluating data produced by applicants, trusting its reliability.

The Everyday Life of Regulation

To get their work done, the RCGM and the GEAC in turn appoint several subcommittees and ad hoc committees. From January to July 2013, I conducted participant observation with one of the committees housed in one of the ministries involved with the regulation of GM crops (there are three such ministries in addition to the Biotechnology Department and the Environment Ministry). Gaining entry to federal ministry offices was exceedingly difficult. Just getting past the security desk at the entrance to ministry offices was a challenge, made worse because the controversy surrounding GM crops had made officers much more guarded. Nevertheless, over months of preparatory summer fieldwork, I persuaded an officer, whom I call Dr. Shilpa, to take me on as an unpaid intern, and in January 2013 I started going to the office regularly.

The ministry, which will remain unnamed, is located in one of the clusters of government offices that dot Delhi's landscape. This particular complex, like many others, has multiple old buildings surrounded by parking spaces full of cars marked with "Government of India" signs. One has to wade through a maze of cubicles, as well as cupboards and cabinets overflowing with files and papers, as one approaches Dr. Shilpa's office. Much to her annoyance, for Dr. Shilpa was very meticulous and methodical with her paperwork, even her office was full of files and documents: the ongoing PIL before the Supreme Court on the matter of regulating GM crops entailed frequent requests for documents, which were being stored in her office.

Dr. Shilpa, with a PhD in the sciences, was a rank below that of joint secretary in the ministry, and she was the member-secretary of one of the committees involved with regulation of GM crops—I am going to call this committee the Committee for Biosafety Assessment (CBA). The CBA was a committee structurally similar to, and a close cognate of, the GEAC and the RCGM. Behind the aggregates of the Biotechnology Department and the Environment Ministry, which represent the Government of India before the public and the courts on the question of GM crops, are actually only a handful of full-time officers. For instance, in the time I worked with Dr. Shilpa, she and her research officer, whom I call Vineet Bansal, were the only full-time ministry officers involved with regulation. Although this was already a lot of work, Dr. Shilpa was frequently assigned other responsibilities as well. Similarly, the GEAC was run by two to three full-time officers of the Environment Ministry, and the RCGM by about three to five officers of the Biotechnology Department, all of whom were frequently assigned additional tasks that were unrelated to GM crops.

The committees typically met once a month, which lent the entire regulatory process a particular tempo.[13] Most of the month was spent preparing for the next meeting and processing the decisions from the previous meeting. The meeting was the only occasion when substantive decisions were made. During the month, we collated all incoming applications for research and trials on GM crops, scheduled them on the agenda for CBA meetings, and sent out the agendas and the accompanying dossiers to CBA members. In addition, the previous meeting's minutes had to be prepared and decision letters written and issued. These were time-consuming tasks, even if repetitive to some extent.

The fact that only a handful of officers worked full-time on regulation at the CBA, as at the GEAC and the RCGM, severely constrained the amount of work they could take on—just keeping track of applications, addendums and corrections to applications, decision letters, minutes of the meetings, and the like was a laborious task. The work was further hampered by the fact that junior officers like Bansal are unfamiliar with both the technical vocabulary of regulation and the English language in general. Often, given the workload, junior officers end up drafting decision letters and agenda notes for the meetings, and their anxiety about language makes them prone to copy and paste text that has previously met their seniors' approval. Sometimes they forget to change particular details while copying text from previous letters, so that, for example, a company seeking permission to conduct field trials in *kharif* (monsoon) season may get a letter that erroneously gives permission for the *rabī* (winter) season. This of course leads to a further flurry of paperwork in an attempt to sort things out, and, on occasion, companies have had to delay trials by a year simply because the tempo of work at the ministries and the monthly frequency of meetings were structurally insensitive to cropping seasons, precise sowing times, and monsoon patterns.

For this reason, public relations or regulatory affairs managers of private seed companies were frequent presences in these offices. Both in the Environment Ministry and the Biotechnology Department, the same set of permanent scientific staff (as opposed to the IAS officers who were transferred in and out) managed regulatory work for several years, sometimes more than a decade. One reason for this was that, after GM crops became controversial, new officers tried to avoid this area of work. By dint of interacting with the same set of officers over many years, corporate managers had forged friendship and camaraderie, especially with male government officers.[14] Corporate managers were also quite savvy in cultivating support staff such as peons through gifts and thus could access documents, minutes, and gossip before they were formally released. Among senior officers and committee members, there were significant individual differences. For instance, Dr. Shilpa generally stayed aloof and maintained a distant but courteous relationship with managers, while a former member-secretary of the RCGM, a senior officer of the Biotechnology Department, was notorious for his backslapping camaraderie with some corporate managers.

Another important aspect of the relationship with companies was that officers of the Environment Ministry and the Biotechnology Department, especially the junior ones, sometimes turned to corporate managers for help—often because of the limited resources available with these regulatory offices. For instance, one day there was an urgent request of the minister for details of all ongoing field trials, and Dr. Shilpa happened to be on leave. The task fell on Bansal's shoulders, who panicked at the prospect of having to answer to the minister. I suggested to Bansal that he could ask RCGM officers for help since they would have the records of all ongoing field trials, but he was wary of reaching out to the member-secretary of the RCGM, who was considerably senior to him. Finally, Bansal decided to call the managers of different companies and ask them for information about their field trials. He explained that corporate managers "are bound to know where they are conducting trials and for which crops." The irony of a government office, responsible for regulating field trials nationally, making ad hoc calls to companies for data was lost on Bansal in his moment of panic. Such occasional trading of favors also cemented social ties between regulatory staff and corporate managers. When Bansal's son got married, he invited not only his seniors at the ministry, but also regulatory affairs managers of a few private seed companies, to the wedding. These ties and a history of interaction play a role in making regulatory officers sympathetic, even against their better instincts, to companies. This is quite a contrast with their attitudes toward anti-GM activists—"troublemakers"—whom they meet rarely and almost always in antagonistic settings.

Having delved into the structure of regulation and its functioning, we can appreciate how the specific historical coproduction of biotechnology, as a scientific activity and as state making, weighs on regulatory design and practice, much as a different, equally specific history weighs on regulatory design in the West (Jasanoff 2005). Setting up two committees, one hosted by the Biotechnology Department (the RCGM) and the other by the Environment Ministry (the GEAC), is a direct consequence of the division of responsibilities enshrined in the Allocation of Business Rules. Virtually all aspects of biotechnology were the preserve of the Biotechnology Department, just as all aspects of environmental protection, and hence the EPA 1986, were the preserve of the Environment Ministry. Thus, the RCGM saw to scientific aspects of regulation—bringing out safety manuals, monitoring ongoing research, and the like. This is why the RCGM is staffed and chaired by external scientists and technical experts, while an officer of the Biotechnology Department, trained in the sciences, serves as the member-secretary. The GEAC saw to both scientific aspects, such as determining which tests need to be conducted and evaluating test results, and legal-administrative aspects, such as authorizing field trials and making decisions regarding commercial release.

A letter from the ministry to the Scientific Advisory Council to the Prime Minister, written in April 2013, notes: "Further, the RCGM and the GEAC fulfill related but distinct regulatory functions. According to Rules 1989, the RCGM is responsible for evaluation of scientific and technical issues associated with the potential environmental and health aspects of GMOs during product-development phase. On the other hand, the GEAC deals with large-scale environmental and health safety assessment of GMOs while ensuring a harmonized approach in the Government of India's policies on GMOs." Because the GEAC is responsible for legal-administration and "harmonizing" an approach to GM crops at the level of the Government of India, it is chaired by an IAS officer and staffed by ex-officio representatives from other ministries and departments. The Biotechnology Department nominates a co-chairperson to the GEAC, and the GEAC, for several years, has been co-opting external technical experts as well, usually from public universities and research institutions. The GEAC is thus a hybrid forum (Callon, Lascoumes, and Barth 2011) of technical experts and policy makers, government officers and external experts. Even though it is a committee with statutory powers, politicians and the Cabinet of Ministers indirectly exercise influence, or at least try very hard to, through the additional secretary serving as the chairperson (see Scoones 2006, chap. 7).

Further, both committees effectively outsource scientific determinations to members, who attend meetings once a month. Only a few full-time officers serve the committees, primarily in the form of preparing agenda notes and minutes and processing decisions, all legal-administrative work. As Secretary Prasad's words quoted above indicate, the Environment Ministry felt out of its depth as far as technical aspects of biotechnology went, and this is why it relied on committee-based regulation to begin with. For various reasons, however, not the least important of which was the inertia exerted by the structure once instituted, neither the Environment Ministry nor the Biotechnology Department augmented its staff strength or resource allocation for regulation over the years.[15] For instance, much of the budget for regulation was allocated to the logistics of convening a meeting each month,[16] and officers serving the committees often had to cobble together resources and funds for things that one might presume are par for the course for regulation—conducting tests on their own initiative, undertaking field trips, and so on. Let us turn to two cases of regulatory disputes to glimpse the interplay of the two documentary modes in the actual functioning of regulation.

Doritos Chips in India Found Laced with Unapproved GM Ingredients

In early 2008 the NGO Greenpeace India lodged a complaint with the GEAC. It claimed that Doritos Cool Ranch Tortilla Chips, manufactured by Frito-Lay for PepsiCo and widely available in India, contained unapproved GM ingredients. At its own expense, Greenpeace claimed to have purchased Doritos chips in New Delhi and had them sent to Eurofins Genescan, a reputed European laboratory, for testing. The report from the laboratory, which Greenpeace provided to the GEAC, showed the presence of herbicide-tolerant (HT) soy, HT corn (Monsanto's NK 603), and insect-resistant (Bt) corn (Monsanto's MON 863) in the chips; none of these GM ingredients had been approved by the GEAC. Before the Parliament and before the Supreme Court, the Government of India had consistently claimed that its regulatory regime was adequate and rigorous, and this was a serious charge of failure.

The GEAC discussed the complaint in its meeting of May 28, 2008. Oddly enough, it asked Greenpeace to explain why HT soy was present in corn chips and also, what the percentage presence of GM ingredients was. The committee also noted that according to Rules 1989, all import consignments with GM ingredients needed to declare that fact at the border, and that importing GMOs and GM products into India without the approval of the GEAC was illegal. Finally, the GEAC also formed a subcommittee to look into strengthening border security measures. As far as Greenpeace's complaint went, however, the GEAC took no action other than to seek clarifications from Greenpeace itself.[17]

The GEAC could not discuss Greenpeace's response until the next meeting, held on June 25, 2008. Greenpeace reminded the GEAC that HT soy could well have been an ingredient of the vegetable oil used to process the chips. It also reminded the committee that percentage content of GM ingredients was not germane to the issue at hand—namely, the presence of unapproved GM ingredients in a food product freely available across India. In light of these clarifications, the GEAC decided to establish a three-member committee to collect samples and have them tested. The GEAC also asked Greenpeace to deposit the samples that the latter had used, as a check.[18]

The next time this matter came up was in the meeting of the GEAC held on August 13, 2008. Greenpeace was unable to produce the samples it had had tested. It claimed that the samples had been damaged when its offices were relocated in Bengaluru. It instead submitted a fresh sample, collected in June 2008. I quote GEAC's response to Greenpeace in full:

> After detailed deliberations on the matter the GEAC opined that the complainant [Greenpeace] has not behaved very responsibly while making such an accusation. The complainant was also not available for presenting their case when given an opportunity by the GEAC in its meeting held on [June 25, 2008]. Since, the M/s Pepsico International clarified [that they] do not use GM crops for manufacturing their products in India and have not authorized any agency to import any of their products from outside having GM processed food, the Committee decided to advise the M/s Green Peace [*sic*] to approach [the] Director General of Foreign Trade [attached to the federal Ministry of Commerce and Industry] for taking necessary action in the matter.[19]

Actually, Greenpeace representatives were present to make their case to the GEAC on that day. After waiting for a few hours outside the room where the GEAC met, they stepped out for twenty-odd minutes for lunch, and that is when the GEAC summoned them. When they returned, the GEAC informed them that they had missed their chance. Greenpeace wrote back on August 29, 2008, asking what the point of going to the Directorate General of Foreign Trade (DGFT) was "when [the] DGFT can check only future imports. What measures will GEAC take on continuing sale of existing products in the market?" Greenpeace did not drop the matter here but pursued it also with the Food Safety and Standards Authority of India, the food safety regulator, and Dr. Anbumani Ramadoss, then the federal minister for health and family welfare. In its letter to the Food Safety Authority dated October 22, 2008, it asked for immediate confiscation of Doritos in the market and an embargo on all imported food products until appropriate testing was conducted for any GM contamination. It also asked that products containing GM ingredients be rejected.

Nothing of consequence resulted from these efforts. The last time this came up before the GEAC was in its meeting on January 14, 2009. Greenpeace appeared before the GEAC and asked what action the GEAC had taken. The GEAC clarified that it had informed DGFT and the Ministry of Commerce that it had not allowed imports of food with GM ingredients. In short, the GEAC did no investigation of its own. The subcommittee that GEAC had decided to set up never saw the light of day. When I interviewed a GEAC member about this matter in July 2013, she said that she suspected that Greenpeace had sourced the packet of chips from abroad. "We told [Greenpeace], send us your samples with receipt, we will collect our own samples . . . and get them tested. For a long time their packet of Doritos chips was lying in my office, but they were not able to produce a receipt.[20]

Greenpeace gave the GEAC the name of the shop in Delhi where it had purchased the chips, along with the name of the importer from whom the shop had procured the chips. Greenpeace also gave the GEAC a new sample of chips, in lieu of the damaged samples.[21] Nevertheless, once PepsiCo declared that it did not use GM ingredients for chips marketed in India, and that it had not "authorized" anyone to import its products from abroad, the GEAC closed the complaint. Before analyzing this further, let us examine the second case.

The Case of GM Mustard Trials in Rajasthan

On August 19, 2011, the eminent biotechnologist, former member of the Scientific Advisory Committee to the Cabinet (SACC), and then director of the Centre for Genetic Manipulation of Crop Plants, Delhi University, Deepak Pental requested a No Objection Certificate (NOC) from the Department of Agriculture, Government of Rajasthan, for conducting field trials of GM mustard. Rajasthan is a state in western India. The requirement of seeking an

NOC from the concerned state government was introduced in 2011. After consulting the agricultural university concerned, Anil Gupta, deputy secretary of the Department of Agriculture, granted the NOC on September 19, 2011.[22] The GEAC too authorized the trial. The field trials were thus undertaken in the *rabī* (winter) season.

This was the time when several states were objecting to field trials of GM crops. In early March 2012, several newspapers reported that field trials of GM crops were under way in Rajasthan. Seeing the reports, the state agriculture minister, Harji Ram Burdak, called Gupta, inquired about the NOC, and alerted him to discussions under way in another file in the same department concerning field trials. This other file had been initiated in July 2011, when several companies had sought an NOC for field trials for GM crops. Since this was the first time the state Department of Agriculture was being asked to approve field trials, the file contained detailed deliberations about the stance Rajasthan ought to take in light of Prime Minister Dr. Manmohan Singh's support for GM crops, and the refusal of states such as Bihar, Madhya Pradesh, and Himachal Pradesh to allow field trials.

The Agriculture Department first decided to consult state agricultural universities and then a broader cross section of scientists, state governments that had opposed field trials, and farmers in order to formulate a position. Bureaucrats were aware that an NOC had been granted to Pental, but they wanted to organize a consultative symposium about January 2012 before determining what to do with respect to other applications. Before the symposium could be held, Ashok Gehlot, then the chief minister (the head of the elected state government) of Rajasthan, received a letter from his Congress party colleague and member of Parliament representing the Nagaur constituency in Rajasthan, Dr. Jyoti Mirdha.[23]

In her letter, Mirdha acknowledged the promises of GM crops in terms of yield improvement, but she then went on to point out the disagreement among scientists on the question of the long-term effects of GM crops on human health and biodiversity. She also observed that the small landholdings in India were unsuitable for cultivating GM crops.[24] She also made critical remarks about the stringency and adequacy of the regulatory regime in India. She concluded by urging the chief minister to "follow the example of some other progressive states and declare Rajasthan GM-free until there is greater clarity on GM seeds and crops."[25] The Agriculture Department did not immediately respond to the letter but decided to take up these issues in the planned symposium. In the meantime, however, a few other companies sent letters seeking an NOC, adding pressure on the government to make a decision.[26]

Finally, Rajasthan's chief secretary, S. Ahmad, stepped in. Concurring with some of Mirdha's observations, Ahmad noted:

> Permitting field trials of transgenic crops is indeed fraught with concerns, the reason being that unanimity does not exist, either in their favor or against them. . . . My own assessment . . . is that we should wait until a national consensus on the question is evolved before we permit open field trials in transgenic crops. In the interregnum, symposia and discussions could be held with all stake holders to help the different camps exchange points of view, find common ground and come to a general agreement on the controversy. It is only, thereafter, that the State government should take a call on this contentious issue.[27]

This note had the concurrence of the agriculture minister. After speaking to the minister, Gupta immediately withdrew the NOC issued to Pental's center. Writing to Pental, Gupta added, "I am also directed to request you that all the plants, production etc. may kindly be destroyed under expert guidance and presence."[28] To Pental's immense disappointment and frustration, a week before the trial was set to end, he had to have it burned and destroyed. Pental sought an intervention from the prime minister and the GEAC, among others, but he did not get any relief because agriculture is a state subject: states have the legislative mandate in the area of agriculture, according to the Indian Constitution. In this way, a scientific determination of uncertainty led the state Agriculture Department to withdraw an NOC previously granted and take the unprecedented step of ordering a field trial of an eminent public-sector scientist to be destroyed. Pental was unable to capture all the data he needed to push GM mustard further along the regulatory process.

The Play of Documents in the Two Cases

One way to read these incidents would be in light of regulatory incompetence and inadequacy, both in terms of checking the illegal flow of GM food into India and in terms of being able to defend a field trial authorized by the GEAC. Then we would miss what is of analytic interest in them: the different modes through which claims are made, adjudicated, and dismissed, and the way claims made in different registers enable and constrain bureaucratic decision making. After all, even an inadequate response is produced through bureaucratic routines. The fissures between scientific and legal-administrative modes of documentation are crucial to gain a deeper understanding of these cases.

When Greenpeace reported the presence of GM ingredients in Doritos chips, it was relying on the scientific mode of documentation. Chips purchased in India stood for food in India. The report from Eurofins Genescan documenting the presence of GM soy and maize pointed to the presence of GM ingredients in Doritos chips, and thereby to the presence of GM food in India. At this juncture, the GEAC decided to deploy both epistemologies—it decided to have samples of chips collected and analyzed on its own; it decided to assemble scientific facts. And it sought clarifications from both Greenpeace and PepsiCo, invoking the legal-administrative mode of seeking representations and testimonies from organizations. It acted only on the latter course of action, however.

PepsiCo's letter stating that it had not authorized anyone to import its products, and Greenpeace's failure to produce its original samples, settled the matter for the GEAC. Instead of conducting an investigation into whether Doritos chips in India actually contained GM ingredients, the GEAC investigated whether Greenpeace had purchased the chips in India by demanding the original samples and a receipt. Again, Greenpeace had informed GEAC about the shop from which it purchased the packets of chips and the importer from whom the shop procured those packets.

This reveals an inconsistency in the way the GEAC conducted this metaphorical hearing. The GEAC was willing to take PepsiCo's assertion at face value—but not Greenpeace's. PepsiCo's declaration that it does not use GM ingredients for its chips in India is no refutation of Greenpeace's case documenting the presence of GM ingredients in Doritos chips. Moreover, the claim that PepsiCo had not authorized anyone to import Doritos chips from abroad may certainly be true, but it is irrelevant. No retailer needs PepsiCo's authorization to import Doritos chips into India. No law in India obligates a trader to seek permission from a manufacturer before importing or exporting its products—such imports and exports are the jurisdictional terrain of the Government of India, not of private companies. The idea that PepsiCo may have been less than forthcoming, or that it may have on occasions imported some of the ingredients from countries allowing GM food, either did not impress the GEAC or was of no consequence to it.

The ease with which the GEAC transformed itself, in this case from a regulatory body to a neutral, arbitrating body, is striking. Loftily, the GEAC became akin to a third party arbitrating between PepsiCo and Greenpeace, investigating both through documentary submissions and finding Greenpeace deficient—in brief, acting in the interested and power-laden ways for which Foucault (1980, chap. 1) critiques courts. To compound the irony, the GEAC asked Greenpeace to follow up with the DGFT about future imports of GM crops—forgetting its own, and not Greenpeace's, statutory obligation under Rules 1989 to address imports of GM food.

In essence, the GEAC responded by trying to establish internal coherence within the world of documents (Hull 2012), with a predilection for preserving the status quo (Gupta 2012). On the one hand, it had its rules and regulations that stated that nobody can introduce GM products into India without the GEAC's permission. PepsiCo's letter reaffirmed this picture. On the other hand, Greenpeace's documents established the presence of unapproved GM food in India, controverting the Environment Ministry's contention before the Parliament and the Supreme Court that the regulatory structure was adequate. Because Greenpeace could not provide its original samples, the GEAC found grounds to disregard its documents. Perhaps burdened by the weight of its own history of denying the presence of illegal GM food in the country (a legal-administrative concern), the GEAC was reluctant to launch an independent investigation, which may have resulted in the embarrassing specter of the Environment Ministry being forced to admit that it had been asleep at the switch. Thus, without independently investigating Greenpeace's allegations, the GEAC dismissed its complaint. In the process, the GEAC effected another astonishing translation: it turned a question of wide public interest, the presence of unapproved GM food in India, into one of the presence of a sample.

Further, once internal coherence was reestablished, it was irrelevant whether those documents corresponded to an actual state of affairs in the country. It would be futile here to observe that the question—whether some packets of Doritos sold in India had GM ingredients—had remained unresolved. In the bureaucratic scheme of things, that question got subordinated to making sure that textual representations conformed to the law, irrespective of their fidelity. The GEAC turned the question of whether Doritos chips had unapproved GM ingredients into whether Greenpeace could substantiate its complaint with the original samples of chips. The legal-administrative mode of constructing truth made the scientific verification of Greenpeace's complaint irrelevant. In effect, the GEAC ended up cross-examining Greenpeace and finding it "irresponsible."

The second case shows how bureaucracies, beholden to history while working within the legal-administrative epistemology, can nevertheless depart from precedent when they switch over to the scientific epistemology. Field trials happened in Rajasthan before 2011–12; even though earlier the GEAC had not required an approval from the state Agriculture Department, the latter had not objected to these trials. The new requirement of an approval led the Agriculture Department to make a fresh assessment of the debate over GM crops. Indeed, the department wanted to organize a symposium because it wanted neither to uncritically say no to GM crops, simply because some other states had done so, nor to say yes, just because trials had happened earlier and because it had given an NOC to Pental. This was a moment when scientific epistemology was at work—the state Department of Agriculture wanted a judicious consideration of different aspects of GM crops and what they might mean for agriculture in Rajasthan. Dr. Mirdha's detailed letter to the chief minister, expressing caution and skepticism about GM crops, led the government to take a position against GM crops. Once the government took this position, it immediately withdrew the NOC and had Pental's trial destroyed. Because the decision not to allow field trials was made through the scientific mode, legal-administrative precedents became irrelevant, as did Pental's stature as an eminent public-sector scientist in India.

Regulation between Science and Legal-Administration

Regulatory practice invariably involves balancing technical reasoning with political imperatives. In the specific case of India, the division of responsibilities and hybridity of the committee structure are neither handicaps nor contradictions of the governance regime for GM crops, as some commentators have observed (Paarlberg 2001, chap. 5; Gupta, Choudhary, and Gheysen 2015), as much as they are an attempt at accommodating scientific efforts within democratic structures of governance. Given that the promotion of biotechnology is a key objective of the Biotechnology Department, environmental assessment and overall regulatory policies for GMOs are, to avoid a conflict of interest, the preserve of the Environment Ministry, which is the nodal ministry for environmental protection. The two epistemologies were thus fused in the very design of the committee structure of regulation, split across different government agencies and involving technical experts, ex-officio members, and civil servants. And as the cases demonstrate, there is an inherent ambiguity lodged between scientific and legal-administrative regimes of truth.[29]

The ambiguity arises from the fact that these regimes construct claims in different ways, and thus there is room to maneuver in their interstices. Claims generated in one mode of documentation can be disputed, discounted, or set aside through those generated in the other mode (as in Pental's case), or truths generated in one mode can fail to make any difference to those sought in the other mode (as in Greenpeace's case). This ambiguity both fosters and constrains democratic participation and politics. It fosters democratic participation by allowing citizens and their groups to produce facts that rival those of the government. And it also constrains participation in at least two ways. First, if claims can be made in the space between the two modes, they can be discounted, too, as Greenpeace realized, to its chagrin. Second, the reliance on documents forecloses claims that are not easily textualized. In other words, a grievance that is experienced but not documented is unlikely to be taken seriously by the state bureaucracy.[30] Activists had long suspected that GM food was entering India, but one had to find such food on one's own and pay from one's own pocket for an expensive laboratory report to get the government to take notice, however cursorily.

This is why it is important to attend to civic epistemologies in analyses of the GM debate, and of technoscientific controversies in general. These documentary squabbles allow us to track the humdrum working of power through which states and the polities of knowledge are constituted and reconstituted. Power is inevitably at stake, given the resources and access required to generate documents and dispute documents (Gupta 2012). Yet these squabbles are not *reducible* to differences in power. The GEAC would perhaps have been in an uncomfortable position if Greenpeace had been able to produce its original samples. Tracking how political contests get textualized, and how they shift registers in the process of struggle, allows us to see the uncertainties, the ambivalences, and the underdetermined aspects of the politics of science. The gaps between the two epistemologies open a generative space for contestation, even as they narrow the spectrum of concerns that elicit a response from the government.

The lesson here may be broadened to the anthropological study of states and bureaucracies, beyond controversies over science. Recent works in the anthropology of bureaucracy have valuably called for the disaggregation of the state (Sharma and Gupta 2006; see also Sivaramakrishnan 1999). The preferred way to do this, however, has been to segment bureaucrats vertically into elites and subalterns (see, for example, Gupta 2012; Mathur 2015). This approach unhelpfully partitions the dynamic and shifting relationships of power and authority among bureaucrats into two homogeneous realms.[31] Yet bureaucracies are not only hierarchically divided, but also horizontally differentiated. Bureaucrats, sometimes at the same hierarchical level, can mobilize different sources of authority, as well as kinds of knowledge (generalists versus specialists, technocrats versus administrators). Even regarding administrators, there is a power dynamic between transferable officers and the relatively long-term staff of an office. How the balance between different sources of power shifts in different circumstances is a question for empirical inquiry; it is not foreclosed simply because some bureaucrats are "elite" while others are "subaltern." For instance, to analyze the GM mustard case, it is not only difficult, but also futile, to map the relative position of Deepak Pental, the chief secretary of Rajasthan, and the chairman of the GEAC on a vertical scale of power and elitism.

Politics of Science-Based Regulation

Finally, close attention to the twists and turns of disputes over GM crops as they unfold in time paints a very different picture of activists, corporations, and governments vis-à-vis accounts that rely primarily on what these groups or institutions say about themselves. For instance, Scoones calls India's biotechnology policy-making and regulatory regime a "technocratic system *par excellence*" (2006, 247; emphasis in original; see also Kuruganti 2006; Shah 2011). Indeed, India's regulatory framework, designed largely by scientists of the Environment

Ministry and the Biotechnology Department, restricts itself to impacts assessment and determinations of biosafety (through the Biotechnology Department and the Environment Ministry) and extramural funding (at the hands of the Biotechnology Department).

This was, again, because of the very way biotechnology was configured as a state science in India. Beyond representation on the committees, the Ministry of Agriculture, the Department of Consumer Affairs, and the Ministry of Health and Family Welfare—as three departments directly involved with crops, food, and health—had very little role to play in the regulatory structure and in policy making. The Department of Consumer Affairs was not represented in the committees at all. Both the Allocation of Business Rules and Rules 1989 framed GM crops as biotechnological products posing environmental hazards, rather than as crops, food, and livelihoods. In early years the ICAR was directly involved neither in agronomic evaluation nor in commercial release. Its role was restricted merely to participation in the GEAC and the RCGM. In May 2003 the Ministry of Agriculture formed a task force on applications of biotechnology in agriculture under M. S. Swaminathan's chairmanship, as a priority-setting exercise. The report, finalized in 2004, remains sidelined. In recent years, under pressure from activists who distrust company-generated data, the GEAC has been asking applicants to conduct field trials supervised by ICAR institutions and state agricultural universities, but that is the extent of the Agriculture Ministry's involvement in the regulation of GM crops.[32] In effect, India's regulatory regime offers no deliberative space to raise more fundamental questions about whether India should venture into GM crops in the first place, and, if yes, which crops and which traits are appropriate in the Indian context. It thus implicitly turns political questions of policy into technical determinations of safety, and, in this respect, the RCGM and the GEAC are indeed technocratic bodies.

It is, however, equally true that even in the realm of regulation, when confronted by an outright technical problem (identifying whether Doritos chips in a particular shop in Delhi have GM ingredients), the GEAC's response is anything but grounded in technical reason. There is a curious role reversal in the cases discussed here. Advocates of GM crops tend to emphasize "science-based regulation." The implicit suggestion is that science is disinterested, whereas opponents have a political agenda in stoking seemingly unscientific concerns. In my analysis, the GM mustard trial was blocked by a scientific determination by the Rajasthan government, while Greenpeace mobilized on the grounds of science, to be thwarted by a legal-administrative consideration. This should alert us both to the politics lurking beneath science-based regulation, and to how activist struggles can equally be anchored in science.

5

Emergence and Deepening of Activism against GM Crops

On a sultry June afternoon in 2013 at central Delhi's Jantar Mantar area, the nerve center of protests in the city, crowds were beginning to thin. Fatigue was setting in as voices turned hoarse from shouting slogans since the morning. The air turned heavily somnolent as people drifted to find a shaded spot to rest after lunch. A corner suddenly erupted with slogans against Monsanto and the Biotechnology Regulatory Authority of India Bill, which aimed to replace the existing committee-based regulatory structure with a single-window regulator. Young men and women, some of whom were wearing the signature white Gandhi cap associated with the newly formed political party, the Aam Aadmi Party, shouted, "Monsanto *Bharat Chhoddo! Bharat Chhoddo!* [Monsanto Quit India! Quit India!]," much as youths two generations before had sloganeered during the anticolonial Quit India movement of 1942. What had sparked the burst of excitement was the arrival of Arvind Kejriwal, leader of the Aam Aadmi Party, then campaigning energetically for the chief ministership of Delhi. Already present on the makeshift stage were two seasoned politicians in an unlikely pairing: Sitaram Yechury, a member of Parliament from the Communist Party of India (Marxist), and K. Govindacharya, associated with the right-wing Hindutva organization Rashtriya Swayamsevak Sangh, the parent of the Bharatiya Janata Party (BJP). Accompanying them were leaders of the Bharatiya Kisan Union (Indian Farmers' Union), among others.

After several rounds of sloganeering and railing against transnationals like Monsanto in colorful and potent Hindi and English idioms, the three politicians—Yechury, Kejriwal, and Govindacharya—held hands in a show of strength and vowed to halt the "invasion" of GM crops and keep the proposed bill at bay. This unlikely coming together of the right, the left, and the upstart Aam Aadmi Party—Kejriwal did not disappoint and took ample potshots at both the right and the left while making common cause with them—was orchestrated by the staff of the Coalition for a GM-Free India (which I will describe in detail later) and Greenpeace India, metropolitan and middle-class activists to boot, who might, according to some interpretations (Chatterjee 2006; Fernandes and Heller 2006), be expected to show disdain for mass and electoral politics.

Studies of the anti-GM movements in India have typically focused on the initial wave of protests surrounding Bt cotton in the late 1990s and early 2000s (Shah 2005; Scoones 2006; Herring 2007a, 2007b, 2010). The standard account goes as follows: the origin of anti-GM activism lies in the framing of "GM crops" as technical and political objects of governance in Europe. This frame then diffused globally through the Cartagena Protocol on Biosafety, setting up administrative "choke points" to which protests could be harnessed (Herring 2010; Scoones 2006). These protests were orchestrated by a relatively thin base of activists, in alliance with international NGOs such as Greenpeace, Genetic Resources Action International (GRAIN), and Rural Advancement Foundation International (RAFI) (Herring 2007a; Madsen 2001; Stone 2012). The protests raised ethical questions regarding moving genes around and patenting them. They targeted Monsanto particularly as a symbol of neocolonial globalization through monopolistic control over seeds, while at the same time capitalizing on regulatory science's inability to provide certitudes about the effects of GM crops on biodiversity, the environment, and the health of consumers and livestock (Shah 2011; Herring 2015). This has happened against the backdrop of widespread reports of agrarian distress and a shocking number of suicides by farmers in the last two decades, many of whom have been (Bt) cotton farmers in rain-fed areas (Vasavi 2012).

Looking at the protests against Bt cotton more comprehensively and also the subsequent ones against Bt eggplant, or brinjal, however, I find that the most interesting aspect about skeptics and opponents of GM crops is not that they have raised "broader" questions of ethics and political economy (Visvanathan and Parmar 2002; Schurman and Munro 2010; Wynne 2007). Rather, they have increasingly fought biotechnology companies on the very terrain where one might expect companies to have a stronger hand—the terrain of regulatory science. In other words, activists have not pointed to the inherent limits of probabilistic science, pace Herring (2007b) and Shah (2011), but have instead fought technical regulatory assessments with counterassessments by drawing on the same body of science and pointing to its weaknesses vis-à-vis its own framework of risk assessment. Second, anti-GM activism in India has highlighted tensions and contradictions in the administration of GM crops under Rules 1989 and the Environment (Protection) Act 1986, rather than relying on regulatory frames from Europe or elsewhere. The Cartagena Protocol is less important to the story—in fact, activism in India predates the Cartagena Protocol. Third, the strength of the activism lies in its loose, somewhat fractious, nevertheless canny coordination among mobilizations that speak multiple languages, rally different segments of the polity, and jockey states against the center (that is, the federal government), departments against departments, and political parties against political parties. Fourth, what enables the coming together of such diverse and even antagonistic segments is the singular and narrow focus on GM crops, while deflecting any consensus concerning the future of agriculture. It is this deft political orchestration that lends anti-GM campaigns their strength and agility (see Scoones 2008), challenging the way we think about popular politics, law, and social movements.

I deliberately pay more attention to mobilizations against Bt cotton and Bt eggplant in India precisely because, as social movements working from a position of weakness, they have tried to link questions of democracy with those of technology in the future of agriculture. The case made by advocates of GM crops is more straightforward about addressing hunger and food shortages through technological interventions (see Pental 2003; Paarlberg 2008).

Emergence of Activism against GM Crops

The initial challenge to GM crops in India emerged from a PIL filed by Vandana Shiva in 1999 before the Supreme Court. Shiva's interest in GM crops arose from that transnational conjuncture in the late 1980s that brought together environmental activists from the North and activists alarmed by the harmful effects of the Green Revolution in the Global South (Schurman and Munro 2010). Shiva told me it was while researching her book on the Green Revolution in Punjab that she started noticing how the chemical industry was venturing into the seeds sector. In the late 1990s she saw Monsanto's advertisements in Indian newspapers promoting Bollgard Bt (GM) cotton, even as neither the Environment Ministry nor the Ministry of Agriculture had approved Bt cotton for commercial release.[1] She told me that this led her organization, Research Foundation for Science, Technology and Ecology (RFSTE), to petition the Supreme Court against the Union of India, represented by the Biotechnology Department, the Environment Ministry, and the Ministry of Agriculture.[2]

This was among the first, if not the first, class-action suit on the issue of sound regulation of GM crops in the world,[3] a tactic that has since been tried in such different countries as Brazil, South Africa, and the United States, with mixed results.

The twists and turns of this case, indeed each case discussed in this chapter, merit more space than is available here, and I will only highlight certain salient aspects. When Shiva filed the PIL through the noted public-minded lawyers Sanjay Parikh and Prashant Bhushan, Mahyco was conducting field trials of Bt cotton in several locations across India under the direction of the Review Committee on Genetic Manipulation (RCGM). In the initial affidavit before the Supreme Court, Shiva posed three principal challenges. As chapter 3 noted, she challenged the permission that the Biotechnology Department granted to Mahyco for importing 3.5 ounces (100 grams) of Monsanto's Bt cottonseeds. She argued that this permission was ultra vires (a jurisdictional overreach) because, according to Rules 1989, only the Genetic Engineering Approval Committee (GEAC) had the power to allow imports and exports.

The second challenge lay in the fact that the Bt cotton field trials that Mahyco was then conducting across India had been authorized by the RCGM and not the GEAC, which was the designated "competent authority" for such trials under Rules 1989. The revised guidelines issued by the Biotechnology Department in 1998 devised a distribution of powers whereby the RCGM can allow small-scale trials, wheras large-scale trials require permission from the GEAC—but these only formalized through "guidelines" what the RCGM had already been doing in practice: approving field trials. As Shiva argued before the Supreme Court, the legal status of these guidelines was unclear, and she urged the Court to set store only by Rules 1989 since they had been enacted under the Environment (Protection) Act 1986.

The third challenge invoked the federal distribution of powers. Shiva argued that the State Biotechnology Coordination Committees and district-level committees were not functioning in the case of many states and districts where Mahyco was conducting trials. She also noted that the GEAC had failed to take village-level (Panchayati Raj) institutions on board, as it ought to have after the passage of the Seventy-third and Seventy-fourth Amendments to the Constitution—which empowered local self-government institutions at the village and town levels. By her raising these issues, the administration of GM crops under Rules 1989, and vis-à-vis the framework of the EPA 1986, was at stake, and not the GM or living modified organism (LMO) framework of the Cartagena Protocol, which entered into force in 2003.[4]

In its replies and counteraffidavits, the Government of India, represented by the Biotechnology Department, denied these charges and defended its actions. Throughout the case, the Biotechnology Department, and not the Environment Ministry, responsible for environmental protection, filed replies on behalf of the Government of India. Shiva did highlight this to the Court. In 2002, when the GEAC approved the commercial release of Mahyco's Bt cotton hybrids, Shiva asked for a stay on the grounds that the processes leading up to the approval of Bt cotton were sub judice (not yet decided), but the stay was not granted. Shiva's strategy to bring the approval of Bt cotton into the picture, however, had an unanticipated consequence. Mahyco's and Monsanto's lawyers, party to the case, pointed out that, under the rules, anyone aggrieved by an order of the GEAC can appeal to an appellate authority. Thus, on November 12, 2002, the Supreme Court ordered Shiva to approach the appellate authority and adjourned the matter until the appeal was heard and decided. In response to Shiva's appeal, the appellate authority, a former secretary of the Environment Ministry, asked the ministry to demarcate the roles and functions of the RCGM and the GEAC more clearly. But he dismissed the appeal itself.[5] Shiva appealed the order back to the Supreme Court, which dismissed the entire PIL in January 2004 on the grounds that it had become "infructuous," or futile.

In 2006, against the backdrop of the regulatory testing of Mahyco's GM (Bt) eggplant, Shiva filed another PIL before the Supreme Court, this time against the Department of Consumer Affairs, the Environment Ministry, and the Ministry of Health and Family Welfare. She again raised the question of inadequate regulation of GM crops, but this time in their guise as food, and asked the Court to direct the Government of India to, among other things, enact rules for labeling of GM food. This was a clever move because, though the Biotechnology Department and the Ministry of Agriculture have opposed labeling of GM food as prohibitively expensive and difficult to enforce, food safety–related issues at that point fell under the purview of the Ministry of Health and Family Welfare and the Department of Consumer Affairs. This PIL succeeded in getting the Department of Consumer Affairs to issue rules for labeling a certain class of GM food in 2013, which was not a minor victory. More recently, the primary food safety regulator, the Food Safety and Standards Authority of India, has begun framing rules for labeling of GM foods, but execution and enforcement remain ongoing challenges (Bhushan et al. 2018).

Shiva is best known outside India for ecofeminism and her activism against capital-intensive, chemicalized agriculture and GM crops. This leads her critics to accuse her of obscurantism and peddling pseudoscience (for example, Aiyar 2002; Specter 2014). An entirely different face of Vandana Shiva is visible in her court maneuvers. The affidavits in the first PIL enumerate details of procedural propriety and regulatory fidelity. These submissions demonstrate detailed comprehension of differences between the multiple regulatory guidelines issued by the Biotechnology Department, as well as painstaking attempts to collect evidence—including scientific papers on GM crops and field data on Bt cotton. The terms Shiva is widely associated with—ecofeminism, biopiracy, seeds of suicide—are absent from the affidavits. Of course, that has much to do with the genre of legal affidavits. But the fact that she chose to go down this route at all suggests a more general point—activism in practice exceeds the terms and frameworks articulated by activists and latched on to by their critics. Consequently, in her first PIL, she raised objections and concerns that might resonate among even those with no particular sympathies for ecofeminism and no aversion to GM seeds. In fact, even those who advocate GM seeds might still share her concerns about procedural propriety and administrative mandates.

The Constitutional Challenge to Rules 1989

The concerns over the structure and scope of regulation were reanimated by two ongoing PILs that were filed a few years after the Supreme Court dismissed Shiva's PIL of 1999. In January 2004 Dr. Suman Sahai filed a PIL before the Supreme Court, which is as yet unresolved.[6] Sahai, an agricultural scientist with a PhD in genetics from the premier Indian Agricultural Research Institute, has held appointments in research institutions in India and abroad. In 1993 she founded the NGO Gene Campaign in Delhi to work on issues of agriculture, food, and biodiversity, and to challenge extension of intellectual property regimes to seeds and to plant and animal genetic resources.

Sahai's involvement with the regulation of GMOs in India predates her activism in the arena of food and agriculture, and in fact it predates even the Gene Campaign. She was a member of the inaugural GEAC when it was constituted in May 1990, though her association with the committee did not last very long. Her most intense engagement, however, began with the proposal to commercially release Bt cotton and GM mustard (developed by a private company) in

India in the late 1990s. From the very beginning, she explicitly distanced herself from other movements against GM crops and Monsanto. For instance, in a blog post titled "Target Monsanto for the Right Not the Wrong Reasons," Sahai (1998) critiqued the uprooting of Monsanto's field trials in Karnataka by the Karnataka Rajya Raitha Sangha (KRRS), or the Karnataka Farmers' Association.[7] In contrast, she argued that the more important concerns with the trials were whether local farmers understood what was being tested and the risks thereof; whether they understood the necessary safety precautions and had consented to the trials with full knowledge of the potential risks; and whether safety precautions had been actually observed and if Indian scientists and monitoring agencies were involved in ensuring stringent and robust trials. In brief, rather than voicing wholesale opposition to either Monsanto or GM crops, she questioned the adequacy of existing safety protocols, availability of experts to competently analyze and interpret data, public awareness, and the fact that applicants were generating all the data and were even paying for the hospitality of monitoring teams. Sahai denies being "anti-GM."

In the early 2000s Sahai repeatedly tried to engage with the GEAC through letters and requests for a meeting. She wrote on multiple occasions to the GEAC asking for all biosafety data—data from field trials, animal feeding studies, toxicological and allergenicity analysis, and so on—for Bt cotton to be made public. Not receiving any response, she wrote another letter, this time with representatives of three farmers' organizations, including Vijay Jawandhia. Jawandhia was associated with Shetkari Sangathana, a farmers' organization in the western Indian state of Maharashtra. In this letter of October 14, 2002, to the GEAC's chairman, the signatories stated:

> We are not asking for a ban or moratorium on GM technology. We are as keen as all other rational and responsible peo-

> ple, that the farmers of this country get a range of superior crop varieties to choose from. However, any varieties you offer the farmers must be thoroughly tested for performance and safety. We are writing to express our concern about the lack of transparency in the functioning of the GEAC and the quite deplorable secrecy that surrounds decision making with respect to GM crops in India. . . . We are writing to demand that all data collected from field trials be made available to the public along with the rationale for the decision taken.[8]

The Shetkari Sangathana has often expressed loud support for GM crops, and the fact that one of its leading members signed onto Sahai's letter points to how she was raising concerns of wider import than those broached by the narrower anti-GM agenda, into which she is slotted too often.

Throughout 2002, Sahai requested the GEAC to release biosafety data for Bt cotton, without any response. She also started posing broader policy-oriented questions about GM crops. In an article written in 2003, she forcefully argued:

> It is clear that priorities for the development of agricultural biotechnologies must be based on indigenous needs and a thorough needs assessment. Yet most developing countries copy the concepts and structures of regulatory and oversight systems straight from the industrial countries, without any effort to incorporate developing country perspectives and sensitivities. Even the research priorities in agricultural biotechnology are based on what the industrial countries have developed, and very little has been done to evolve an indigenous set of priorities based on the needs of small farmers and local agricultural production systems. . . .

> India is an important agricultural country with significant concerns about food security and the livelihoods of millions of small and subsistence farmers. A targeted and informed biotechnology policy can help to solve some of India's agricultural problems. (Sahai 2003)

In 2003 the Gene Campaign organized a conference, "Relevance of GM Technology to Indian Agriculture and Food Security," and formulated twenty consensus recommendations that Sahai forwarded to the Biotechnology Department. The department rebutted each of those recommendations. For instance, responding to the recommendation to conduct a socioeconomic impact assessment before making a decision on a GM crop, the Biotechnology Department trivialized the issue and made it about profitability analyses by seed companies. I report some of the recommendations with the department's responses in Table 4.

Stonewalled by the government at every step, Sahai took legal recourse. The PIL that she filed in 2004 before the Supreme Court took up the deeper issues signaled above. In fact, to my mind, more than Shiva's first PIL and another PIL filed in 2005, Sahai's 2004 PIL presented the most significant constitutional challenge to the regulatory regime in India. Sahai's core claim was that the Rules 1989 were arbitrary and unconstitutional and not in consonance with Article 21 (Right to Life) in the Indian Constitution.[9] Further, they had not kept pace with developments in environmental jurisprudence in India; they failed to address principles that had been affirmed by the Supreme Court on a number of occasions, such as precautionary principle, sustainable development, the "polluter pays" principle, intergenerational equity,[10] and the right to information and community participation.

To substantiate the claim of arbitrariness, Sahai drew the Court's attention to the fact that Rules 1989 did not provide qualifications for

Table 4. Some Recommendations from the Gene Campaign in 2003 and Responses from the Biotechnology Department

Recommendation	*Response*
A comprehensive biotechnology policy should be developed in consultation with all stakeholders.	It is not felt necessary that a separate National biotech policy should be developed.
There should be a consultative and participatory process to prioritise crops and traits for genetic improvement through biotechnology with the goal of addressing the needs of small farmers and Indian agriculture.	The Ministry of Agriculture has already set up a task force to look into the issues.[a]
A cost and risk benefit analysis must be conducted before deciding on a GM product.	The cost and risk benefit analysis is the basic fundamental of seed business and there should not be any apprehension with such GM crops.
Develop a stringent protocol to assess environmental and ecological impact.	The Protocol to assess environmental and ecological impact for risk assessment and risk management are already inbuilt in the EPA and they are not less stringent than anywhere in the world.
Make GEAC more competent, transparent and accountable.	GEAC is comprised of all stakeholders pertaining to various administrative ministries and is thus competent.
Post data on research and development of GM crops and products on websites and local newspapers.	Posting of data on R&D on GM crops and products on website is not a practical suggestion.
An annual review of all decisions on GM products must be presented to the Parliament.	Submission of GEAC decisions to Parliament is not a practical exercise.
There should be a moratorium on *commercial cultivation* of GM crops until the regulatory system is demonstrably improved. Research on GM crops, however, should continue.	There is no need for a moratorium on commercial cultivation of GM crops as research in this field aims at benefit to the farmers at large with benefit to the society. The regulatory procedures that exist today are good enough.

a. This was the task force under M. S. Swaminathan's chairmanship.

membership of the regulatory committees, and that the GEAC was staffed by ex-officio members (such as the director general of the Indian Council of Medical Research) who may not have been competent in the regulation of GMOs. Further, subject specialists, such as soil scientists, entomologists, agronomists, toxicologists, allergy experts, ecologists, and social scientists, were entirely absent from the GEAC. Other lacunae she pointed out included lack of transparency and public participation mechanisms, lack of accountability, lack of penal provisions for violations of rules, and lack of protocols or expertise to assess the socioeconomic effect of GM crops. In essence, Sahai exposed the absence of any substantive regulatory framework at the heart of Rules 1989. The Indian government denied these contentions.

Sahai asked the Court to direct the Indian government to (a) bring Rules 1989 in consonance with various provisions of the Constitution, especially Article 21 (Right to Life), which includes the Right to Environment and Human Health, failing which the Court declare Rules 1989 unconstitutional; (b) set up a "high-powered committee" to formulate a national policy on GMOs through a multi-stakeholder consultation process; and (c) observe a moratorium on various permissions, approvals, and trials concerning GMOs, until the rules were amended and a sound regulatory and monitoring system was put in place. She emphasized the last demand especially for those crops for which India is a center of origin or diversity.

The case, however, got pushed away from these constitutional matters to far more technical and logistical matters with the filing of another PIL on the same issue in 2005. But I would like to describe some of the developments Sahai's PIL triggered. First, the Biotechnology Department undertook a hasty exercise in framing a national biotechnology development policy, for which it invited Sahai to serve on the expert committee; Sahai resigned after a few meetings, citing lack of transparency in drafting the policy (Sahai 2006).

Because of both the PIL and the respect Sahai enjoyed among a section of agricultural scientists and policy elites close to the ruling Congress Party–led United Progressive Alliance (UPA) government, the Planning Commission asked Sahai in March 2006 to chair the Task Force on Biodiversity and Genetically Modified Organisms for the Eleventh Five Year Plan (2007–12). The task force included agricultural scientists, biotechnologists, ecologists, policy experts, and social scientists. The final report that the task force submitted devised a policy framework to bring together and integrate concerns regarding GMOs, agro-biodiversity conservation, agrarian livelihoods, and farmers' rights. It was very critical of the ad hoc approach of the Environment Ministry and the Biotechnology Department. In essence, the report called for a policy for GM crops devised through consultation with multiple stakeholders. It saw this policy as directing biotechnology research and research on GM crops in ways that were in line with the needs of India's diverse and complex agriculture. It was critical of the model whereby the Biotechnology Department and the Environment Ministry confined themselves to assessing the safety of products prioritized and developed entirely outside their supervision, and it wanted the Biotechnology Department to take a more active role in shaping the research and development agenda for GM crops. It called for a moratorium on commercial release of GM crops until the regulatory system was improved—research, however, could continue. I quote some sections from the report, not only to offer a flavor of its logic and recommendations, but also because the very same themes keep appearing in the debate over GM crops in India, in different forums, at different junctures.

> The policy framework for proper management of GMOs is located within a wider biotechnology policy, agricultural policy, [science and technology] policy, and environmental policy.

Proper management of GMOs will be confined to printing ink and paper unless and until policy dialogue among different compartments of the Indian bureaucracy that shapes or has an impact on Indian agriculture, is facilitated.

The Government of India, through its Department of Biotechnology must initiate this process, and a comprehensive policy for GMOs be developed within two years.

The national policy on GMOs should follow the recommendation of the M. S. Swaminathan Task Force on Agrobiotechnology. . . .

- To start with, a comprehensive biotechnology policy approved by stakeholder consultations must be put in place. . . .
- A policy must be developed for transgenic varieties for which India is a center of origin and diversity, particularly rice. Commercialization of GM rice should be deferred until a body of data is built up on its safety under Indian conditions. . . .
- There should be a consultative and participatory process to prioritize crops and traits for genetic improvement through biotechnology with the goal of addressing the needs of small farmers and Indian agriculture.
- Herbicide tolerance trait will displace agriculture labor which does manual weeding, destroy vegetation that is used by rural communities as supplementary food, fodder and medicinal plants and disallow multiple cropping systems. State level and District level committees must be in a position to assess these contexts—of labour supply and demand constraints and estimate

where and how GM crops with these traits can be cultivated. . . .

- The GM crop research agenda must be sensitive to India's trade interests. It would be foolish to indulge in Bt Basmati and jeopardize the Basmati export market to Europe. . . .
- Review the policy of promoting GM crops vs Organic crops, assessing the [unique selling point] of particular agriculture zones like rain fed areas, hill states and mountain ecosystems. (Planning Commission 2007, 14–16)

As I wrote earlier, the thrust of Sahai's PIL on constitutional and policy-oriented matters was pushed in a different direction because of the filing of a second PIL on the issue of regulation of GM crops in 2005.[11] Aruna Rodrigues, an economist and management consultant based in the central Indian town of Mhow, spearheaded the PIL, filed by a group of individuals.[12] The veteran public interest lawyer Prashant Bhushan represented them before the Court. In her initial affidavit, Rodrigues marshaled some of the same arguments as Sahai, and she, too, sought a moratorium on the release of GM crops until adequate and stringent biosafety testing mechanisms, and those for incorporating inputs from the public, were put into place. Unsurprisingly, the Supreme Court merged the two PILs. In subsequent affidavits, however, Rodrigues and Bhushan began focusing on narrower issues of field trials and biosafety protocols, forcing the Supreme Court to weigh in on the nitty-gritty at a remove from constitutional matters.

This resulted in several contradictory interim judgments from the Supreme Court. For instance, in May 2006 it ruled that all field trials could be authorized only by the GEAC, essentially putting an end to the practice of the RCGM's approving small-scale trials. Then, in September 2006, the Court ordered the GEAC to withhold approvals for all field trials. In May 2007 the Court allowed certain ongoing field trials to continue but ruled that all GM crops under testing should be isolated from their non-GM variants by at least 650 feet (200 meters), to reduce the possibility of accidental pollination of non-GM variants by the GM crop. Isolation distances, however, are crop-specific. That distance is more than sufficient for mustard and not enough for, say, eggplant. It also ordered that all applicants submit a validated protocol that could detect the presence of the GM event[13] at a level of detection of 0.01 percent: sensitive enough to detect, for example, one GM rice grain among 9,999 conventional rice grains.

This section of the ruling from May 2007 is a particularly stark illustration of how confused the Court itself was as far as the details of biosafety tests and trials went: "As regards these four species of Bt cotton varieties, the GEAC may give permission for commercial use, subject to the usual conditions imposed. GEAC should also satisfy itself that events are not further genetically modified so that no further species are created by such modification. GEAC should also verify whether these species by commercial use create any toxicity or allergenicity to any of the users in organic conducted with these varieties of Bt cotton." The PIL got mired in a swamp of technical details and confusion. At various points, the judges themselves protested that the Court was not competent to rule on details of biosafety assessment.[14] In 2008 the Court allowed the GEAC to consider applications for approval of GM crops, but it appointed M. S. Swaminathan and Pushpa Bhargava as observers to the GEAC—acceding to a request from the petitioners.

Undoubtedly, the confusion and vacillation in the rulings threw the regulatory system into chaos, as dossiers accumulated before the

GEAC or were not considered until the sowing season had already passed. Even among environmental activists, there was some consternation about the increasingly narrow issue of field trials that was occupying the Court. Nevertheless, there were two significant developments that emerged from the heightened judicial attention to the issue of biosafety. First, on a petition by Sahai, the Court ordered all the biosafety tests conducted on Bt cotton to be made publicly available through the Environment Ministry's website. This met the longstanding demand of many groups and opened up the scientific case for Bt cotton to be subject to wider scrutiny. Second, in 2012 the Supreme Court set up a Technical Expert Committee of six scientists vetted by both the petitioners and the Government of India to break the impasse. These triggered developments outside the Supreme Court, to which I now turn.

Mahyco used the same Bt gene sourced from Monsanto to develop a transgenic Bt eggplant, or brinjal. By virtue of the pesticidal protein coded for by the Bt gene, Bt eggplant is said to be resistant to lepidopterous pests such as the eggplant fruit and shoot borer (*Leucinodes orbonalis*), and Mahyco claimed that farmers could save on the amount of pesticides they had to spray. Bt eggplant started moving up the regulatory ladder around 2001 and underwent large-scale field trials starting in 2007, by which time it was clear that the GEAC would soon have to decide on its commercial release. Meanwhile, GM mustard, developed by Deepak Pental at Delhi University, and GM rice were also moving forward in the regulatory process.

In 2006 several groups working in different states and regions on issues related to agriculture, environmental justice, and rural livelihoods, such as the Centre for Sustainable Agriculture in undivided Andhra Pradesh, Thanal in Kerala, Kheti Virasat Mission in Punjab, and Greenpeace India, among others, came together as the Coalition for a GM-Free India. On June 15, 2006, the coalition met with the federal environment minister, A. Raja, and demanded that the GEAC provide evidence of the effective functioning of regulatory mechanisms, respond to technical objections to some of the studies done with Bt eggplant, and withhold permissions for field trials until fundamental questions about farmers' and consumers' rights to choice, to safe food, and to participation in regulatory policies and decisions about GM crops were satisfactorily answered through public debate.

The GEAC also came under fire from Pushpa Bhargava, appointed as an invitee by the Supreme Court in 2008. Bhargava told the press in May 2008 that the "lack of data on health and bio-safety [of Bt eggplant] is shocking" (Jain 2008). Further, using the newly legislated Right to Information Act, 2005, Greenpeace India and subsequently the Gene Campaign filed requests seeking the biosafety data on Bt eggplant that Mahyco had submitted to the Biotechnology Department and the Environment Ministry. Because both Mahyco and the Biotechnology Department opposed this request on the specious grounds of hurting the former's competitive market position (Aga and Choudhury 2018), ultimately Sahai petitioned the Supreme Court. In August 2008 the Supreme Court directed the GEAC to post all biosafety data on Bt cotton and Bt eggplant on its website and make them publicly available.

Making biosafety data publicly available had three major consequences. First, esoteric debates over field trials and biosafety, which were until then confined to the Supreme Court, spilled into wider forums, including transnational public spheres. Second, on the back of the contention over science, groups mounted pressure on elected politicians, rather than just the bureaucracy. Third, younger activists took the battle to the streets and to social media, and, most consequentially, they rallied states against the federal government.

Public Contests over Science

> Ravi Chandran, a self-professed farmer from Tamil Nadu, in a tweet: "The anti GMO activist's biggest strength [is] Superstitions of the people. The vested interest activists thrive by nurturing such superstitions."
>
> Neha Saigal, campaigner, Greenpeace India: "You are slightly confused, the strength is science and that will not change despite biotech propaganda."
>
> —*Tweets exchanged between @FarmerRaviVKV and @NehaSaigal24, February 14, 2014*

As soon as the full biosafety data were released, Aruna Rodrigues contacted several scientists and asked them to comment on the biosafety dossiers. At Rodrigues's behest, four scientists outside India—Gilles-Éric Séralini, Judy Carman, Jack Heinemann, and Doug Gurian-Sherman—responded with serious critiques of the dossiers.[15] Rodrigues filed the critiques before the Supreme Court. For instance, Jack Heinemann pointed out that the experiments conducted to establish the number of transgene inserts in Bt eggplant were inconclusive, leaving open the possibility of more than one transgene insert, or insertion of vector DNA along with the transgene—ideally, a transgenic should have only one copy of the foreign gene. This is one among several examples that make specific criticisms from within the paradigm of regulatory testing. Whatever their views on GM crops in general, what these four scientists provided were, first and foremost, technical critiques of the biosafety data and tests; these were criticisms of the way tests had been designed and conducted and the way inferences were drawn on the basis of inadequate and faulty data.

Under attack on the technical front, the GEAC constituted a second expert committee to review the biosafety data of Bt eggplant. The report of this committee, released on October 8, 2009, stirred the hornet's nest further. Along with reviewing the biosafety data, the committee was also tasked with addressing the critiques provided by the aforementioned scientists, along with comments from Bhargava and Kavitha Kuruganti. Kuruganti is one of the leading advocates of sustainable agriculture in India, has been associated with the NGO Kheti Virasat Mission (Mission for Agrarian Heritage) and the umbrella group Alliance for Sustainable and Holistic Agriculture (ASHA), and has worked intensively with the Coalition for a GM-Free India. In its final report, the expert committee dismissed all concerns and criticisms and cleared the way for the commercial release of Bt eggplant. Following the favorable report, the GEAC, in its meeting of October 14, 2009, decided to approve Bt eggplant for commercial cultivation. Upon nudging by Environment Minister Jairam Ramesh, and in a move contrary to its statutory nature, however, the GEAC left the final decision to Ramesh.

In a unique public exercise between October 2009 and February 2010, Ramesh released the second expert committee report, organized public hearings in seven cities, and invited anyone interested to offer feedback. He also sought comments from notable scientists, state governments, and a range of experts and political leaders in India and abroad. Some farmer groups supported Bt eggplant, while others opposed it. Kavitha Kuruganti wrote an excoriating critique wherein she accused the second expert committee of being unscientific, riven with conflicts of interest, and having failed to analyze the data thoroughly. She found the report unscientific on several counts. For instance, she observed that the actual Bt gene inserted in eggplant was chimeric, a gene synthesized by combining nucleotides from cry1Ac and cry1Ab genes,[16] while some of the animal feeding and other studies were conducted with the pure cry1Ac protein (a protein that had been manufactured synthetically, and not the one actually expressed in Bt eggplant). She also faulted some of the statistical analyses and their interpretation. Further, she raised questions of co-optation of regulation: she charged the second expert committee with being compromised by conflicts of interest because some members were themselves developing GM crops and some others were associated with the same program that was promoting Bt eggplant in partnership with Mahyco. She also pointed out that the chairman of the committee, Professor Arjula R. Reddy, had himself admitted to the media that long-range research, required to assess the safety of Bt eggplant, had not been conducted (Chakrabarti 2009). Similarly, Aruna Rodrigues wrote a response detailing technical deficiencies in the biosafety assessment, with input from researchers like David Schubert of the Salk Institute, in California, and the renowned expert on plant lectins Árpád Pusztai.[17] Vandana Shiva too weighed in with criticisms of the biosafety assessment, while warning of threats to biodiversity and food sovereignty.

The second expert committee report was also vigorously critiqued by other scientists, such as Johannes Manjrekar (Microbiology Department and Biotechnology Center, the Maharaja Sayajirao University of Baroda), David Schubert (Salk Institute), David Andow (Department of Entomology, University of Minnesota), and Gilles-Éric Séralini and Jack Heinemann, mentioned earlier. The Centre for Social Medicine and Community Health of the Jawaharlal Nehru University in New Delhi passed a resolution calling for a moratorium on GM crops until their safety was established. Several scientists also supported the decision to commercialize Bt eggplant, such as Deepak Pental (Delhi University), G. Padmanaban (Indian Institute of Science Bangalore), Keshav Kranthi (Central Institute of Cotton Research Nagpur), J. Gowrishankar (Centre for DNA Fingerprinting and Diagnostics Hyderabad), Raj Bhatnagar (International Centre for Genetic Engineering and Biotechnology New Delhi), Nicholas Storer (Dow Agro Sciences), Desiree Hautea (University of the Philippines),

A. M. Shelton (Department of Entomology, Cornell University), and the World Food Prize laureate Gurdev Khush.

Already this scientific dispute was becoming a trial of strength that was based on numbers, a decision-making procedure from the realm of democratic politics and not regulatory science. Two letters were particularly decisive. Ramesh had asked both M. S. Swaminathan and V. L. Chopra for their views. Neither supported the decision to immediately release Bt eggplant. Swaminathan asked for an assessment of chronic effects of consumption of Bt eggplant, as well as the potential effect on eggplant biodiversity in India—given that India is a center of eggplant diversity. Chopra spoke of the need for independent and above-reproach regulatory mechanisms. He also emphasized that the government should prioritize the crops and traits taken up for transgenics development, echoing a key contention made by Sahai and other activists.

> Government should take the initiative of specifying what traits and crops it will like to see modified through transgenic approach because while the technology CAN make a difference, it should be guided for application strictly according to national needs and priorities. . . . It needs to be recognized and appreciated that food is more than an issue of nutrition and safety: among other things, it is an endowment of culture, a potent instrument of social inter-action and a component of lifestyle whose exercise in terms of choice is jealously guarded and strongly defended. Anything that endangers these requirements will meet with strong resistance in society.[18]

Once the dogged fight to make biosafety data publicly available was won, thanks to the Supreme Court order, the struggle on the scientific front spilled out of the courtroom, as scientists and others from India and abroad weighed in, either in favor of or against Bt eggplant. If contests over science, increasingly public, constituted one significant strand of the debate over GM crops, these larger questions were also articulated directly and indirectly in political terms.

Deepening Political Struggles over GM Crops

The contests over technical aspects of GM crops occurred against the backdrop of campaigns critical of Bt cotton, along with several audits of Bt cotton that had been conducted by different groups in cotton-cultivating states beginning in 2002. As mentioned earlier, after 2006 many of these groups came together as the loose Coalition for a GM-Free India. The group is loose enough for one of its members to confidently assert to me that Suman Sahai was very much a part of it, even as Suman Sahai denied to me any association with "these Johnnies-come-lately." These groups, by virtue of their work, had already established channels of communication with their respective state governments and had more of a base among citizens than Suman Sahai or Aruna Rodrigues or the scientists who were clashing over regulatory science. Their experience of rallying people to the streets ("*raste pe utar aayenge*") and their finger on the pulse of state-level politics constitute the second significant prong of the fight against GM crops.

Some of the first set of protests came from farmers' groups in rice-growing areas, who were anxious about the risk of contamination from GM rice trials, which could jeopardize their exports to Europe and other markets averse to GM food. States such as Kerala and Uttarakhand, where there were already strong constituencies advocating organic agriculture, also saw protests. In 2006 the Bharatiya Kisan Union (Indian Farmers' Union), led by the agrarian populist Mahendra Singh Tikait, organized a major rally of about 30,000 farmers, named Kisan Kumbh (*Kisan* is the Hindi word for farmers) after one of the most important Hindu festivals, in the northern Indian city of Haridwar in Uttarakhand state. On the banks of the river Ganga, Haridwar is considered holy by a large number of people. At the conclusion of the rally, Tikait, Devinder Sharma (the co-petitioner in Aruna Rodrigues's PIL), and other farmer-leaders met with Chief Minister N. D. Tiwari and demanded that the Uttarakhand government declare the state "GM-free" in order to realize its vision of an organic state (Coalition for a GM-Free India 2006). They also warned Tiwari about the grave risks of Bt eggplant—and GM seeds in general—and secured his assurance that he would not allow GM seeds in the state.

Similarly, groups advocating organic agriculture in the southern Indian state of Kerala, such as Thanal (another member of the coalition), were petitioning their chief minister to ban GM seeds in the state. This culminated in the state government writing a letter asking the federal Ministry of Agriculture to declare Kerala a "GM-free zone." In India, under the federal distribution of powers, agriculture is a state subject; state governments have the power to legislate on agriculture. By virtue of the Allocation of Business Rules for the Government of India, GM crops had been framed as a biotechnology product requiring regulation from the point of view of environmental hazards. Even the PILs, by invoking Article 21 (Right to Life), worked largely within this framework. By taking their demands to state governments, however, activist groups effectively broadened the framework—the politics of GM crops was no longer only that of biosafety and environmental risk, but also that of agricultural production and livelihoods, a matter that could not be left to the Environment Ministry and the Biotechnology Department alone.

In November 2008 Kavitha Kuruganti wrote a strongly worded letter to the federal health minister, Dr. Anbumani Ramadoss, himself a medical doctor, pointing out that his ministry's representatives to the GEAC were not raising health-related concerns; they were barely attending GEAC meetings.[19] Ramadoss's political party, Pattali Makkal Katchi, has a base among lower-caste agricultural laborers in the southern Indian state of Tamil Nadu. It was one of the first political parties in India to explicitly take a position against Bt cotton, and GM seeds more generally, for having "ruined" many farmers (*Hindu* 2007). In December 2008 an organization calling itself Doctors for Food & Bio-Safety wrote a long letter to Ramadoss. The letter, signed by six medical doctors,[20] asked the Health Ministry to intervene with the GEAC and press for a moratorium, given the grave health concerns regarding GM crops. The letter also asked the ministry, which had had a department for Ayurveda, Yunani, and other South Asian medical systems since 1995, to protect eggplant and other plants considered medicinal in indigenous healing systems. This anxiety was also shared by many right-wing religious groups, including Hindu nationalist groups. In the same month, Ramadoss gave a fiery speech (in Tamil) in Kancheepuram, Tamil Nadu, denouncing GM crops and vowing not to let Bt eggplant in (*Hindu* 2008). Following up on these petitions, the Health Ministry wrote a letter to the Environment Ministry asking the GEAC to "stop the release of Bt [eggplant] and other GM foods . . . with immediate effect" until consumers' concerns and health-related issues were addressed.[21]

These tactics and the traction they were getting in the states and in the federal government compelled Environment Minister Ramesh to intervene in the GEAC's decision to approve Bt eggplant. As he told me in August 2014: "Otherwise, there would have been hell to pay. I would have been defending in Parliament a decision in which I had no role." After assuming the responsibility for deciding the fate of Bt eggplant, Ramesh invited comments from state governments, too, since agriculture is a state subject. All the state governments that responded to him expressed apprehensions, and no state supported Bt eggplant—not even Gujarat, then under Narendra Modi, which had firmly stood behind Bt cotton. Because of opposition from the states, and a lack of consensus among scientists, Ramesh declared an indefinite moratorium on Bt eggplant, pending further and adequate regulatory testing, among other stipulations. In addition, he emphasized a "cautious, precautionary principle-based approach" and stated that he did not find a persuasive case in favor of Bt eggplant in terms of India's food security (Ramesh 2010; see also Ramesh 2014; Visvanathan 2014).

Another decisive turn in this emerging federal-state tension came in 2011, when some Bihar-based NGOs raised a hue and cry about discovering an illegal GM maize field trial by Monsanto in Samastipur—the GEAC had allowed field trials in two other locations in the state. Maize is one of Bihar's key agricultural commodities, and a furious Nitish Kumar, the chief minister, called Ramesh and insisted that the Environment Ministry immediately withdraw the GEAC's permission and investigate the matter. He also asked Ramesh to consult state governments before allowing field trials. Kumar was upset enough to personally call Ramesh, rather than write a letter, which is more usual. Ramesh shot off a letter to the GEAC, saying: "Bihar [chief minister's] phone call reinforces my belief that biotech regulation, particularly in the field of agriculture, cannot be a purely scientific enterprise. . . . There are political considerations that will come into play and I use that term in its best people-oriented sense" (Parsai 2011).

Immediately afterward, Madhya Pradesh, ruled by the BJP, which was in opposition to the federal government, wrote a strongly worded letter to Ramesh expressing "shock" about the GEAC having allowed trials of GM maize in the state. The letter said: "Government of Madhya Pradesh has taken a decision to prohibit all environmental release of GMOs and keep the state totally free of GM food. We would also request you to reconsider the policy on GM in the national scale and declare a moratorium on all GM food crops" (Sethi 2011). The pressure to take a stand against GM crops probably came from the BJP's grassroots farmers' organization, the Bharatiya Kisan Sangh (Indian Farmers' Organization) which, along with the Swadeshi Jagran Manch, has often made common cause with anti-GM activists in opposing transnational firms and providing critiques of GM crops.[22] On Ramesh's instructions, in July 2011 the GEAC decided to seek No Objection Certificates (NOCs) from state governments before allowing field trials in those states.

The Bt eggplant moratorium and the demand for NOCs from the states, coupled with confusing directions from the Supreme Court, hamstrung GM crop developers further. They were already irked by the GEAC's insensitivity to time and seasons for conducting field trials. The additional requirement of securing NOCs from state governments made conducting trials extremely difficult. Sometimes, by the time an NOC came, the season was already over and the GEAC's season-specific permission had lapsed. The requirement of an NOC opened another front for activism, as groups in several states exerted pressure on the state governments not to issue NOCs for GM crop field trials. By its very structure, this demand cohered with an inertial bureaucratic response, tending to preserve the status quo (Gupta 2012). The status quo had the states uninvolved in field trials: there was no precedent, no mechanism, and no designated "competent authority" to issue NOCs. All states had to do to acquiesce to activist demands was archive the requests for NOCs without doing anything about them. Doing nothing was easy for state bureaucracies and satisfied the activists, and the state did not necessarily have to take a formal and articulated stand against GM crops.

Activism against GM crops had broadened in scale and deepened in terms of social bases from the early days when Vandana Shiva and Suman Sahai petitioned the Supreme Court and the federal government, and the Karnataka Rajya Raitha Sangha burned field trial plots. The younger generation of activists, like those with Greenpeace, the Coalition for a GM-Free India, and regional environmental and agrarian movements, incorporated the tactics of street protests, which have a long history in Indian politics. Thus, in 2008 the Coalition for a GM-Free India, in association with the Our Seeds Campaign (*Hamara Beej Abhiyan*), launched the "I Am No Lab Rat" movement against Bt eggplant. It reached out to students, film stars, and others and organized protest marches in different cities. It used creative ways to make consumers aware of GM foods; for example, activists bicycled around dressed as vegetables and invited famous chefs to cook the "world's biggest" (nearly 750 pounds) roasted, mashed non-GM eggplant dish (*baingan bharta*) in September 2011—offering some of it to Prime Minister Manmohan Singh and the rest of it to underprivileged people. For the last few years, coalition members have been organizing "Monsanto Quit India!" protests on August 9, the anniversary of the anticolonial Quit India movement of 1942, and making efforts to draw support from political parties as well. Different groups have tried to bring the transnational "March against Monsanto" to India, organizing cycle rallies and marches in several Indian cities.

Thus, even as proceedings before the Supreme Court increasingly started turning on narrow technical details of regulatory testing, broader issues of policy and public participation were articulated outside the courtrooms, in the streets and political rallies, and before state- and national-level politicians. The multiplication of repertoires and sites of contestation has also been inflected by regional variations and the schisms in the federated landscape of Indian politics. For instance, the demand by Tikait to keep Uttarakhand "GM-free" at a rally designated as Kisan Kumbh in the "holy city" of Haridwar mobilized the trope of religious purity, which is quite different from the demand to go organic in Kerala, where a fierce controversy has been raging for several decades over the deleterious consequences of the pesticide endosulfan (Joseph and Irshad 2015), even as both campaigns exploit the fact that states rather than the federal government are empowered to legislate on agriculture. There are also more contingent factors to reckon with—for instance, the fact that the Manmohan Singh government (2009–14) was riven by internal dissension (Baru 2014) and multiple centers of power, which allowed Ramesh more leeway than is usually available to a junior minister. Even though his decision to impose the moratorium on Bt eggplant did not go down well with some of his senior Cabinet colleagues, including Prime Minister Singh, he remained unyielding.

Finally, the shift from cotton, a fiber crop, to eggplant, a food crop, was decisive in deepening the concern about GM crops in the second cycle of protest. Even though Bt cottonseeds are crushed to extract edible oil, government regulators consider it exclusively a fiber crop. In the case of a food crop, the debate could no longer be restricted to implications for farmers and biodiversity. The question of food and associated issues of health opened up the debate to wider segments of society and moved it beyond relatively esoteric concerns like agronomic profile and effects on biodiversity. On the plank of consumers' health, doctors were able to muscle in to the debate, even as activists pressured the Ministry of Health to get involved. Far from there being any unified debate across all GM crops, specificities of the crop in question and its intended uses matter, as does the trait in question, as I elaborate in the next chapter. Different types of crops open up different matters of concern through which one can demand a say in the GM debate.

Widening the Base through Multifocal Campaigns

In trying to reach out to uncommitted citizens, activists have been quite savvy in taking advantage of the reach of social media in India, whose penetration is steadily deepening, and which political parties, especially the BJP, are serious about. Though their social media efforts are typically made in the English language, they can still reach a large number of Indians who may read and follow English better than they can speak or write it themselves. For instance, Valentine's Day in India has over the years become a day of clashing with the patriarchs of society, if not in public places, than at least from the safety of a computer or smartphone. On February 14, 2014, Greenpeace India and some members from the Coalition for a GM-Free India launched posts on Twitter saying, "We Don't Love You," addressed to federal ministers advocating GM crops and Prime Minister Manmohan Singh (see figure 1). The exchange between Neha Saigal and Ravi Chandran quoted earlier was from this Twitter campaign.

On February 19, 2013, the Twitter handle @the_BigBattle, which was the self-proclaimed weekly Twitter debating platform, organized a debate titled "#GMFood: Helpful or Harmful?" Anyone could participate, provided one hashtagged GMFood. Neha Saigal (Greenpeace India), Devinder Sharma (co-petitioner in the Rodrigues PIL), Dr. G. V. Ramanjaneyulu (Centre for Sustainable Agriculture), Sridhar Radhakrishnan (Thanal and the Coalition for a GM-Free India), and Ravi Chandran were invited to respond to questions and participate in the debate. The panel was skewed toward naysayers to begin with, and then Ravi Chandran did not come online. In the best tradition of Twitter, there was very little dialogue—the conversation featured some facts along with a melange of rumors and half-truths, charges and countercharges. Supporters of GM crops were in a minority but nevertheless made their presence felt. According to Greenpeace India, this small Twitter campaign managed to reach about 900,000 users, though it is unclear how many of them were in India.

Campaigners were also active in trying to get political parties to take positions against GM crops, especially before national and state elections. For instance, in 2013, when the Congress-led federal

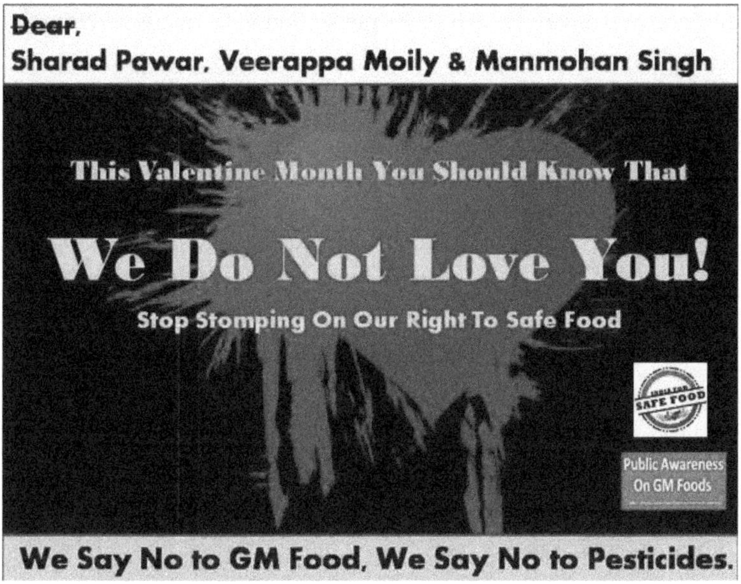

Fig. 1. Post by Neha Saigal, Greenpeace India, on Twitter on February 14, 2014. Manmohan Singh was then India's prime minister, Veerappa Moily the environment minister, and Sharad Pawar the agriculture minister.

government decided to allow some field trials, P. Muralidhar Rao, the national general secretary of BJP, tweeted, "What was [the] hurry for Congress led UPA to clear [the] GM crops field trials which [is] highly controversial just before Loksabha elections?" Neha Saigal, Kavitha Kuruganti, Rajesh Krishnan (then the convener of the Coalition for a GM-Free India) immediately commended him, on Twitter, for "standing for the people of the country" and "taking an anti GM position." Perhaps encouraged by this, Rao then launched 140-character tirades against the Congress-led government for being anti-farmers and pro-companies.

It would certainly be a mistake to overstate the importance of this electronic activism, though this was accompanied by strong regional and national alliances with street power and with traction before the courts. But even electronic activism can translate into popular pressure. When the government tried to introduce a new, single-window independent biotechnology regulatory authority (the Biotechnology Regulatory Authority of India), whose composition, mandate, and powers made activists see red, they launched a signature campaign against the authorizing bill, which collected 460,000 signatures (Tembhekar 2013). Greenpeace India then presented the petition to the Parliamentary Standing Committee on Science and Technology, Environment and Forests. Standing committees are permanent committees comprising members of Parliament from different parties. They report to the Speaker and assist the Parliament and the government in legislating bills and scrutinizing government programs and performance. In the face of fierce opposition, the government had to backtrack, and the bill lapsed in 2014.

Similarly, the March against Monsanto of 2013 inspired former Cabinet Secretary T. S. R. Subramanian (2013) to pen a column on the dangers of field trials of GM crops. Subramanian had little to do with either farming or biotechnology, but given his erstwhile stature as the most senior civil servant in the country, his words carried weight in the government and the bureaucracy. Similarly, former Supreme Court Justice V. R. Krishna Iyer, former federal Election Commissioner J. M. Lyngdoh, and former Chief Justice A. P. Shah of the Delhi High Court, along with several notable scientists, have called for abundant caution before allowing field trials of GM crops (Parsai 2013). There is no doubt that anti-GM activists have had considerable success in galvanizing support and exciting the imagination among different segments of the citizenry about the potential risks of GM crops and food, even as many other social movements, fighting harder and sometimes more important battles, struggle to mobilize people other than those immediately affected by a policy.

The Interplay of Technical Critiques and Popular Politics

The anti-GM movements speak in multiple voices and project multiple agendas and commitments, but, underlying the dizzying array of details about specific campaigns, there is a method to this carnival of protests. Thanks to the loose coordination provided by the Coalition for a GM-Free India, the anti-GM campaign rides on the back of environmental and agricultural movements in different regions of the country. In fact, there are very few exclusively GM-focused movements in the country. Nearly all of them work on GM-related issues as part of a broader program of environmental and agrarian activism. This is what lends the anti-GM campaign clout with regional political parties and state governments (as in Kerala, Madhya Pradesh, Tamil Nadu, and others). These movements provide the campaign its salty vernacular idioms and allow it to plumb the emotive depths of populism. Needless to say, these groups are not always concerned with fidelity to scientific facts about GM crops; they routinely get carried away by the logic of their own idioms and metaphors. Devinder Sharma described to me in June 2013 an episode from the controversy over GM "terminator seeds," which yield sterile seeds in the next generation because of Gene Use Restriction Technologies (GURTs) and so farmers cannot resow them. Sharma was once struggling to translate GURTs to Hindi. A state-level politician came to his aid and suggested to him "*Beejon ki nasbandi*"—or the sterilization of seeds, cleverly comparing GURTs to the deeply unpopular forced sterilization programs during the Emergency years, 1975–77.[23]

The work of articulating thoughtful, technical critiques is done by the likes of Kavitha Kuruganti, Rajesh Krishnan, and other members of the Coalition for a GM-Free India, along with scientists painstakingly recruited by Aruna Rodrigues. With the help of dissident scientists such as Suman Sahai, Pushpa Bhargava, and Gilles-Éric

Séralini, and drawing on transnational networks of anti-GM activists such as Third World Network, the Coalition for a GM-Free India challenges regulatory mechanisms in India, creating ever more hurdles for GM crops in the form of regulatory testing. Advocates of GM crops understand this politics of waiting all too well, as one developer of Bt eggplant said to me in July 2011, "Yes, let's keep testing and testing for the next fifty to a hundred years, by which time this technology will anyway have become obsolete." This is what makes it hard for the government to pin down anti-GM movements. If the government makes a scientific case for the safety of specific GM crops, the movements deploy scientific critiques and the weight of scientific authority—for instance, a petition signed by over one hundred scientists, including vice chancellors of universities—to dispute the case (Nandi 2013). When advocates make a political (usually Malthusian) case to allow GM crops or at least their field trials (for example, Prakash et al. 2014), anti-GM movements challenge them on populist grounds of encroaching on people's right to safe food, or allege that "corporate greed" is preying on India's farmers, often targeting multinationals to whip up nationalist outrage. Thus, anti-GM mobilizations have one foot firmly planted in the terrain of science and the other in the fertile ground of agrarian and consumer populism.

The campaign critical of GM crops consists of regional environmental and agrarian movements with street power, coordinated at the national level by social-media savvy, English-fluent activists who can gauge the mood of India's growing middle classes and who also connect with transnational anti-GM movements. One of the best illustrations of this dialectic was what happened when Veerappa Moily, who took charge as environment minister in December 2013, allowed the GEAC to function after a long hiatus. As he suavely argued to the press in February 2014 in New Delhi, the GEAC was a statutory body and hence he was only making sure it functioned as it should, obliquely critiquing his predecessor and Congress party colleague, Jayanthi Natarajan, who had informally disallowed its meetings. Of course, activist groups responded with petitions and letters. But the most spectacular success, tuned to the cycles of 24/7 news, came when large numbers of irate farmers belonging to the Karnataka Rajya Raitha Sangha and South Indian Coordination Committee of Farmers' Movements surrounded Moily's residence in Bengaluru and shouted slogans, threatening violence. Moily's suaveness vanished, and he desperately tried to placate the crowd, in full glare of television cameras, by denying that he had personally approved field trials (*DNA* 2014).

A more serious success of the orchestration of technical critiques backed by political appeals has been the meticulous attention that the issue of GM crops has received from the Parliamentary Standing Committee on Agriculture, in 2012, and the Committee on Science and Technology, Environment and Forests, in 2017. Both committees, comprising politicians from the ruling and opposition parties, unanimously came down on the regulatory regime and the ad hoc approach to GM crops. They also strongly recommended overhauling the regulatory regime and instituting labeling mechanisms for GM foods.

The point is not just about interactions among different institutions and arenas of protest, but also about the ease with which actors crisscrossed what scholars might consider "elite" and "popular" realms of politics. We have already encountered the example of Devinder Sharma, who is a co-petitioner with Aruna Rodrigues in the Supreme Court and also a part of the farmers' rally led by Tikait in Uttarakhand. To take another example, the scientific critiques of regulatory dossiers that Rodrigues placed before the Supreme Court are also deployed by activists as they try to garner support from politicians and political parties, and successes here are in turn reported to the

Supreme Court. Events that unfolded in one arena drew on and fed into those unfolding in other arenas. Developments across sites were thus interactively and dialectically related.

This does not imply, and it is scarcely the case, that there are no tensions within these loosely coordinated groups. Many young activists with the Coalition for a GM-Free India are uncomfortable with Vandana Shiva's more bombastic statements and are skeptical of her exaggerated profile as the spokesperson in the West for India's sustainable agriculture movements. Many activists were wary when Sahai and Rodrigues filed their PIL before the Supreme Court, having observed how the Court ruled against the *Narmada Bachao Andolan* (Save Narmada Campaign) in 2000.[24] Despite these tensions and contradictions, one must acknowledge the hard work of mobilizing different segments of society, coordinating among them, and keeping abreast of scientific literature on GM crops, not the easiest thing to do even for practicing biotechnologists. Nevertheless, there are certain structural features of anti-GM activism that allow an overlapping consensus to emerge among disparate groups.

The Specific Opportunities and Constraints of a Movement on a Technical Issue

The only consideration before releasing a GM crop is biosafety and, therefore, activists have to contest the assessment of biosafety. In March 2013 Kavitha Kuruganti and the Coalition for a GM-Free India released a compilation of abstracts from peer-reviewed scientific journals that highlighted the risks of GM crops and presented this booklet to regulators within the Biotechnology Department (Coalition for a GM-Free India 2013). This led one senior officer involved with the RCGM to reflect that activists were getting ahead in terms of science. Only within the structure of Rules 1989 does this unusual tactic acquire meaning and significance. The emphasis on scientific critiques and scientists in the campaigns against GM crops is one measure of the distance between the anti-GM movements and previous, well-studied environmental movements, such as those against forest logging (Dungdung 2015), the Bhopal gas tragedy (Jasanoff 2007; Narain et al. 2014), and the Sardar Sarover Project (Baviskar 2004; Oza et al. 2017). This is most directly a consequence of the very structure of policy making involving GM crops in India—which is to say, there is scarcely any policy making other than regulation, despite two decades of demands from activists and even the government's own task forces, such as the one chaired by M. S. Swaminathan and the one chaired by Suman Sahai. Since all the "choke points" (Herring 2010) for interrupting or influencing decisions about GM crops are regulatory, anti-GM movements have to be able to make arguments that are grounded in regulatory science. This is also the reason a PIL in the Supreme Court has to be grounded in inadequacies of regulatory science, and why even appeals to the environment minister to overrule the GEAC have to have a strong foot in the failures of regulatory science.

Pace Herring (2010), it is not the Cartagena Protocol, but Rules 1989, as an embodiment of the settlement on GM crops between the Biotechnology Department and the Environment Ministry, that produce the deep dispute over technical aspects. Not only does activism against GM crops in India predate the Cartagena Protocol, but its focal points have to do with concerns particular to India's federal politics and the trajectory of the PILs. Herring (2015, 160) is correct in pointing out that in debates over GM crops, it is not a unitary "Science" in question, but rather state science: "science filtered, weighted and selected through political processes constituted by or aimed at the state" (see also Jasanoff 2005). Yet one can agree with this claim without accepting the corollary that Herring offers, namely, the very inability of science to offer certitudes implies that there is endless potential for doubt and infinite scope for challenging regulatory science.

For instance, Kuruganti's criticism about using the pure cry1Ac protein for testing, when Bt eggplant incorporates a chimeric gene, is a specific criticism about the way a certain test was conducted. The test could have been conducted with the synthetic or actual protein coded for by the chimeric gene. Kuruganti's criticism was thus not about the inherent limitations of probabilistic risk assessments, but, rather, about specific ways in which they were conducted. Similarly, it is possible to satisfy dissident scientists' demand that the copy number (the number of copies of the foreign gene inside the host genome) be conclusively established to be one—and, indeed, Mahyco scientists are doing the tests for accidental presence of vector backbone and partial copies of the gene insert for their newer GM events. At least some of the criticisms that skeptics and opponents have offered can be addressed from within the domain of regulatory testing.

Precisely because this has not happened, the Coalition for a GM-Free India and a figure like Suman Sahai, who has no objection to GM crops *in principle*, end up on the same side. To my mind, the import of state science is a little different from how Herring reads it. As the examples in this chapter attest, engaging with state science does not require anyone to work at the overarching level of whether GM crops are safe or unsafe, harmless or harmful. It is enough to puncture holes in humdrum regulatory dossiers by asking such questions as whether there were statistically enough rats in the toxicity studies or whether the copy number was indeed one. This is why all the very many reports of "overwhelming consensus" among scientists globally about the safety of GM crops are irrelevant. The nub of the matter is not GM crops in general, but specific biosafety dossiers placed before the GEAC for particular GM crops.

The reliance on technical critiques of GM crops allows for participation in two ways, both slightly different from participation typical of democratic politics. First, the credibility of technical critiques does not depend on the number of supporters their authors can claim. Whether Pushpa Bhargava is electable or whether he has a mass following is irrelevant to the merits and demerits of his criticisms of biosafety dossiers. Second, participation is not bound by place or any identity, whether ascribed or chosen. Everyone is a potential consumer of GM food, if it is allowed, and therefore anyone can ask that his or her opinion be counted. Thus, the usual politics of representation that characterizes local, regional, or group-based movements, against, say, dams or land acquisition, pales in the matter of GM food. This is equally an implication of the fact that regulatory decision making depends not on science but on state science. State science in the hands of the Environment Ministry and the Biotechnology Department is sovereign over a national space and therefore the "public" (Dewey 1927; Latour 2004), for decision making over GM crops extends to the entire nation (Jasanoff 2005). This was less so for Bt cotton, which was not recognized as food.

This also offers clues to the very real constraints of participation. First, an adequate grasp of the technical issues involved is necessary if one wants to participate in the rarefied debates over details such as genes, proteins, vector backbones, pollen flow, and so on. Even a former Cabinet secretary like T. S. R. Subramanian has to quote from scientific reports in his columns. Second, the strong emphasis on technical aspects keeps open the possibility that a strong-willed minister or government might, rightfully, decide to go ahead with a certain GM crop, the risks notwithstanding, as happened in the case of Bt cotton. Ultimately, this may prove to be the Achilles' heel of the turn to science by the anti-GM campaign. As activists battle over field trials and biosafety protocols, fundamental questions about public participation in agenda setting for agricultural biotechnology, which Sahai and others have raised for more than a decade, recede further from the horizon of the debate.

Technical disputes do not exhaust the politics of GM crops. This is where the street smarts of agrarian and environmental movements come in. Even if the regulatory structure offers very limited choke points, democratic politics invents and multiplies choke points by capitalizing on the tensions and contradictions of a federal structure. This is what activists sought to accomplish through legal and political interventions.

In the legal realm, Vandana Shiva's second PIL exemplifies this best. By taking the Department of Consumer Affairs and the Ministry of Health and Family Welfare to the Supreme Court, and by keeping the Biotechnology Department out of the PIL, she effectively forced these two offices to get involved in GM crops. The political realm works a little differently from both the legal and the technical realms. In the political realm, the power to rally numbers and evocative idioms, the appeal of place, and membership in a community matter immensely. A figure like the late farmer-leader Mahendra Singh Tikait can cast GM crops as a threat to purity in the "holy city" of Haridwar in a way that scientists like Pushpa Bhargava or Suman Sahai cannot. Similarly, getting states to withhold permissions for field trials, or getting them to declare themselves "GM-free," has dealt a crippling blow to GM crop developers. At one level, these are strategic maneuvers to place roadblocks in front of GM crops. At another, more fundamental level, however, these are attempts to renegotiate the compact between citizens and the state.

The premature and limited settlement of GM crops as a biotechnological object that could pose some environmental hazards, effected in the 1980s, is what is being pried open through these attempts. Asking state governments to formulate a point of view on GM crops, forcing the Health Ministry to intercede where food and medicinal plants are involved, or encouraging the Environment Ministry to organize public hearings expands the scope for public participation and deliberation. These maneuvers turn Bt eggplant from an "environmental hazard" to food, to an ingredient of Ayurveda and other medicinal systems, and each new definition potentially widens the debate to a new public (Dewey 1927), opening up new ways of apprehending GM crops.[25]

Partha Chatterjee's (2006) influential formulation of popular politics would have us distinguishing these publics on the basis of whether they are part of political or civil societies. In a similar vein, legal scholars mark a distinction between use of law (and legal institutions) and social movements (and extralegal institutions) (Rajagopal 2003). But more useful than carving out distinct realms of political action is looking at how different groups respond to GM crops, and how their interactions drive the politics of GM crops (Scoones 2008). Analytically, it is more important to notice the process by which meanings and definitions associated with a particular GM crop (or any other object of controversy) shift, allowing new subject positions to speak up. When the subject position can draw on a history of protest, the tropes for articulating a concern are more easily available and recognizable in society—for instance, the way the KRRS (and farmers in general) can mobilize the "sons of the soil" rhetoric to rail against Monsanto and to demand concessions from the government, or the way someone like Suman Sahai or Aruna Rodrigues can deploy the PIL to turn the GM dispute into a constitutional question. When the subject position does not have a long history of protest to draw on, new tropes have to be creatively invented or old ones adapted. For instance, framing Bt eggplant as food has allowed a constituency of doctors to become vocal, along with allowing the Coalition for a GM-Free India to launch critiques from the vantage of food safety, effectively challenging the idea of toxicologists having the final word on consumers' concerns.

It is also in the nature of issues to generate broader coalitions and mixed methods of protest. The combination of canny democratic wrangling allied with sharp critiques of state science has worked to the advantage of opponents of GM crops, at least for now, but this is, by definition, enabled by the singular focus on GM crops. Although many activists in the Coalition for a GM-Free India are committed to rural and agrarian reconstruction and poverty alleviation through shifting away from industrial agriculture toward more sustainable and equitable models of cultivation, these commitments are not necessarily shared by movements like the Bharatiya Kisan Union that provide the coalition its roots in the hinterlands. Herring (2015) is right in observing that part of the difference between the trajectories of Bt cotton and Bt eggplant lies in the fact that the interests of cotton farmers are better organized and integrated with the textile industry than those of eggplant farmers. That said, the fact that many state governments and political parties dominated by landed farmers are shying away from GM crops should make one wary of unqualified claims about the benefits of GM crops per se to farmers.

Democracy and Popular Politics

> The need for transparent and accountable systems is very great otherwise [GM] technology will get mired in controversies to the extent that it could fail to reach those farmers that it has the potential to help.
>
> —*Suman Sahai (2003)*

Eighteen years after Sahai wrote these prescient words, Ramesh's moratorium on Bt eggplant remains in place—it has survived two other federal environment ministers after Ramesh, and the Narendra Modi government, which has been in power since 2014, has not revoked it. Meanwhile, several states, including Gujarat, which had firmly stood behind Bt cotton, have prohibited field trials. Some states have done this for all GM crops, whereas others have done so only for GM food crops. In addition to the Parliamentary Standing Committee reports mentioned earlier, the majority report of the Technical Expert Committee, appointed by the Supreme Court in the Rodrigues and Sahai PILs, highlighted glaring lacunae in the regulation of GM crops. It also found HT crops unsuitable for Indian agriculture, going a step further than the Task Force on Biotechnology for the Eleventh Five Year Plan under Sahai's leadership, mentioned earlier. Despite repeated censure, however, there has been no comprehensive overhauling of regulatory structures and policies.

The singular focus on keeping India "GM-free" is narrower than the globalization debates that divided farmer movements in the 1990s (Omvedt 2005). The attempt to keep GM seeds out of the country is happening when farmers are increasingly purchasing seeds and other inputs from the market and cultivating hybrids that need to be purchased afresh every season. Some of the criticisms made of GM crops—such as dependence on corporations—can be applied to non-GM hybrids, pesticides, and other synthetic chemical inputs as well. The final part of the book grounds the GM debate in the everyday realities of cultivation and agribusiness profits.

PART THREE

Remaking Agrarian Capitalism

6

Profiting from Seeds: GM Crops and Agribusiness Capital

Farming for profit is risky. Outside a few vertically integrated, specialized industries such as tea (Sen 2017), companies would rather sell inputs to farmers and purchase commodity crops from them than themselves take up the task of farming through laborers (see Singh 2002). It is also cheaper to get farmers to exploit themselves, their household labor, and hired laborers than to bring them onto corporate payrolls (Breman 2007; Harriss-White 2012), especially in countries like India where large-landholding, dominant-caste farmers are a political force to reckon with. If companies can extract profits by selling things to farmers, what kind of things are these? In the main, seeds, agrochemicals, and machinery. Each of these intervenes in agriculture in a different way. But at an overarching level, all of them displace animal and manual labor and shared knowledge systems.

The way machines such as tractors and threshers displace animal and manual labor is well known (Vasavi 1999). Purchasing seeds does away with the delicate, skilled work of on-farm breeding, recovering seeds from the harvest, and conserving heirloom varieties, tasks that are done by women expert farmers in many parts of India (Haldule 2012).[1] Agrochemicals are more ambiguous in terms of their effect on labor. Herbicides quite straightforwardly displace the work of manual weeding, which land-poor daily wagers, often women of Adivasi and marginalized caste groups, perform. Some fertilizers and stimulants can be applied manually. At the same time, using synthetic fertilizers is simpler and less cumbersome than on-farm nutrient recycling and crop rotations. Pesticides, too, can be applied manually, though their use interrupts agro-ecological knowledge systems and pest-management practices that rely on polyculture and biodiverse farming (Altieri and Nicholls 2005; Deb 2009; Gliessman 2015).

In India, as in the rest of the world, the three industries—agricultural machinery, seeds, and agrochemicals—developed separately. I will focus only on seeds and, secondarily, on agrochemicals to the extent they relate to GM traits. In the West, chemical companies such as Monsanto and Bayer have horizontally integrated into seeds, and herbicide-tolerant seeds have allowed synergies between the chemicals and the seeds businesses. In India, the two industries (seeds and agrochemicals) are still distinct[2] because of the way domestic agribusinesses have evolved.

The Structure of the Private Seed Industry in India

Kloppenburg's (2004, xv) complaint about the relative lack of scholarly attention to "the parallel development of plant breeding and the seed industry" in the United States holds broadly true for India as well.[3] The colonial government in the late nineteenth century initiated organized "agricultural improvement." The targets of agricultural improvement were primarily crops key to the colonial political economy like cotton and jute. Some research was undertaken, however, on cereals like paddy and wheat as well. The institutional settings for this were research stations at places like Dharwad and Pusa, Bihar, coordinated by a central authority located in Delhi—the Imperial Council of Agricultural Research, which became the Indian Council of Agricultural Research, or ICAR, after independence (Kumar 2006).

With the exception of some fibers and cereals, agricultural research did not singularly focus on improved seeds and varieties, as it did in the United States in the nineteenth century. Many scientists in India looked at farming holistically, examining practices of mixed and intercropping as well as building soil health (Saha 2013). Consequently, even as late as 1960, there was no organized seed industry in India (Rao 2004, 847). Farmer-saved seeds and farmer-to-farmer exchanges were the predominant mode of generating seeds each season. This was to change with the launch of the Green Revolution.

The introduction of the Green Revolution in the 1960s involved the release of so-called high-yielding varieties and hybrids of paddy and wheat, developed by the ICAR. The production of hybrid seeds necessitated organized production. The responsibility fell primarily on the shoulders of the public sector, notably the ICAR institutes, but also the National Seeds Corporation, established in 1963 to produce, process, and market hybrid seeds. Unable to meet the demand for the new seeds, however, public-sector institutes started contracting out seed multiplication and distribution to the private sector.[4]

Private seed companies thus took off, multiplying and distributing public-sector seeds. As late as the 1980s, the seeds produced by the private sector were those bred by the public sector. Moreover, the public-sector varieties were bred from landraces cultivated by farmers in different regions, with traits backcrossed into them from the varieties bred by international agricultural research institutes. Since the public sector lacked the institutional capacity to deliver on the promises of state-led agricultural development, it necessarily had to partner with the private sector. On the other hand, domestic companies needed to access public-sector germplasm—living genetic resources such as seeds or tissues used for plant breeding—for their seed-multiplication programs. Also, sheltered from foreign competition, domestic seed companies could play the volumes game of seed multiplication without investing in risky and long-lead-time research and development. There were other reasons, too, why the private sector was lagging behind in breeding. Because of the land ceiling act, private breeders did not have enough land to multiply their own seeds, and there was a prohibitive customs duty on the import of equipment required for breeding (see Barwale 1987, cited by Rao 2004).

Private breeders got a major boost in the late 1980s for several reasons. First, the National Seeds Programme Phase III (1990) offered concessional loans to private breeders. Second, in 1987, the Indian government reclassified the production of hybrid seeds and agricultural biotechnology products in its industrial policy, which allowed large and foreign companies to invest in the seeds sector, as discussed earlier. Third, in 1988 the New Policy on Seed Development was introduced. The policy allowed import of seeds of coarse cereals and pulses and oilseeds for a period of two years by seed companies having foreign collaborations. The crops in which imports were allowed were those in which public-sector breeders had met with less success in developing high-yielding varieties and hybrids, and ones in which major international programs were not invested. Also, the Plants, Fruits and Seeds Order, 1989, was passed, allowing import without a license, of seeds and planting material for vegetables, flowers, ornamental plants, and fruits for sowing and planting (Rao 2004, 848). Last, pushed in part by the Biotechnology Department, the seed industry was liberalized further in the New Industrial Policy of 1991. Certified high-yielding hybrids and certified high-yielding plantlets developed through tissue culture were put on the list of industries for automatic approval of foreign technology agreements and 51 percent foreign equity investment. For such collaborations and joint ventures, licensing (seeking permission from the government) was no longer required. As I pointed out earlier, this is what allowed the western Indian seed company Mahyco to partner with Monsanto for the introduction of

Bt cotton. All these developments led to a steep jump in the number of private seed companies undertaking research and development. There were only three such companies in 1970. By 1985 there were nine, and by 1995 the number had shot up to forty (Arora 1995, cited by Rao 2004).

The seed industry in India thus traversed a very different trajectory from that in the United States. Unlike its American counterpart, the Indian public sector did not have the capacity to provide farmers with seeds directly. Consequently, the private-sector seed industry did not need to compete with that in the public sector, but could merrily ride on its coattails by multiplying and bulk-producing public-sector varieties and hybrids, without much capital or research investment. Thus, the first entrants into the private seed industry were large landholding commercial farmers looking to capture value through in-house seed production, and later entrepreneurs from the trading and mercantile castes who saw an opportunity to make small profits in short lead times without significant investment.[5] These were also the caste groups that had access to capital and land for seed multiplication. They built their germplasm collection through the seeds that they received from state agricultural universities and the institutes of the ICAR. Moreover, the fact of accessing public-sector products (and the promises they entailed) through the private sector created the conditions whereby farmers could demand that the private sector behave more like the public sector, and that the state regulate private-sector production and sales in much the same way it regulated those of the public sector.

After the 1990s, with the decline of the Ministry of Agriculture, domestic seed companies by and large turned to foreign collaborations for new technologies, germplasm, and products. The conjunctures by which seed companies arose in India can be seen through the story of Badrinarayan Barwale, the figure behind many of the principal seed companies in Maharashtra, the founder of Mahyco, and the winner of the World Food Prize in 1998.

The Case of Badrinarayan Barwale

The terrain on both sides of the highway from Aurangabad to Jalna in Maharashtra is flat. Every once in a while, one encounters factories along the highway, in addition to seed companies, their warehouses, and research farms, the most arresting of which is Mahyco's R&D center in Dawalwadi, near Jalna. Many of these seed companies, and Mahyco directly, owe their beginnings to Badrinarayan Barwale.[6] Barwale was born in 1931 into a *Marwari* family in Parbhani,[7] which was then under the royal principality ruled by the Nizam (sovereign) of Hyderabad and is today in Maharashtra. Owing to a quirk of fate, he was adopted by a distant relative who was a wealthy cloth merchant in Jalna. Jalna, in the Marathwada region of Maharashtra, has a favorable climate for plant breeding. Also, landholdings there are less fragmented than in the *ryotwari* areas of western Maharashtra,[8] allowing for land parcels in the tens and hundreds of acres. In the years leading to independence from British rule, in 1947, Barwale was active in politics and even served time in prison for his dissidence.

In independent India, Barwale began with seed multiplication in the 1950s. His operations snowballed when he got hold of Pusa Sawani okra seeds from the distinguished breeder at the Indian Agricultural Research Institute, Dr. Harbhajan Singh, also known as the Indian Vavilov, after the Russian geneticist and botanist Nikolai Vavilov. First Barwale tried to sell the okra that he had cultivated on his own parcel of land, but he quickly suffered some losses caused by crashing prices. It was then that he decided to recover seeds from the okra and sell the seeds instead. He soon realized that there was a market for good seeds waiting to be tapped by enterprising seed multipliers, since government warehouses were unable to cater to the demand for improved seeds. By 1966 Barwale had started his own nursery for seed production and was building a sales network through word-of-mouth referrals among farmers and through leaflets.[9] Barwale's business got a further boost from the technical cooperation under way between the Rockefeller Foundation and the Indian government under the auspices of the Green Revolution. Mahyco became the first company in Maharashtra to produce the hybrid maize seeds that were developed under the Green Revolution program. Thereafter, Mahyco ventured into hybrid sorghum (*jowar*) seeds, procured from the Rockefeller Foundation.

By the late 1960s and 1970s, a few companies like Mahyco had started some research efforts by hiring trained agricultural scientists, sometimes those retiring from the public sector. As a risk-mitigation strategy, companies kept both proprietary and public-bred varieties and hybrids in their product mix. Taking inspiration from Barwale, several other family members and former employees of Mahyco also ventured into the seed business, many of which are also located in the Aurangabad-Jalna area. For instance, Nath Seeds was started by Satish Kagliwal, who is related to Barwale; Sheetal Seeds was started by Suresh Agrawal, who is Barwale's nephew.

At the same time, a majority of seed companies in India have been averse to major investments in research and development, preferring to play the volume-driven market for bulk-produced seeds on contract from the public sector. This may have less to do with risk appetite than with the availability of working capital and necessary cash flows to sustain long-term research programs—my interviews with founders of seed companies revealed considerable anxiety about servicing debt obligations, which tells us that these companies are more akin to small businesses than Indian equivalents of Monsanto. Even in 2014, when Mahyco had long been one of the most respected seed companies in India, with operations in multiple countries, Barwale emphasized the importance of "knowing how much a [500-million-rupee] loan costs, what it means if this loan is repaid to the bank a day early or one day after it was due" (Paul 2014). The problem of working capital is more acute for most other firms, which are smaller than Mahyco. Seed companies are neither in the league of giant transnational agribusinesses like Bayer and Dow, nor in the league of large Indian firms that have few qualms defaulting on loans in the billions of rupees.

Most companies were unable to scale up research and development because they lacked the breeding skills that Barwale had and the technical know-how that his daughter and son-in-law brought to Mahyco, as the founder of another Jalna-based seed company told me. Mahyco bucked the trend, in part because Barwale's daughter, Usha Barwale Zehr, had a distinguished career in agronomy and plant breeding. Trained at the University of Illinois, she worked on sorghum and millet breeding at Purdue University before she returned with her husband, the late agronomist and biotechnologist Brent Zehr, to Jalna to steer the company's research programs. This is a recent trend among seed companies in India. The children, often sons, of founders are undertaking higher education in agricultural sciences in Europe and the United States to start marker-assisted breeding and biotechnology programs for their companies upon returning to India. Very few, however, have invested in R&D and, more specifically, in GM crops on the scale that Mahyco has.

Thus, as Usha Barwale Zehr mentioned to me in 2014, over 80 percent of the 350-plus companies registered with the private seed companies' umbrella association, the National Seed Association of India (NSAI) are traders who bulk-produce and sell seeds on contracts. They run small-scale operations catering to farmers in a small radius around the company. The strength of these companies is their relationship with their limited customer base. While speaking to me, she recalled how farmers would come to their house to ask for seeds directly from her father. Similarly, a young scientist hailing from rural Maharashtra told me in September 2014 that one reason he felt very proud about working for Mahyco was that he had grown up hearing about Barwale's seeds from his family and other farmers in the village. The regional specialization of seed companies also has to do with the fact that varietal testing and registration happens both at the state and federal levels. On the one hand, this means that seed companies have to maintain good relations with agriculture bureaucracies at the state and federal levels. On the other, it also means that seed companies in a particular state have an advantage over those from elsewhere trying to enter that state, because of long-standing relations with the state agricultural bureaucracy, along with recognition among farmers.

For those few seed companies that have ventured into research and development through independent, proprietary breeding programs, the parental lines have largely come from the public sector and international agricultural research institutes.[10] For a long time, even these research initiatives were in the realm of hybrids—which offer natural intellectual property protection since seeds saved from the harvest do not breed true. Hybrids rely on the empirical finding that the progeny of two elite, inbred varieties show some characteristics that are better than those of either parent. Hybrids are selected to yield more than their parent varieties. The yield advantage of hybrids (called hybrid vigor) does not last beyond the first generation, and for this reason farmers cannot save and use hybrid seeds from one generation to another without compromising on yield and other characteristics—they need to purchase fresh seeds every season. Starting from the mid-1990s, a small number of companies among those with independent research programs have ventured into expensive and long-lead-time biotechnology research. This was also the point when transnational companies like Monsanto expanded their presence in the Indian market—Monsanto picked up a 26 percent stake in Mahyco in 1998. Before turning to transnational companies, let us briefly look at some market indexes for seeds in India, which explain transnational agribusinesses' interest in the Indian market.

India is the fifth-largest market for seeds globally, with an annual turnover of about U.S. $2.5 billion in 2013 and healthy growth rates of about 11 percent per annum (Subramani 2013; see also *Economic Times* 2012; *Business Standard* 2015). Private companies account for less than 20 percent of the total seeds market (Subramani 2013). Much of the seed business is in the unorganized sector (Sahai 1993), and in the organized sector, the public sector accounts for close to 51 percent of the market share. In certain niches, though, such as hybrid vegetable seeds, there is a near-total dominance by the private sector. Considering that small landholders are increasingly switching over to hybrids, even for field crops (rice, wheat, cotton, and so on), the industry is very optimistic about growth prospects, which makes India an attractive market for transnational businesses. Private players have tried to capture those areas of the market space for seeds where the presence of the public sector is weak: vegetables, fruits, horticultural crops. They have also invested in cereals. Their preferred vehicle to capture market space is hybrid seeds. Few of these small players have integrated backward into research and development and assumed dominant positions in regional pockets. The implication of this industry structure is that there are significant barriers to entry both for a regional player trying to expand into another region, and for a new player trying to enter the country, even if that new player is a deep-pocketed transnational agribusiness. The barriers to entry are not simply regulatory or policy-induced, but ecological too—a new entrant needs locally adapted germplasm to develop seeds for India's different agro-ecological zones.

The changes in the policy environment in the 1990s led to large domestic companies such as ITC and Godrej, and transnational companies such as Monsanto and Syngenta, entering the seed sector (Pray and Ramaswami 2001) in a big way. They worked through joint ventures and through buying out seed companies along with their germplasm, scientific expertise, and experience in dealing with farmers and governments (Pray, Ramaswami, and Kelley 2001; Murugkar, Ramaswami, and Shelar 2007). What opportunities might genetic modification open up in this landscape of commercial competition? The next two sections answer this question from the standpoint of GM insect-resistant (Bt) and herbicide-tolerant (HT) crops. The two traits entail different pathways to growth in the private seed industry in India. For insect-resistance, I draw on the case of Bt cotton.

Conflicts among Seed Companies in the Market for Insect-Resistant Bt Cotton

Bt cotton confers one kind of advantage to transnational agribusinesses and another to domestic agribusinesses. A company vending Bt cotton differentiates itself from its competition with considerable first-mover advantages, given the steep regulatory hurdles involved in commercializing a GM crop. From 2002 until 2004, Mahyco was the only company authorized to sell Bt (Bollgard) cottonseeds, which offered it a near monopoly. Bollgard refers to the first-generation Bt (cry1Ac gene) construct belonging to Monsanto. I say "near monopoly" because there was, at the same time, a robust but unreliable market for smuggled Bt cottonseeds (Murugkar, Ramaswami, and Shelar 2007; Herring 2007b). Until then, Mahyco had been primarily a vegetable seed company; in cotton, the hybrids of rival companies were superior (Ramasundaram and Vennila 2013), yet for two years Mahyco was the only company offering Bt cotton legally. One reason for the rapid proliferation of ecologically suitable though illicit hybrids was that Mahyco's Bt "MECH" hybrids did not perform particularly well. These illicit Bt strains of cotton notwithstanding, there is no doubt that its monopoly over legal Bt cotton allowed Mahyco to gain a market share in cottonseed sales that it would scarcely have been able to on the strength of its non-GM hybrids. It was only in 2004 that Mahyco faced competition when the Tamil Nadu–based company Rasi Seeds received approval for commercializing its Bt (Bollgard) cotton hybrids. This was followed in 2005 by the release of Andhra Pradesh–based Nuziveedu's and Maharashtra-based Ankur's Bt cotton. The crowding out of non–Bt cotton from the market was noted with much consternation among activists as more and more companies partnered with technology vendors, principally Monsanto, to release Bt cotton.

Initially, companies charged between 1,600 and 1,850 rupees per 1-pound (450-gram) packet of first-generation Bollgard Bt cotton seeds. In comparison, a similar-sized packet of non-GM hybrid cottonseeds cost 350–500 rupees at that point, and non-GM cotton varieties were even cheaper. Companies justified the inflated price on the grounds that they had to pay a licensing fee or royalty (also called trait fee) to the providers of the Bt construct such as Monsanto. It is also true, though rarely admitted publicly, that companies wanted a share of the savings on pesticides that they felt would accrue to farmers (Menon and Uzramma 2017, chap. 5).

Whether the Bt trait actually reduced pesticide-related expenses for farmers remains a controversial question; a recent long-term review suggests that it did not (Kranthi and Stone 2020). What is more evident is the dominance in the cotton market that a few companies managed to gain through Bt cotton. Whereas competition was extremely stiff in the market for non-GM cotton hybrids, with the advent of Bt cotton only seven or eight companies managed to corner 75 percent of the market. Of those, three or four companies saw a meteoric rise in their annual turnover—for instance, Rasi Seeds was about a 1.1-billion-rupee company before it launched its Bt cotton hybrids in 2004; by 2012 it had grown to about 4.5 billion rupees, 70–75 percent of which was contributed by Bt cotton. Similarly, the Aurangabad-based Ajeet Seeds grew from about 750 million rupees to 2.5 billion rupees over a decade. Before it launched its Bt cotton in 2006, it had a market share of 3–4 percent in cotton, which grew to 10 percent by 2012 (Mukherjee 2013).

Nowhere did the entry of Bt cotton change the landscape of cultivation as profoundly as in northern India. In the cotton tracts of Punjab, Haryana, Rajasthan, and western Uttar Pradesh, even commercially inclined farmers principally grew varieties bred largely by public-sector institutions (Singh and Kairon n.d.). In 2005 the GEAC permitted the release of Bt cotton hybrids of Mahyco, Rasi, and Ankur seed companies in this North Zone, and in subsequent years many more companies released Bt cotton hybrids here. This led to widespread abandonment of cotton varieties across the North Zone. As the veteran cotton breeder and former member of the GEAC, B. M. Khadi (n.d.), noted, "One clear impact of Bt-cotton on Indian agriculture appears to be the replacement of large tracts of varietal areas of north India, with Bt-hybrids, since the technology is available in India only in the form of hybrids." Even accounting for the spread of illegal hybrids, this was a major breakthrough for companies, all of which initially were from outside the North Zone, and dealt a blow to public-sector cotton breeding efforts.

Most companies mentioned earlier licensed the Bt gene from Monsanto Mahyco Biotechnology Limited (MMBL), for which MMBL charged a stiff licensing fee, effectively a royalty or a trait fee. MMBL is a (50:50) joint venture between Monsanto and Mahyco. Monsanto had the Bt construct, and it also owns a 26 percent stake in

Mahyco. From 2002 to 2005, MMBL earned between 726.50 and 1,250 rupees on every packet of Bt cotton that was sold.[11] Thus, MMBL demanded 45–67 percent of the price of a packet of Bt cotton seeds for a single gene construct that Monsanto had developed around the late 1980s and early 1990s. In 2005 about 1.3 million packets of Bt cottonseeds were sold in India, and this earned Monsanto and Mahyco anywhere from 944 million to 1.63 billion rupees (U.S. $21–36 million), as trait fees.[12] In effect, the Bt gene allowed MMBL to capture a share of the all-India market for seeds through a product that required no new investments beyond the costs of regulatory approval. Further, without launching major breeding programs, without itself taking Bt cotton through the regulatory hoops (Mahyco handled regulatory approvals), Monsanto was able to corner at least 22.5 to 33.5 percent of the value from Bt cotton sales,[13] while Mahyco made money from Bt cotton sold by MMBL's licensees, who were all Mahyco's competitors.

This arrangement was hardly beneficial to MMBL's domestic licensees. Also, Monsanto was in a position to disproportionately affect the fortunes of rival seed companies. With no viable Bt construct available from the public sector, and those from alternative sources performing unreliably, companies had little choice but to license it from MMBL, and MMBL's refusal meant a company could not launch its Bt cotton product. In essence, MMBL was able to effectively enjoy the benefits of patent protection (Peschard and Randeria 2020), even though it does not have a patent on Bollgard Bt cotton in India. This relationship of MMBL and its domestic licensees began to come under stress starting in 2006 because of pressures from an unprecedented source.

In 2006 the state government of Andhra Pradesh filed a case against Monsanto before the Monopolies and Restrictive Trade Practices (MRTP) Commission for "exorbitant pricing of Bt cotton seeds." The MRTP Act 1969 authorizes the MRTP Commission to investigate and take measures against the concentration of economic power in the hands of a few economic players that result in monopolistic practices and, in general, practices that restrict market competition.[14] While referring the matter to the MRTP Commission, the state agriculture minister, N. Raghuveera Reddy, claimed that he was acting at the behest of cotton farmers. He added that he was against neither companies nor technology, but he found the royalty charged by Monsanto totally unjustified. "Bt cotton seeds worth Rs. 129 crore were sold since 2002 till date in the state, of which Rs. 79 crore accrued as royalty to Monsanto. . . . Exploitation of farmers through exorbitant royalty for an insect-resistant technology is uncalled for. Monsanto . . . neither gives the source material [seeds] nor transfers the gene into the hybrid seed. The multinational company just shares its technology with domestic companies for production of Bt cotton seed for a huge royalty" (quoted in *Business Standard* 2005). The charge of restrictive trade practices was all the more serious given that Monsanto did not and does not have a patent for its first-generation Bollgard Bt cotton in India. Effectively, the commitment to farmers' welfare and the compact between technology, development, and public welfare, variably effective but ever available as a political launchpad, came to haunt the happy dominance being enjoyed by Mahyco and Monsanto.

The MRTP Commission found the technology fee to be "too high for the Indian market" (Chandrashekhar 2006) and ordered that prices be lowered. Monsanto sought relief from the Supreme Court, but the Court refused to intervene in the matter. Thus, the Andhra Pradesh government fixed the price of a packet of Bt cottonseeds at 750 rupees, and governments in many major cotton-growing states, such as Maharashtra and Gujarat, followed suit. To lower the price, MMBL had to swallow a drastically reduced trait fee of 150 rupees per packet. Monsanto, worried about other states taking inspiration from Andhra Pradesh, threatened to withhold second- and third-generation products from the Indian market unless it was assured of no government interference there. This narrative of a "free market" has immense traction in the United States but very few takers in India precisely because the domestic private sector developed while holding the hands of the very state now being asked not to interfere. Monsanto's threat indicates both a misreading of the Indian landscape, as it did in Europe earlier (Schurman and Munro 2010), and its very different historical trajectory vis-à-vis Indian companies. Thus, despite Monsanto's threats, in 2006, Mahyco and a few other companies released hybrids containing Monsanto's second-generation stacked Bt gene, named Bollgard II cotton. These hybrids were priced at 925 rupees and included a higher royalty of 225 rupees (Damodaran 2015). This triggered another round of action from the state governments.

Andhra Pradesh enacted new legislation—the Andhra Pradesh Cotton Seeds (Regulation of Supply, Distribution, Sale and Fixation of Sale Price) Act, 2007. Following Andhra Pradesh, Maharashtra too enacted new legislation to regulate corporate Bt cottonseeds—Maharashtra Cotton Seeds (Regulation of Supply, Distribution, Sale and Fixation of Sale Price) Act, 2009.[15] These acts gave the state governments sweeping powers to regulate the price of Bt cottonseeds.[16] Thus, states brought down the price of Bollgard II Bt cottonseeds to 750 rupees per packet and lowered the price of first-generation Bt cotton to 650 rupees per packet, forcing MMBL to lower the royalty to 150 rupees and 100 rupees for Bollgard II and Bollgard Bt cotton, respectively.

Lower prices for Bt cottonseeds are certainly in the interest of farmers, but so are several more transformative measures, which do not get as much attention from the government. What was decisive here was the interest of domestic seed companies. As the senior journalist Latha Jishnu (2010) noted, "It is an open secret that Indian partners of Monsanto [company] were behind the campaign to get the trait fees reduced because it was reducing their margins." The price controls hit MMBL's royalty hard. Whereas they were earning anywhere between 726.5 and 1,250 rupees per packet before 2006, after price controls those earnings were reduced to 150 rupees.

Some domestic companies soon upped the ante and started withholding payments of the trait fee to MMBL. In 2015 MMBL sued eight domestic seed companies for having withheld payments of over 4 billion rupees (about U.S. $62 million). The domestic seed companies charged that they were unable to honor their contracts with MMBL because of price controls introduced by the state governments. They claimed that between 2010 and 2015, they had paid Monsanto 16 billion rupees in excess of the trait fee set by the government (NSAI 2015). Monsanto felt especially frustrated because the companies were already in possession of the GM event[17] and thus could not be stopped from selling Bt cotton year after year, even as licensees withheld royalty payments. Monsanto also charged the industry association, NSAI, for lobbying of domestic firms. For the past few years, the NSAI has been headed by M. Prabhakar Rao, the president of Nuziveedu Seeds, one of India's biggest players in the seeds sector and a leading player in the market for Bt cottonseeds. Nuziveedu Seeds is also one of the companies sued by Monsanto for their failure to pay royalties, and Rao is considered close to the right-wing Rashtriya Swayamsevak Sangh, the ideological parent of the ruling Bharatiya Janata Party.

This was only the beginning of a larger storm brewing over the transnational firm. On December 7, 2015, the Modi government, whose ideological commitments are often glossed as neoliberal, issued an order under the Essential Commodities Act 1955. This order uniformly fixed the retail price and trait fee for all varieties of cottonseed, including Bt cotton, effective March 2016. This move was spurred by Rao in alliance with the right-wing Bharatiya Kisan Sangh, or Indian Farmers' Organization (Bhardwaj, Jain, and Lasseter 2017), which is close to the BJP and has at different points made common cause with anti-GM activists, as mentioned in the previous chapter. Even as the NSAI hailed the order, Monsanto (through MMBL) immediately challenged it before the Delhi High Court and the Karnataka High Court. The NSAI inserted itself into the matter and opposed Monsanto's motion before the Delhi High Court, and both the High Courts have so far refused to stay the order.

The Modi government has also opened another front against Monsanto. In December 2015 the federal Ministry of Agriculture asked India's fair trade regulator, the Competition Commission of India, to investigate alleged monopolistic practices of Monsanto, at the behest of the NSAI and farmers' groups associated with the ruling BJP. This was followed by a formal complaint by Nuziveedu Seeds. Similar complaints were then filed by the farmers' group All India Kisan Sabha (All India Farmers' Assembly, affiliated with the Communist Party of India), the NSAI, and the state government of Telangana, the state where Nuziveedu is headquartered. In May 2019 the Competition Commission found evidence that MMBL was abusing its dominant position in the market for Bt cottonseeds. It found that MMBL was charging high trait fees even though it was "merely a licensing entity with very limited fixed costs" and without any research and development activity. It also criticized Monsanto for excluding certain companies, and for distorting competition and indulging in price discrimination just to extract as much surplus as possible from farmers purchasing Bt cottonseeds (Sally and Singh 2019).[18]

Even while the investigation was on, in March 2016 the Modi government brought down the price of a 1-pound (450-gram) packet of Bollgard I Bt cotton seeds to 635 rupees—and zero trait fee. The price of a similar packet of Bollgard II Bt cotton was fixed at 800 rupees and the trait fee at 49 rupees. In March 2019 the two figures for Bollgard II Bt cotton were further slashed to 730 and 20 rupees, respectively, and from March 2020 the trait fee was zero.

Analyzing the Controversy over Bt Cotton at Different Levels

India is the only country in the world where the Bt trait is available exclusively in hybrids. In every other country, companies and the state have made Bt cotton available in varieties (Suresh, Ramasundaram, and Chand 2011).[19] Considering that varieties are cheaper to multiply and hence cheaper to purchase, and that their seeds can be saved for the next cultivating season, varieties are of greater interest than hybrids to most farmers. A survey among farmers conducted by the large landholder farmer and policy commentator Ajay Vir Jakhar's Indian Farmers' Society (Bharatiya Krishak Samaj) with the Centre for the Study of Developing Societies (CSDS), New Delhi (CSDS 2014), found that farmers expressed a preference for GM varieties rather than hybrids. The report says on page 51, "Asked if GM seeds were good for profitability, 20 per cent said it should be used for higher farm profitability; whereas 42 per cent *did not want hybrids* to be used and 38 per cent had no opinion" (emphasis added). Because enforceable contracts restricting the saving and multiplication of seeds by farmers (as in the United States) are politically difficult in India, private companies, both domestic and transnational, would rather concentrate on GM hybrids, which assure them of sales every season. The enthusiasm among companies for hybrids has been such that they have released over five hundred hybrids in a country with twenty agro-ecological zones (Choudhary and Gaur 2010). In this regard, the failure of the public sector to release even a single viable Bt cotton variety or hybrid is particularly disappointing and has cemented the total dominance of the private sector in the cottonseed market.

There is another aspect of the proliferation of Bt cotton through hybrids that merits attention. It was only with Bt cotton that hybrids swept through North India. As Pulla (2018) notes, "From 2002 to 2011, the area under cotton hybrids rose from 2% in north India and 40% elsewhere to 96% across the country." Hybrids offer a significant yield advantage over varieties. This should make us skeptical of studies that measure the success of Bt cotton in terms of yield improvement—the yield improvement at the national level is inevitable when varieties are replaced by hybrids, and such improvement would have happened even with conventional non–Bt hybrids. The appropriate study to measure the impact of Bt cotton would compare its performance with that of its non–Bt hybrid or close (near isogenic) non–Bt variant. This is the analysis that would isolate the contribution of the Bt trait in the overall performance of the GM crop. In nearly two decades of the debate over Bt cotton, this relatively straightforward experimental evaluation has not happened (Ramasundaram and Vennila 2013, 697). Further, the adoption of Bt hybrids has also had adverse effects on cotton biodiversity, replacing sturdier, older varieties with more fragile, longer-staple hybrids (Menon and Uzramma 2017, chap. 5).

Different levels of analysis of Bt cotton bring to light different facets of the controversy. At the level of the crop, Bt cotton codes for a protein that is toxic to lepidopterous pests or bollworms. Initially, Monsanto and seed companies charged a hefty premium for this trait, claiming that farmers stood to gain much more from the reduction in pesticide use than the premium they would pay for the seed. In reality, however, bollworm attacks may wax and wane from season to season—in those seasons when pest incidence is low, Bt cotton offers no advantage over its non–Bt equivalent. In other words, regarding bollworm attacks, purchasing Bt cotton is akin to purchasing insurance—and not a very good insurance at that, for Bt hybrids in India show large variability in terms of the expression of Bt toxin in different parts of the plant and at different points in the season—the expression of the toxin is the lowest in parts most susceptible to bollworm attacks (Kranthi et al. 2005). The uneven expression makes the crop more susceptible to pest attacks than Bt cotton in other countries (Pulla 2018). The variability stems from another uniqueness of Indian Bt cotton—all Bt hybrids in the country are hemizygous—they get the Bt gene from only one parent. Because of the uneven expression, farmers are forced to spray pesticides even for bollworms.

Farmers spray pesticides for a number of other pests that afflict cotton. Moreover, given that the retail and marketing of corporate agrochemicals are geared toward increasing sales, village-level retailers have every incentive to push pesticides irrespective of whether the farmer is growing Bt or non–Bt seeds (see Aga 2019). Finally, bollworms are bound to become resistant to the specific Bt protein, rendering the GMO ineffective and forcing farmers to resort to toxic cocktails of pesticides. India is already seeing cases of fatalities among farmers from exposure to lethal pesticides—in an especially harrowing case, at least fifty Bt cotton farmers lost their lives and over a thousand were poisoned in Vidarbha (northeastern Maharashtra) in 2017 (Hardikar 2018a). In recent years, Nuziveedu has begun declaring a breakdown of resistance to pink bollworms on its seed packets while continuing to charge the same premium prices. The warning on the back of a packet of Nuziveedu's Bt cottonseeds shown in figure 2 says, "The **Pink Bollworm** (PBW) has developed **resistance to Bt proteins**[;] as a result **Bt cotton cannot give protection against PBW**." Further, these warnings are in English, which most farmers cannot read (see Choudhury and Aga 2019).

Fig. 2. Front and back of a packet of Nuziveedu's Bt cotton seeds. Photographs by Chitrangada Choudhury, July 2019.

Several studies report that Bt cotton use has reduced pesticide consumption (see, for example, Krishna and Qaim 2012; Herring and Rao 2012), whereas others have struck important cautionary notes on the adequacy of the evidence (Stone 2012; see also rejoinders by Herring 2013 and Rao 2013) and questioned if pesticide reductions translate to better health and environmental outcomes (Venkata et al. 2016; Flachs 2017). Keshav Kranthi (2011), then the acting director of the ICAR's Central Institute for Cotton Research in Nagpur, pointed out that the combined effects of new pesticides, new seed treatment chemicals, new hybrids, along with the Bt construct, explain aggregate trends in cotton cultivation and pesticide applications, making it even harder to isolate the effects of the Bt trait. Kranthi (2012) further notes that by 2012 pesticide applications had returned to pre-GM levels. In a recent review, Kranthi and Stone (2020, 194) scathingly observed that, seen over a two-decade period, the benefits of Bt cotton have been "modest and largely ephemeral," as pesticide consumption steadily increased beyond pre–Bt cotton levels and yields stagnated.

The evidence on the cost of seeds is, however, unambiguous—it has gone up sharply with Bt cotton (Ranganathan, Gaurav, and Halder 2018; Kranthi and Stone 2020). In sum, farmers wanted Bt varieties and profitability; instead, they got Bt hybrids and higher upfront investments on seeds in anticipation of savings on pesticides, which have not materialized.[20] This is one reason that the Standing Committee on Agriculture of the Indian Parliament noted (2012, 378), "In case of transgenics . . . in India, the experience of last decade has conclusively shown that while it has extensively benefitted the industry, as far as the lot of poor farmers is concerned, even the trickle down [benefit] is not visible." Moreover, yield is not generally a good proxy for profitability for farmers; bumper productions tend to depress prices that farmers receive. These dynamics are likely to plague Bt eggplant too. Under pressure from activists, the Environment

Ministry commissioned an ex-ante assessment of "economic benefits" of Bt eggplant. The study predicted that consumers would benefit much more than farmers because of a decline in retail prices (Kumar, Prasanna, and Wankhade 2010). Curiously, the study is silent about seed costs for farmers. If these were as high as for Bt cotton, farmers might not see any benefit at all.

At the level of Bt cotton hybrids, promoted by different seed companies through gene constructs sourced primarily from Monsanto, we see a new dimension of the debate. In a massively fragmented market, Bt cotton has allowed a few domestic companies to increase their market share and achieve market dominance. The second aspect is the conflict between domestic seed companies and Monsanto. This tussle is being waged over specific pricing and licensing arrangements mediated through the state and federal governments, the courts, and regulatory agencies like the Competition Commission of India. In this scuffle, two major farmers' organizations—the All India Kisan Sabha, backed by the Communist Party of India, and the Bharatiya Kisan Sangh, backed by the right-wing BJP—have rallied with a section of domestic companies led by NSAI against Monsanto, and they decisively brought seed prices down in their mutual interest. The nationalism and nativism of the BJP and Prime Minister Modi have translated into a strong intervention on behalf of domestic seed companies—setting royalty terms by government order.[21] This is unlike the earlier state government legislation, which capped the retail price but left the royalty for MMBL to renegotiate with its licensees.

This compact between the government and domestic seed companies, led by Nuziveedu, which convinced transnational agribusinesses and their partners like Mahyco to leave the NSAI in 2016, may come back to haunt the private seed industry. A powerful precedent has been set for government regulation of prices and licensing terms.

Monsanto is famous (or notorious) for its advocacy of free-market principles. Its global power notwithstanding, it is unable to prevent state and federal governments from interfering in royalty arrangements, usually left to private negotiations, and is so far unable to get any significant relief from India's courts.

The Case of Herbicide Tolerance (HT)

HT crops are immune to the herbicides glyphosate and glufosinate, and they are thus especially profitable to companies like Monsanto that sell HT crops and the herbicides to go with them. The Indian subsidiaries of transnational agribusinesses like Bayer and Dow are taking their HT crops through the regulatory process, along with Mahyco and a few other companies. These firms have introduced the HT trait in crops like cotton and rice. In fact, some companies have illegally released HT cotton (Choudhury and Aga 2019) for some years, and a few farmers' groups have demanded that the government legalize the crop. The herbicides to go with these HT crops are manufactured not only by Monsanto but also by many domestic companies that retail it at cheaper rates than Monsanto and offer better margins to retailers (see Aga 2018).

The fact that many companies that manufacture herbicides also manufacture pesticides challenges the oft-repeated rumor that agrochemical companies are secretly funding anti-GM activists because they fear a drop in pesticide sales due to the Bt trait. Agrochemical companies and seed companies have no conflict of interest as far as HT crops are concerned. In fact, worldwide, the adoption of HT crops has gone hand in hand with steeply increasing application of herbicides.[22] HT crops are thus a win-win for both agrochemical companies and seed companies. Strictly speaking, it is in the interest of agrochemical companies to oppose Bt crops and call for the release of HT crops, rather than endorse a blanket opposition to all GM crops. If such nuances are likely to be lost in the rough-and-tumble of popular politics, then agrochemical companies have an interest in welcoming GM crops because the commercial potential of HT crops has proven to be greater than that of Bt crops worldwide. These speculations apart, given the fact that anti-GM activists are often the same as or closely allied to environmental activists opposing the use of synthetic chemical inputs in agriculture (Scoones 2008), it is unlikely that the agrochemicals industry would ally with anti-GM activists to keep out those crops that will spur the sale of herbicides in India. As Kavitha Kuruganti of the Coalition for a GM-Free India said to me once, "The pesticide industry and the biotech lobby see a common enemy in us."[23]

If one needs to be a little skeptical of rumors about the pesticide industry funding the anti-GM campaign, one also needs to appreciate why many seed companies would rather not have the Indian government release HT crops. For instance, Jagdish Pandit (real name disguised), one of the most senior breeders and biotechnologists in Krupa Seeds (real name disguised), a leading private seed company based in Maharashtra that competes with Mahyco, elaborated the labor-displacing consequences of HT crops along with why most seed companies, in his opinion, would prefer that the government not allow HT crops. Since our conversation was happening against the backdrop of Mahyco's proposal to commercialize Roundup Ready Flex (RRF) cotton, which is herbicide-tolerant, we ended up talking about RRF cotton, but his remarks apply to HT crops in general. He insisted on showing me a picture (figure 3). This image was mounted in an interior room, which suggests it was perhaps something more than a public relations exercise. I have not encountered such an image in any of the public-sector agricultural research institutions that I have visited. As Dr. Pandit explained:

About 70–80 percent of our agriculture today is run by women, the menfolk are gone [as migrant labor to urban India]. . . . Agriculture today is not just crops, it is a couple of animals—cows, buffalos, some goats. Why is this so? Because landholdings have become 1.5 acres, 2 acres . . . sometimes there is water, sometimes not. . . . Farmers use these animals to give them their daily bread, in the sense they might get some milk. If they sell this milk, they may get one, two, three hundred rupees. This is their livelihood, not farming. Through farming they may make some money, they may not. . . .

The second source of income [for them] is going out as labor. [Children], grandma, mother-in-law, daughter-in-law—the full team goes for weeding. And not just for weeding, also to bring some weeds back as fodder. If three people work like this, they bring at least three hundred rupees home, another one or two hundred rupees from selling milk. Five hundred rupees every day translates to fifteen thousand rupees per month, which is a decent income [for] the rural household. [Farming] is not the major source of income anymore, mainly because there is no irrigation, and [farmers] don't have the money [for] luxury pesticides and seeds. This is 70 percent of our agriculture.

Now, when you bring in RRF, first and foremost you are going to take away their livelihood. Second, suppose you and I are brothers. You have two or three acres and I have two or three acres. There is no wall, the crops are [adjacent]. You have RRF and I don't. You spray [herbicide], and I lose my crop too. It is not possible to stop glyphosate. . . .

Third, when Bt [cotton] had come . . . on average [MMBL] charged [a steep royalty] for [several] years. Now, when RRF comes, what is going to happen? If RRF comes,

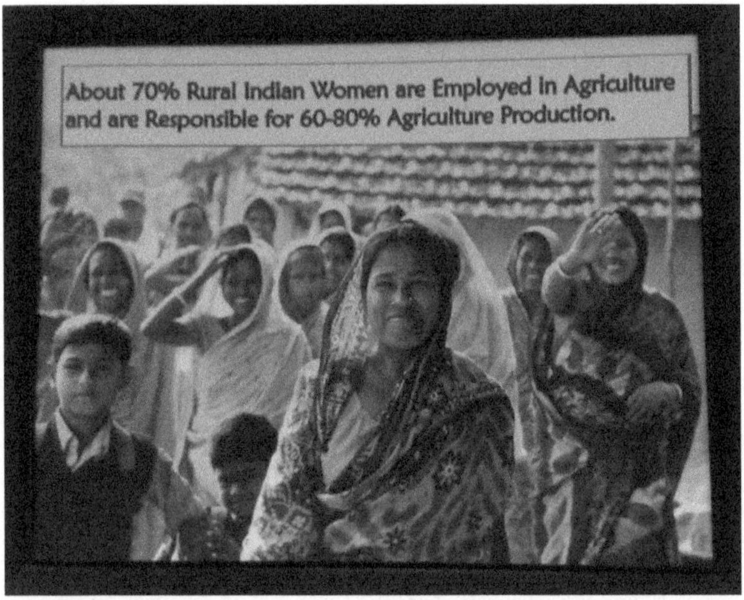

About 70% Rural Indian Women are Employed in Agriculture
and are Responsible for 60-80% Agriculture Production.

Fig. 3. Poster mounted in an interior room of Krupa Seeds.

> it'll be the Monsanto-Mahyco product which will be released first. [Even as a licensee of the RRF gene from Monsanto-Mahyco, I cannot release my product until at least two years after Monsanto-Mahyco release their product]. [In that time], my market is finished. This is why no seed industry is supporting [MMBL] for RRF. Everybody is quiet.[24]

Even in the specific case of GM cotton, the political stakes associated with a trait yet to be released are different from those associated with a trait already released. Most large domestic companies have already incorporated the Bt gene in their proprietary hybrids, and there is no easy way for MMBL to stop them from selling Bt cotton. This leads to political maneuvers through which domestic companies try to increase their profit margins—refusing to pay royalties and seeking government intervention to bring royalties down. The Roundup Ready Flex trait, however, is yet to be released. Only a few transnational companies have the trait in their possession, and there will be enormous first-mover advantages if this trait gets regulatory approval, especially if the government decides not to regulate licensing terms.

Second, Dr. Pandit captures so much of the apprehension surrounding HT crops in India. His views may seem remarkable for a corporate scientist, but, as I have repeatedly argued, a sharp opposition between public and corporate sectors is not to be found in India. As the Ministry of Agriculture has declined in prestige and importance, Dr. Pandit is one of many senior scientists to leave the ICAR and join private industry. These scientists have been motivated by a range of reasons, not the least of which is the chance to actually see their research translate into something of use for farmers, unhindered by the red tape of government institutions. Thus, even as the ICAR and scientists of the Department of Biotechnology enthusiastically back HT crops, we have an ex-ICAR scientist referring to agricultural innovations' influence on gender relations and equity. When I asked him if Krupa planned to develop its own RRF cotton hybrids with Monsanto's gene, he said in a resigned tone that the company had to in order to be competitive, but he felt personally the government should not allow HT crops. Similar points against HT crops were emphasized by a majority of the Technical Expert Committee of the Supreme Court as well.

What Dr. Pandit described to me was borne out in my fieldwork with farmers. Farmers who can afford expensive or "luxury" chemicals, as Dr. Pandit described them, prefer spraying herbicides to hiring laborers, often lower-caste or Adivasi (indigenous) women, or weeding themselves. In October 2013 in the Nashik district of Maharashtra, where I conducted field research with farmers, I was talking one evening to Yogesh, a medium landholding farmer. We were in his tomato plot, slightly smaller than an acre. While talking about herbicides, Yogesh remarked to me that they were very useful. "Weeding this plot [through laborers] will cost 3,000 rupees, while the cost of spraying herbicide is only about 300 rupees."[25]

HT crops will displace labor directly, and they will increase the consumption of herbicides. Similarly, Bt crops involve the farmer's paying a premium upfront to seed companies,[26] in anticipation of some savings on pesticide purchases and labor expenses for spraying—that is, if the Bt plants work exactly as promised; and when they don't, as in the case of Vidarbha in 2017, farmers end up purchasing expensive seeds upfront and lethal pesticides later (Hardikar 2018a, 2018b). The talk about an Evergreen Revolution notwithstanding, the dominant GM crops are labor-displacing and keep the farmer dependent on external sources of synthetic chemical inputs and knowledge (Aga 2019), and thus more of the same as the Green Revolution. In the Green Revolution, it was mechanization and chemicals that displaced labor, more acutely on large farms that could offer economies of scale to capital investment. Most of the GM crops commercialized worldwide are geared to the level of the seed for large-scale industrial farming of commodities (Glover 2010; Stone 2010; for a dissenting view, see Qaim 2009).

Although Bt and HT crops constitute most of the development work on GM crops happening in India, some laboratories, including those in the public sector, are conducting research on other traits, such as drought tolerance and male sterility for hybrid production, as in Delhi University's GM mustard, discussed earlier, which is herbicide-tolerant.[27] Available details about these traits are too sketchy to allow even a brief analysis. It is theoretically possible, however, to have GM traits that are not labor-displacing—for instance, the drought-tolerance trait may not displace any labor.

The Perils of Neglecting Rifts within Agribusiness Capital

There are four ways in which the GM debate in India has surged ahead of that in other countries, in terms of asking far-reaching questions about technology governance and democratic politics. First, the historical development of private seed companies in India in a complementary, rather than an antagonistic, relationship with the public sector is key to understanding the terms through which farmers access Bt cotton, and why governments are willing to legislate market interventions as deep as fixing prices and royalties. To talk of the GM debate as a global struggle of farmers versus transnational agribusinesses is to work implicitly within the framework of the rise of agribusinesses in the United States, whereas the Indian case is more representative of the very different conditions that obtain in the Global South.

Second, GM crops represent different opportunities and constraints for domestic vis-à-vis transnational firms, and thus seed companies do not necessarily share an interest in advocating GM crops. Critical scholarship on corporate food regimes and "supply-chain capitalism" tends to take the unity of purpose and interest among agribusinesses for granted (Patel 2007; Tsing 2009; Fitting 2011; Heller 2013). GM crops, however, present one gambling chip between transnational agribusinesses trying to make it in a new market and small domestic companies trying to hold their own. They are, at the same time, a crucial gambit in the struggle for competitive advantage among domestic seed companies. Further, GM crops have also served to place the private sector at a distinct advantage vis-à-vis public-sector breeding programs. Monsanto first tried to sell Bt cotton through the ICAR, but it was rebuffed by V. L. Chopra, then its director general. It was at this juncture, in the late 1990s, that Monsanto and Mahyco started negotiating a partnership tied to Bt cotton. The Bt gene offered a distinct advantage to each company. It allowed

Monsanto to capture value in the Indian market for seeds without major investment in its own cotton breeding programs—it could tap into the programs and experience of Mahyco. For Mahyco, it offered a ploy to increase its market share and expand into regions and the cottonseed market where its presence was weak.

Third, to understand the political dynamics surrounding GM crops, we have to disaggregate the crop and notice shifts between varieties and hybrids, and the products of one company vis-à-vis the products of another. The clearest evidence of what we lose if we fail to disaggregate Bt cotton is provided by the fate of cotton varieties in northern India. If we say only that Bt cotton swept through northern India, we miss the fact that, as a consequence, cotton hybrids replaced varieties. To then measure yield improvements is to compound the error because yield improvements are inevitable when hybrids, GM or non-GM, replace varieties.

Another illustration concerns distress among Bt cotton cultivators in arid Vidarbha because of crop failures, spiraling debt, and resistant bollworms. Advocates of Bt cotton aver that the blame lies with water-guzzling hybrids rather than the Bt gene per se (Herring and Rao 2012, 50; see also Byatnal 2012).[28] This is at best a deflection because it exculpates neither the state government for having allowed hybrids, which even senior cotton scientists considered ecologically "inappropriate" for the region,[29] nor the ICAR for having failed to release a Bt cotton variety—which virtually all public-sector scientists agree is the need of the hour (Suresh, Ramasundaram, and Chand 2011). It also does not reckon with the deeply unequal relationship between companies and farmers, through which the latter access technologies like Bt seeds, as I highlight in the next chapter (see also Flachs 2017; Aga 2019). Consider again that when polled by the CSDS (CSDS 2014, 51), a large number of farmers expressed disapproval of GM traits in hybrids, preferring them in varieties. This nuance, so important for agriculture, renders it meaningless and futile to ask whether farmers want "GM crops" without specifying whether one is talking of varieties or hybrids, and under what pricing and royalty arrangements. Finally, while GM traits differ in the way surplus is extracted from agriculture, GM crops, by themselves, neither ameliorate the uncertainties of agriculture nor reduce the dependence of farmers on external sources of expertise.

7

Merchants of Knowledge: Petty Retail and the Gambles of Agriculture

One afternoon in August, while I was talking to Ganpat inside his shop, a farmer approached the shop counter and asked:

Farmer: Do you have Manjari [a brand of hybrid eggplant] seeds?
Ganpat: Yes, I do.
Farmer: How are they?
Ganpat: Very good. Manjari is good, otherwise Ajay is also very good. Try Ajay. How many packets do you need?
Farmer: Give me three.

Rapid increase in the number of farmers and acreages cultivating Bt cotton seeds is testament to Indian farmer's faith and trust in this technology.

—Jagresh Rana, director, Mahyco Monsanto Biotech Limited (quoted by Prabu 2010)

For advocates, the wide adoption of GM crops by farmers has clinched the debate. In India, seed companies, social scientists, many agricultural economists, and pro-GM activists contend that over 90 percent of cotton acreage being under Bt cotton is conclusive proof of its popularity and success among farmers.[1] In this view, to question the inference is to cast aspersions on farmers' intelligence and agency.

A whole range of commentators, from the senior journalist Harish Damodaran of the leading national daily, the *Indian Express*, to the former deputy chairman of the Planning Commission and top policy maker in the Congress-led UPA government (2004–14), Dr. Montek Singh Ahluwalia, assured me that "farmers are not fools" when I asked if we could read Bt cotton cultivation statistics so simply.

Matters, however, are not so straightforward, nor do they turn on farmers' intelligence. Dubious is the argument that when farmers purchase seeds, they are participating in a referendum on GM crops at large. Exercising choice in any meaningful sense entails access to the knowledge about different products and the autonomy to transact a sale on the basis of that knowledge. I question whether both these conditions obtain by illuminating how and on what terms farmers access and purchase agricultural inputs. This chapter brings to light something that partisans in the GM debate consider unimportant, namely, the relations through which farmers will access, cultivate, and sell GM food crops if and when they are commercialized. Although no one cultivated GM crops in the areas of western Maharashtra where I conducted field research, unless we understand these relationships, and the scope for collaboration and coercion coded in them, we understand little about farmers' engagement with new technologies (see Shah 2005; Witt, Patel, and Schnurr 2006; Lapegna 2016).

Since the nature of the encounter between farmers and agribusinesses is at stake in the GM debate, this chapter is about the people through whom farmers interact with transnational and domestic agribusiness capital in their everyday lives. Specifically, I focus on that node which serves as the point of sale to farmers: the petty retailer of seeds and agrochemicals such as fertilizers, pesticides, herbicides, fungicides, and micronutrients. How a sale of an input is transacted, who the petty retailers are, and how they relate with farmers are not mere anthropological curiosities. These questions are central to the story of industrial capital in agriculture.

Until the 1990s, there were few pesticides and fungicides available in rural markets; these were manufactured by Indian companies and sold in market towns and district headquarters. With the expansion of transnational agribusinesses in India since the 1990s, new and many more chemicals, manufactured by Indian and multinational companies like Monsanto, Dow, BASF, Bayer, Syngenta, and DuPont (Monsanto was acquired by Bayer in 2018), have become available. Shops retailing these have slowly expanded outward from market towns and district headquarters, going into smaller and smaller villages. Significantly, certain sections of farming households in western Maharashtra are taking advantage of these opportunities in the expanding retail space, as I demonstrate below.

This makes petty retailers important for a reason beyond their role in sales of seeds and inputs. These figures are largely absent from popular and policy writings on Indian agriculture, which often offer a narrative of crisis and all-round distress. Detailed attention to the transactions between farmers and retailers, however, reveals aspects of agrarian India that qualify this narrative (Ramachandran, Rawal, and Swaminathan 2010). Even as certain farmers have been driven to suicide by neoliberal policies in agriculture (Shah 2012; Vasavi 2012), others have sought to capitalize on the opportunities created by the same policies (Jodhka 2006, 2012). This troubles the populist notion that farmers as a bloc are under threat from an undifferentiated industrial capital. Instead, such dynamics call for a subtly shaded picture of agrarian change and the shifting configuration of not only constraints, but also opportunities.

In the Lap of the River Godavari

I conducted fieldwork in the agrarian villages to the west and south of Nashik city in the Nashik district of western Maharashtra. Close to the source of the river Godavari, this is a major area for the production of vegetables and fruits, including eggplant. It is blessed with abundant rainfall, easy access to groundwater, and fertile black cotton and red laterite soils. My principal field sites were Khedgaon, a large village, and its closest market town, Pimpalgaon.[2] Since the Bt eggplant debate turned on the problems of eggplant cultivation, especially pesticide applications, I was keen to observe how synthetic inputs feature in the lived reality of farming.

Marathas constituted the dominant landholding caste in both Khedgaon and Pimpalgaon. There were also Dalit and Adivasi (indigenous people) residents. Among them, the few who farmed cultivated undulating lands with poor access to irrigation. Given the rich, water-retaining black cotton soil and the heavy rainfall, paddy, along with millets, was traditionally cultivated in this area in the monsoons. During the winters (the *rabī* season), farmers grew onions and potatoes. Village elders recount that in the 1980s, the state completed several major and minor dams, and irrigation become widely available. This was also the time access to electricity expanded in this region. With the arrival of irrigation, crops such as grapes, sugarcane, and vegetables began to be cultivated across a wider socioeconomic base of farmers. Today, even those with less than five acres of land cultivate grapes for domestic and export markets, provided they have some access to water and capital, since grapes require large quantities of inputs.

The other major shift that has occurred in the last three decades is the progressive domination of private-sector hybrid seeds in vegetables, which has contributed significantly to the high cost of vegetable farming. Although hybrids result in higher yields, they require many more inputs and greater care. The wide adoption of hybrids has coincided with the decline of public-sector extension efforts and state-provisioning of rural credit across India (Shetty 2009; Ramakumar and Chavan 2014), and with the expanding footprint of transnational and domestic companies, which supply more and newer chemicals. These intersecting regional and national dynamics have ramped up the consumption of synthetic chemical inputs in the area since the 1990s: between 2000–2001 and 2017–18, the total consumption of pesticides, herbicides, and fungicides in Maharashtra has more than quadrupled, from 3,570 tons (3,239 metric tons) to 17,161 tons (15,568 metric tons) (Indiastat 2017; 2019).

While speaking to farmers in Khedgaon, I asked them where they purchased seeds and how they decided which chemical to spray on their crops. Invariably they referred me to the *dukaandar*, or the retailer of inputs. This led me to retailers and brought into view a line of inquiry largely absent in the critical scholarship of contemporary agriculture. In the monsoon season of 2013, and then again in 2014, I interviewed ten retailers in Pimpalgaon and in villages around Nashik city, and I spent several hours across seven months in the shops of three retailers.

The Krushi Seva Kendras, or Agricultural Service Centres

Somnath is the proprietor of Pooja Krushi Seva Kendra (almost all retail shops are named Krushi Seva Kendra, or Agricultural Service Centre) and the principal retailer serving my farmer informants in Khedgaon.[3] Born in 1983 to a family of Maratha cultivators, Somnath hails from a village in Dindori block (a subdistrict unit) of Nashik district. While his elder brother looked after their two acres of land where they grew grapes for export, Somnath got a diploma in agriculture, followed by an undergraduate degree in horticulture from the Yashwantrao Chavan Maharashtra Open University in Nashik city. In 2003 he joined the sales and marketing team of Syngenta, where he was assigned the sugarcane region of Niphad, in Nashik district. As a sales and marketing agent, he worked among farmers as well as retailers, promoting chemical products.

Not keen on working for a private company for too long, he decided to open a shop in Pimpalgaon, where he had some relatives. As he said to me one evening at his shop: "[In Niphad] there were already very strong retailers. I could not have established myself. At that time there were few retailers here. Growth was just beginning here. . . . Grapes were only 5–10 percent here, today they are 80 percent. . . . This was not a developed pocket then, it was on the path of progress . . . and so I picked this pocket." Somnath raised around 600,000 rupees from his family, without taking a loan, and started Pooja Krushi Seva Kendra in June 2006.

Pooja Krushi Seva Kendra is one among about twenty-five petty shops in Pimpalgaon[4]—bear in mind that even petty shops can have an annual turnover of 10–15 million rupees.[5] Consider bigger and swankier shops like Vikram Agro Services, with names in English. Although they are single-story structures like the petty shops, their larger area and sheen qualify them as "malls" in farmers' parlance. As I entered Vikram Agro Services one afternoon, I immediately spotted Rajubhau, the proprietor. A bespectacled man in his fifties with graying hair, wearing a formal shirt tucked into trousers with a smart belt, he had the air of a middle-class corporate executive.

Rajubhau belongs to a large Maratha family that owns about six acres of land. He recalled that it was very difficult to feed the family from the proceeds of the vegetables that his parents cultivated. Rajubhau got an undergraduate degree in law and a graduate degree in commerce, but he could not get a government job, for which there was a "craze" then. He rued that his "open category" Maratha caste got in the way of getting a government job.[6] So he joined a small manufacturing unit in Nashik's industrial area, in the finance department. Although he had a job, he used to feel insecure, fearing that the private company might close down any day. He kept saving money and started stocking a few bottles of chemicals at home. Thus began the retail business from his home. This was about two decades ago. In 2007 he finally left the job to work full-time on his retail business. Today he is not only a retailer, but also a wholesaler to other retailers. He is also grooming his son, Vikram, for the business. Vikram, who is in his twenties, has finished a graduate degree in agriculture and an MBA in agribusiness management, the latter from the prestigious Symbiosis College in Pune, the state's second-largest city and a prominent education hub. Somnath and Rajubhau are but two examples, but they point to the general trend.

Situating the Retailer

Since the 1990s, Marathas, typically small and semi-medium (and not large) farmers, have ventured into petty retailing, usually sourcing capital from the small surplus generated by agriculture along with some loans.[7] Among retailers I met, landholding sizes ranged from two to six acres. Descriptively, they are the poorer among K. Balagopal's "provincial propertied class." As he wrote, "A typical family of this provincial propertied class has landholding in its native village, cultivated by hired labour, [sharecroppers], tenants or farm-servants and supervised by the father or one son; business of various descriptions in towns—trade, finance, hotels, cinemas and contracts—managed by other sons; and perhaps a young and bright child, who is a doctor or engineer or maybe even a professor in one of the small-town universities" (Balagopal 1987, 1545). I say "poorer" because the retailers I interviewed had their families still laboring on farms. This is not the class of large, capitalist farmers who found opportunities for consolidation of their power and wealth through control of cooperative institutions, local self-government bodies, credit societies, sugar factories, or electoral politics (Baviskar 1980; Breman 2007), and diversification into agro-based industries (Damodaran 2008). These large, capitalist farmers galvanized the new farmer movements of the 1970s and 1980s around their particular interests (Brass 1995). In sum, retailers have arisen from among petty agricultural commodity producers of the provincial propertied class, at the edge of capital accumulation.[8]

Thus, as transnational and domestic capital penetrates deeper into rural areas, petty commodity producers, typically smallholders of the dominant farming castes, have tried to capitalize on the associated opportunities. While at the district and state levels, *Jain* and *Baniya* merchants hailing from Gujarat and Rajasthan (*Marwari*), with generations of mercantile experience, handle the trade,[9] for perhaps the first time at the village level, Maratha petty commodity producers are venturing into the retail business. In the process of selling inputs to farmers, the latter come to depend on retailers in three ways—provision of credit, troubleshooting knowledge, and access to markets for their produce.

Provision of Credit

When I probed the challenges of running the retail business, Somnath touched on some themes that I had heard across my interviews with retailers.

SOMNATH: This is a 100 percent credit business. If farmers do not pay on time, then it becomes difficult to make payments to my creditors.

ANIKET: You need to settle accounts monthly or maybe [every] two months, and once you offer credit to farmers, they will not be able to make payments until they harvest their crops. So how do you manage your business?

SOMNATH: I am always under pressure [*kayam gaadi load var rahate*]. It is difficult even to tell you how I manage. It's terrible.

Different retailers extend credit to different degrees, depending, in part, on their risk appetite, their economic position, and pleas from farmers. A lot depends on the historical relationship between the farmer and the retailer on the one hand, and the retailer and companies on the other. That said, all retailers reported that companies had become very "tight" in the last several years. Companies insisted on monthly settlements and required payments to be made by check. Moreover, for some years now, transnational corporations in particular have been asking for blank checks from retailers as guarantee of payments. Matters were less stringent in terms of timing some years ago. This has a bearing on the terms retailers impose on farmers when they buy on credit.

Typically, retailers offer the largest discount when their fellow Maratha farmers, regular customers, buy with cash. In general, though, they appraise their customers before they quote a price, and some negotiation is virtually guaranteed. Dhananjay, a retailer outside Nashik city, told me that he never divulges prices on the phone to unfamiliar customers; he insists that they come to the shop, so that he can size them up before quoting a price.

Retailers prefer cash, but it is almost impossible to sell only in cash. Grapes and vegetables are very inputs-intensive, and around late October, farmers start running short of cash because of mounting expenses for inputs, as well as purchases for the festival of Diwali, which falls in late October or early November each year. Perhaps because of climate change, the monsoon season has also become more erratic in this region, and it is not uncommon for rains as late as the end of October and into November,[10] a time when grapevines are particularly vulnerable to fungal attacks. Farmers have to douse the ripening grape buds with fungicide as soon as rainfall stops. Even twelve hours' delay can devastate the crop. This was forcefully brought home to me late one evening when, suddenly, it started pouring, and I

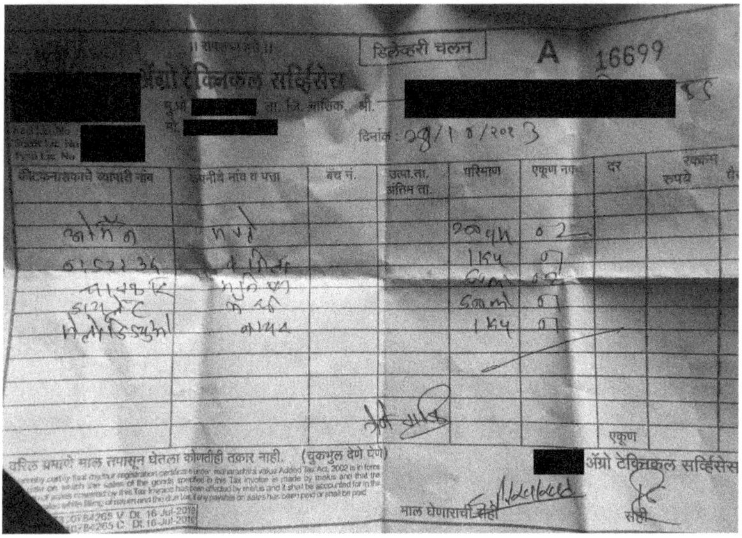

Fig. 4. Receipt showing inputs bought on credit. The far right column for prices is blank.

decided to wait out the rain in Somnath's shop. As soon as the rain stopped, the roads were full of grape farmers rushing to purchase fungicides. Within minutes, Somnath's shop was full, and there was a queue outside. Such rainfall imposes an enormous burden on grape farmers' pockets. For these reasons, this is when *udhari,* or buying on credit, peaks. Even if retailers want to transact only in cash, pleas for credit from regular customers are difficult to decline.

When Maratha farmers buy on credit, the retailer gives them a receipt but does not write the price on the receipt (see figure 4). He quotes a price only when the farmer returns to settle the bill. The price he quotes depends on the time interval between the purchase and the full payment of the bill. As Dhananjay explained, "If my purchase cost is 800 rupees, and the MRP [maximum retail price] is 900 rupees, I will sell it for 850 rupees in cash. If it's on credit, then I will sell it for the MRP. The margin between my purchase price and the MRP is what I have to play with." The MRP is the printed price on a product. Since companies insist on monthly settlements, generally retailers start asking for the MRP if the bill is settled more than a month after the purchase. From the point of view of the retailer, this makes sense as he manages a complex credit-driven business, but for the farmer this effectively amounts to usurious lending. Paying 850 rupees in cash versus 900 rupees after a month implies an effective interest rate of 71 percent per annum. Ganpat, a retailer, said to me explicitly, "Anyway [a farmer] takes credit at 5 percent per month, why should it be any different when he takes credit from me? I too have to run a business." Ganpat was referring to the widespread, informal, noninstitutional moneylending, which comes with an interest rate of anywhere between 5 and 10 percent per month, depending on one's caste and one's standing with the moneylender.

In Table 5 I list a few examples of the prices that retailers offer on a cash-and-carry basis and on credit, and the annualized interest rate implied by the difference. These are indicative—the cash price offered, the period after which the retailer will charge the MRP, and the length of time for which a farmer could delay repayment in full depend on the retailer's impression of whom he is selling to, their history of transactions, and the bargaining power of the farmer, based on his caste, landholding, crop mix, and standing in cooperative and local self-government institutions and political parties. For instance, a farmer with eight acres of grapevines may be perceived as more risky and less creditworthy than one with six acres of tomatoes and eggplants, since grapes are harvested only once a year, are much more capital-intensive than tomatoes and eggplants, and are highly susceptible to fungal attacks.

From the point of view of farmers, they get locked through credit to particular retailers. The more a farmer takes credit from one

Table 5. Annualized Interest Rates Implied by the Difference in the Cash Price and the Maximum Retail Price (MRP)

Item	*Cash price in rupees*	*MRP in rupees*	*Annualized interest rate (when paid after one month)*	*Annualized interest rate (when paid after two months)*
Ivory radish seeds (1 can)	350	415	223 percent	111 percent
Roundup herbicide (500 ml)	180	200	133 percent	67 percent
Doom (Dichlorvos 76%) pesticide	525	550	57 percent	29 percent

retailer, the more he gets locked to that particular retailer. This is because another retailer will be much more reluctant to open a credit line to a new person,[11] and in a small market town, retailers know most farmers and whom they go to for credit. Credit, however, is not the only mechanism that ties farmers to particular retailers. They are also constrained by their need for troubleshooting knowledge and access to markets for their produce.

Provision of Troubleshooting Knowledge

When farmers spot symptoms of diseases, pest attacks, or fungal infections on their crop, they invariably consult retailers. They also reach out to field marketing agents of large agrochemical companies, who frequently tour villages in this region and who recommend products for purchase from retailers (Aga 2019). Very often farmers go to shops with a specific need or a problem, sometimes with a sample cutting of the infected plant. The retailer then gives them a chemical remedy, or more often a cocktail of chemicals. Retailers thus serve as a crucial source of knowledge and troubleshooting advice for farmers.

This is why I call them merchants of knowledge.[12] To appreciate the delicacy of this transaction, consider the following exchange I observed at Somnath's shop.

FARMER: Do you have anything to get tomato to flower?

SOMNATH: [*To his assistant*] Arey, give that . . . give Daikin one kilogram. And Hans one liter.

SOMNATH: [*Turning to the farmer*] Do you need pesticide? Are there leaf miners [a class of pests that consumes leaf tissues]?

FARMER: I have applied medicine [*aushadh*]

SOMNATH: Which one?

FARMER: Korasin [DuPont's Coragen]. . . . No, [there are no] leaf miners.

SOMNATH: Trust me and apply some pesticide, if there is a miner hiding somewhere, it'll die. Leaf miners will not come. There is a light and inexpensive pesticide here [*adding a packet of pesticide to the bag*].

FARMER: Is this for flowering?

SOMNATH'S ASSISTANT: Yes, this is for flowering. Each of the three is for two tips [105 gallons, or 400 liters].

FARMER: I need sixteen pumps [referring to the spraying container that one straps to the back].

SOMNATH: Will you spray with a pump?

FARMER: One and a half tips [80 gallons, or 300 liters].

SOMNATH: Look here, I will explain. One tip is [53 gallons, or] 200 liters. Put in half the powder, half the bottle, and [the] full bottle [*pointing to the three chemicals he had sold*]. Now what's left with you? Half the powder, half the bottle, and a full bottle. Now put half of each. When you have [80 gallons, or] 300 liters, some amount of chemicals will remain, but that cannot be helped.

One must pay attention to a few important things in this exchange. First, the farmer came to Somnath asking for a stimulant for tomato. Somnath used the opportunity to ask him if he wanted a pesticide, and if the tomato crop had leaf miners. The farmer replied that he had already applied DuPont's powerful pesticide, Coragen, and confirmed that he had no leaf miners. Nevertheless, Somnath asked him to apply another dose of an inexpensive pesticide. He said if there were any leaf miners hidden somewhere, they would die. Thus, Somnath managed to sell the farmer a pesticide he never wanted and did not ask for. Further, the farmer asked Somnath for the dosage. So, not only did Somnath sell him a pesticide he did not originally want, Somnath was also the authoritative source for how much to use. Although dosage is mentioned in English and a few regional languages on bottles and packets, farmers and retailers tend to ignore it.

Retailers try different techniques of persuasion with different farmers. A few minutes after the incident above, I noticed another delicate transaction, in which Somnath managed to veer a farmer away from what he originally asked for and toward what Somnath wanted to sell him, like Ganpat in the vignette at the beginning of this chapter. These transactions are sensitive to the farmer's position with respect to the retailer. Sometimes farmers are assertive and refuse to take anything beyond what they ask for. Sometimes they say they have already applied a pesticide or fungicide, at which point the retailer asks them which one. If farmers can name the pesticide, then the retailer offers another one, saying it is different, more powerful, or more appropriate for the problem. Quite often, however, farmers cannot name what chemical they have used, in which case the retailer asks them to err on the side of yet another dose. In general, though, the retailer has to balance his interest to sell more with the necessity of not coming across as too keen or aggressive.

After many hours of observation, I started noticing a pattern whereby, in the absence of any strong countervailing pressure, retailers would try to push domestic companies' products onto farmers. I asked Somnath and other retailers about this, and they told me that "multinational products" offered very low margins vis-à-vis domestic products, and so retailers had an incentive to push the latter. Transnational companies employ their own sales and marketing teams to promote their products and direct farmers to retailers for sales (Aga 2019). Domestic companies generally do not have the resources to invest in sales and marketing teams, and so they rely on retailers to market their products. This became clear to me in the following exchange between Somnath and a marketing agent for a domestic company with a pesticidal product, Larva Fighter. I asked the agent how his company competes with large Indian and transnational corporations selling rival pesticides. Somnath responded before the agent could.

SOMNATH: Why will they compete? They will take me to a hotel, take me to a dance bar.[13]

ANIKET: You mean they will take the retailer . . . ?

SOMNATH: Who else? Otherwise why am I here? And then will I sell [rival product from the house of Tatas] or Larva Fighter [*winking*]? You need two things. First of all, the product. When you give a product, it must be good. And then the question is, do farmers know about your product? Once demand among farmers is created, then I don't have to use my mind. . . . If a farmer is already asking me for a product, then I don't need to advertise. But when I do need to advertise, then the company has to give me better margins. So the money I make from selling four bottles of [DuPont's] Coragen, I can make from selling two bottles of Larva Fighter.

Over time, I consistently observed that retailers would push domestic products whenever they could. When I met him in September 2016, Ganpat explained to me why he prefers pushing domestic products over those of transnational companies: "With multinational [companies'] products, margins are small, and because results are good, farmers don't come back for more chemicals quickly. Domestic companies offer higher margins, and the results are not as good, and so farmers have to come back sooner for more purchases." Nor was Somnath's talk of dance bars and hotels an exaggeration. Domestic companies find it cheaper to offer monetary and nonmonetary incentives to retailers than to recruit marketing teams to advertise village to village.

The logic of margins and incentives governs the sale of seeds, too. Quite often farmers simply ask for good or new eggplant seeds or maize seeds or describe some physical characteristics like "seeds for the thorny [*kateri*] eggplant," and then it's up to the retailer to push seed brands that he wants to sell. Sometimes farmers buy the brands he recommends, and sometimes they purchase a few packets of those brands that performed well in their fields the last season, if they remain available, along with a few packets of brands the retailer recommends. Brands of vegetable seeds came and left the market frequently, though less rapidly than the Bt cotton brands in Stone's (2007) study—this preempted farmers' capacity to choose on the basis of past experience. It was common for my informants to ask retailers for a certain brand of seeds and to be told that it was no longer available.

One reason farmers are dependent on retailers for technical advice is that there is virtually no state extension service providing technical support. Although there is an extension unit of the ICAR about 5 miles (8 kilometers) from Khedgaon, none of the farmers I met during my fieldwork sought technical advice from the extension staff, nor did any extension staff visit Khedgaon. Moreover, the extension staff focused on cereals, oilseeds, and pulses, rather than horticultural crops such as grapes and tomatoes. The extension staff was constrained by the varieties and technologies available from state agricultural universities and regional ICAR institutes, whose research programs for vegetables pale in comparison to those of private seed companies. A second reason is that farmers seek solutions to problems as they arise within the specific micro-ecological conditions of their fields—for example, why two rows of tomatoes were paler than those in the rest of the field, or how to address the slope of their field. No one has clear answers at this level of specificity. Friends, neighbors and kin, marketing teams of transnational agrochemical companies, as well as the package of practices that some of the younger, educated farmers access online with their mobile phones, provide broad-brush solutions in the form of chemical applications. Further complicating matters is the fact that farmers identify some chemicals by their brand name (Coragen and Karate, for instance), some others by their chemical compounds (such as cypermethrin), and others simply by their function (for example, *kitaknashak*, or pesticide). In this context, the retailer, situated at the point of sale, is in a position to exercise influence over what farmers buy by making sense of and tailoring, rightly or wrongly, these bits of information to the specific requirements and conditions that the latter report. In the fields many of my farmer-informants would confidently assert to me that they knew what was best for their crop. Yet in shops they would appear much less sure of themselves, and they would often defer to the retailer (see Flachs 2019).

The confusion and gaps in knowledge among farmers allow the retailer to push products he wants to push. For instance, I saw farmers simultaneously buy the same fungicide under two different brand names, made by two different companies. A few of my farmer-informants did this to diminish the risk of one of the two being fake or inactive. Others told me that they were buying two distinct products, which they were not. Glenn Stone (2007) notes a similar confusion in the case of Bt cottonseeds in Warangal, south India. I also encountered occasions of outright duping. For instance, Gokul, a grape farmer, went to his retailer for fungicides, but the retailer palmed off domestic insecticides instead, and Gokul was none the wiser. In contrast, one evening when I was sitting in Somnath's shop, two men walked in. From the way Somnath immediately stood up, adopted an extra-ingratiating tone, and shook hands with them, it was clear that they were rich farmers. They wanted fungicides for their grapevines, and Somnath tried to push domestic copper sulfate on them. They laughed, firmly pushed the copper sulfate back toward Somnath, and insisted on a "multinational product."[14]

Another implication of the difference in margins is that retailers, overtly and covertly, start bundling products, especially to infrequent customers. Many farmers told me that their retailers insisted that they buy certain products together, as a package. I asked Ganpat about this after several months of interacting with him, and he told me that he saw no point in selling something that earned him a mere five to ten rupees, and so he bundled low-margin products with high-margin products.

Providing technical inputs frequently leads to conflicts between farmers and retailers. On several occasions, farmers came back and argued that the retailer's advice and product had not worked. Sometimes they even demanded a refund or refused to pay off their debt to the retailer. In all such cases, retailers firmly absolved themselves of any responsibility. They insisted that they could scarcely help it if, for example, it had rained too much, or too little, or if it was too sunny, or too cloudy, and so on. In brief, there was always a competing explanation for their advice not having worked. This rarely satisfied farmers, but they felt unable to challenge the retailer in the absence of an alternative source of advice and diagnosis. Further, they felt constrained by their dependence on the retailer for subsequent purchases of inputs. Farmers also worried that if they fought with one retailer, all the other retailers in the market might boycott them.

Provision of Access to the Market

Finally, farmers also depend on retailers for access to markets for their produce. Traders purchase grapes directly from the farms, and tomato traders from northern India set up camp in Pimpalgaon from October to early December. For all other crops, the farmers have to take their produce to the nearest agricultural produce market yard, or *mandī* in Nashik city, wait there for it to be auctioned, and collect the money from the commission agent (*adathi*)[15] before they can return home. This can easily take half to a full working day. Therefore, many farmers, especially those who do not own transport vehicles, sell their produce through retailers. In the last decade, retailers have struck agreements with commission agents in the market yard at Vashi, a city outside Mumbai, and sourced boxes of vegetables from farmers on their behalf. The retailer sends minivans to the farm gate, where the farmer keeps the produce packed and ready. A few days later, the farmer can collect cash from the retailer, along with the *pukka*, or proper receipt. The receipt lists the rate at which the produce was auctioned at Vashi, as well as the deductions—a commission for the agent, transportation charges, and a 3 percent commission for the retailer, among others. As Sandip, a retailer, told me, the 3 percent commission is entirely "risk-free," to be made "just by sitting in the shop." This arrangement inverts the very purpose of the Agricultural Produce Marketing (Regulation) Act's insistence on open auctions. Open auctions were meant to ensure transparency and to thereby get the best rates for farmers, even if this did not work well in practice. In the arrangement above, however, farmers have no way of knowing what prices their crop actually fetched at Vashi.[16]

In this way, the retailer also becomes a banker of sorts for the farmers. During harvest season, when farmers come to collect their receipts and money, the retailer makes claims on the money in lieu of the credit he has extended. Or sometimes he adjusts the cash against their immediate purchases. And then sometimes farmers deliberately leave their money with the retailer, saying that if they take it home, they may end up spending it. While many Maratha farmers in Khedgaon told me that they were free to sell their produce through any retailer, and not exclusively through their creditor-retailer, a few also mentioned that they felt obligated to sell through their creditor-retailer, even if they thought that some other retailer would get them better rates.

For all these reasons, the figure of the retailer embodies a dense hub of social and economic relations in agrarian life. Moreover, it would be wrong to see these relations as mere transactions. The retailer's shop is a place for exchanging news, reading the newspaper, drinking a cup of tea while waiting for the bus to Nashik city, gossiping, and discussing political developments. Further, the retailers are often from the same or neighboring villages and are related to some of their clients through birth or marriage.

Differentiation without Consolidation among Farmers

Petty retailers hardly feature in the GM debate.[17] The observations above, however, highlight the significance of the petty retailer in mediating farmers' access to new corporate-sector technologies and, more broadly, in the trajectory of agrarian change. Industrial capital and farmers transact with each other through complex mediations, and at the bottom of the agribusiness supply chain is the retailer. Figures like Somnath and Rajubhau belong to a small section of Maratha farmers who have invested surplus capital generated from agricultural petty commodity production, or from salaried jobs, or from loans taken from kin and caste relations, and ventured into petty retail. Many retailers continue to keep one leg in farming, often with the help of the labor of family members, especially women of the household. A few have, over the years, slowly pulled back from direct involvement in farming, as their retail business has stabilized—Rajubhau is an example of a farmer who has pulled back entirely from farming.

In this way, retailing for domestic and transnational agribusinesses offers avenues for upward mobility to Maratha farmers. As more and more villages see such shops open, we can see retailing as a vehicle for farmer differentiation.[18] More precisely, the Maratha petty retailer represents a further differentiation among landed dominant-caste farmers. In western Maharashtra, as in some other irrigated areas of India, the process of differentiation has been going on since at least the colonial times (Guha 1985), which saw the advent of cash-crop cultivation. While the capitalist farmers have consolidated their power and wealth through electoral politics and control of cooperative societies, banks, sugar factories, and so on, the deeper penetration of agribusiness capital in rural areas, the turn to petty commodity production, and the decline of public-sector extension and rural lending have together offered opportunities for accumulation to those farmers who could not break into influential positions in cooperative societies and sugar factory boards. With access to some surplus, these farmers have augmented their petty agricultural commodity production with retailing—which can be seen as one step up the agricultural inputs value chain. The nature of the business, and the political economy of contemporary agriculture, however, is such that upward mobility remains unstable and transient.

Petty retail is very risky. Retailers extend credit to farmers on the one hand, and take credit from companies on the other. But the two credit lines operate on different schedules. Farmers cannot repay fully until harvest time, and harvest may be delayed because of weather, or markets may be down because of gluts or export restrictions. For instance, Kasturi (2014) analyzes enormous fluctuations in the market for vegetables in Maharashtra, which highlight the uncertainty that farmers encounter even, or perhaps especially, in good monsoon years—bountiful harvests usually tend to depress prices. Companies operate on the linear time of quarters and fiscal years. They do not operate by agricultural seasons, which dominate the lives of farmers.

Retailers end up mediating the two time lines. They have to manage their operations in a manner that ensures that they have sufficient cash flow to honor the monthly settlement that companies insist on and to meet their day-to-day expenses, even though farmers can pay off most of their debts only at harvest time. Coordinating these two schedules successfully is thus a risky task, requiring astute accounting skills, as well as judgment in terms of how much credit to extend and to whom. As many retailers told me, managing inventories and credit was crucial to staying afloat.

Here lies the crux of the difficulty with running the retail business. Several retailers told me that if a farmer were to default on payments owed to them, they could not easily seize his assets or land. This, again, points to their sociopolitical situation—retailers have neither the political muscle nor the collective organization to forcibly collect debts from defaulting farmers. Ganpat explained the conundrum: "If my credit goes up, say in a month, I have extended credit to the tune of [100,000] rupees. Will I be able to sleep at night? It's not easy recovering [100,000]. Farmers are full of excuses . . . seeds did not germinate, market was down, and of ten customers, one or two usually turn out to be scoundrels. You have to be prepared for that. The important thing is that you should never allow the gun to go into the hands of farmers. The gun should stay in your hands."

Retailers have to be careful never to extend so much credit to farmers as to become seriously vulnerable to the threat of default. In the context of Punjab, where commission agents lend to farmers somewhat like retailers in my study, there have even been reports of agents committing suicide on account of defaulting farmers (Chaba and Jagga 2016). As already mentioned, retailers in small market towns do not open a new credit line to a farmer they associate with another retailer. Of late, they have begun to share details of defaulting farmers with retailers in nearby villages and towns through WhatsApp groups and other social media platforms. Even with their regular customers, they insist on small partial payments at frequent intervals before the harvest season, intensifying their demands for repayment once harvests begin. The anxiety to remain afloat also sometimes nudges retailers to resort to underhand measures, such as selling spurious, dated, and expired stock, and black-marketing of seeds—issues that have cropped up on multiple occasions in the case of Bt cotton in India. In a particularly galling case, in October and November 2017, over fifty Bt cotton farmers in Vidarbha succumbed to death, and over one thousand farmers suffered serious illnesses on account of poisoning by pesticides. As ecologists and some activists had anticipated, the insect-resistance of Bt cotton cracked under a ferocious attack by pink bollworms. Farmers, desperate to save the expensive crop, turned to retailers in anguish. And retailers ended up selling them lethal pesticides, some of which were illegal, in deadly combinations, which led to this horrific tragedy (Hardikar 2018a, 2018b). Such incidents sharply expose the travesty of reading sales simply as choice and call for investigations of retailers' incentives, constraints, and influence over farmers.

Without an easy recourse to coercive power, retailers can only flex the dependencies to collect their debts from farmers, while being careful about how much and to whom they lend. This aspect of retailing—managing risk and credit—is precisely where they lack historical experience as first-generation merchants. In the words of one Maratha retailer, "Unlike *Marwaris*, we don't know how to patiently recover money. We Marathas . . . our style is to abuse the farmer, fight, and snap all ties with him. But that does not get our money back. *Marwaris* know how to get their money back." *Marwaris* refers to all-India mercantile and trading castes hailing from Rajasthan, also involved in moneylending.

Companies too are aware of retailers' vulnerability, and they therefore try to minimize their risk exposure by insisting on stricter settlement terms. But, given their importance to farming, farmers too try to cultivate retailers through the usual method of forging kin and marital relations. For example, one of the most respected farmers in Khedgaon had "given his daughter" in marriage to Somnath. These ties come with their own obligations and norms, which cut both ways. While farmers deploy the idioms of kinship to try to get better credit terms, retailers modulate them to exert pressure, garner sympathy, and threaten social and moral sanctions to recover their due in a timely manner.

Buffeted by obligations from companies as well as farmers, retailers run a precarious operation. The intensifying vagaries of weather and market volatility have deepened their risk, and it is not uncommon for retailers to go bust. Somnath told me that in the course of a decade in Pimpalgaon, six of twenty retailers had closed shop, and ten new retailers had come in. Rajubhau, who services retailers in many blocks of Nashik district, told me that he had seen as many as 80 percent of retailers go bust over a decade, to be replaced by new entrants. A small number of credit extensions at the wrong time, or to the wrong people, can snowball into collapse.

The Gambles of Agriculture

The GM debate turns farmers' purchase decisions into a referendum on technology. Partisans leave little room for considerations of how and why farmers end up purchasing the seeds and chemicals they do. Such transactions find salience and meaning, however, only through everyday interactions between farmers and retailers. These in turn draw attention to certain key, interrelated aspects of the changing political economy of agriculture in India that bear on the GM debate.

Arising from Maratha petty agricultural commodity-producing households, retailers are the vehicle for the deepening penetration of agribusiness capital in western Maharashtra, even as this intensifies indebtedness. The expanding market for agricultural inputs has opened opportunities for upward mobility, income diversification, and enrichment for farmers, however limited and tenuous. Thus, the petty retailer, at the bottom of the agribusiness supply chain, is both farmer and agent of industrial capital. It is through him that farmers purchase seeds and chemicals, which figures aggregate to generate the adoption statistics of technologies and products. This troubles the notion that farmers' choice can be neatly inferred from sales figures, a point also borne out by studies related to Bt cotton in South Africa (Witt, Patel, and Schnurr 2006) and Burkina Faso (Dowd-Uribe and Schnurr 2016). Rather, what sales figures capture is companies shaping retailers' incentives and retailers steering farmers' purchase decisions, more than farmers exercising autonomous choices. They reflect farmers' choices as modulated and shaped by retailers. Both farmers' knowledge of what is being pushed on them and the capacity to resist retailers' influence are tenuous. At any rate, they cannot be taken for granted, as figure 2 suggests. This also accounts for some of Glenn Stone's (2007) powerful findings from Warangal, a region in what was then Andhra Pradesh, where petty commodity production is as extensive as in western Maharashtra. The fads for different brands of Bt cottonseeds that Stone observed were likely to have been shaped by what retailers in the region were trying to push on farmers. The lesson couldn't be clearer: farmers' engagement with GM crops cannot be understood without taking into account, at a minimum, retailers' interests and incentives with respect to GM seeds and associated inputs.

If the emergence of petty retailers challenges neat accounts of technology adoption, it also qualifies the critical literature on corporate food regimes (McMichael 2013) and food sovereignty (Patel 2009). This literature frames trajectories of agrarian politics and change in terms of a stark opposition between transnational industrial capital and the peasantry. My findings qualify this narrative frame in two ways. First, the literature tends to paint both agri-inputs industries and industries that rely on farm outputs with the same brush, without parsing the differences between the two (for example, Patel 2007; Weis 2007). Though the two types of industry share the logic of appropriating agrarian surplus, they do not appropriate it in the same way. Industries that rely on farm outputs seek to direct and control practical aspects of production through contract farming, vertical integration, payment terms, and so on. Companies manufacturing pesticides or chemical fertilizers do not need to directly control farm practices in their quest for greater sales and profits. They can capture a share of farmers' wallets through managing the mediating figure of the retailer and his incentives and constraints. Thus, farmers do not perceive as clear a conflict of interest with agri-inputs industries as with buyers of their produce. The conflict with agri-inputs industries gets figured, in practice, as bargaining, negotiations, and arguments with retailers.

Second, retailing opportunities have arisen on account of both transnational and domestic capital. Indeed, the friction between them, one facet of which I described in the previous chapter, is an important source of profits for retailers, as they chase higher margins offered by the latter. In other words, more than antagonisms between agri-inputs businesses and farmers, the tensions within different blocs of capital help explain some strategies by which retailers accumulate.

From the vantage of the Maratha petty retailers, heterogeneous agri-inputs capital presents another complex of constraints and opportunities in the long history of peasant differentiation.

One implication of the emergence of the farmer as petty commodity producer lies in farmers' increasing exposure to market risk, coupled with the intensifying risk of crop failure as a result of climate change (Vasavi 2012). Commercial farming is becoming akin to a gamble. Farmers may have a good year followed by several bad years and then another good year—without any systematic pattern. In fact, while conducting fieldwork in 2013, I noticed that purchase prices would fluctuate by as much as 22 percent for every crate (about 45 pounds, or 20 kilograms) of tomatoes within the span of an hour. Prices for tomatoes in my fieldwork area went through the roof in 2013 because unseasonal rainfall had routed the crop elsewhere in the state. In 2014, however, prices crashed, and many farmers were forced to dump their harvest by the roadside.

There is thus a thick fog of uncertainty that farmers experience—it has become very hard to predict what price a crop might fetch in the market. In addition, farmers often cannot fathom why crops are not growing well, or how to address the increasingly aggressive pest and fungal complexes, made worse because of climate uncertainty. As Maratha farmers negotiate these uncertainties and the attendant risks, they can effectively reach out only to retailers, who not only provide some advice and troubleshooting knowledge, but also absorb some of the farmers' risk by extending credit.

This dependence on the retailer for knowledge stems from larger shifts that have taken place in India in the last three decades. First, as I mentioned earlier, more and more farmers are raising unfamiliar crops, such as grapes, tomatoes, and bell peppers, in which their accumulated experience across generations is thin. Coupled with ecological shifts and climate change, this means farmers' shared knowledge base has collapsed; it is no longer helpful to diagnose the problems of cultivation they confront (Aga 2019; Aga and Choudhury 2019). This is the deeper issue, though not the only one, at the heart of the agrarian crisis (Vasavi 2012). Second, the state has scaled back the provisioning of agricultural credit. Finally, the state has effectively privatized agricultural extension by allowing retailers to reclaim the space vacated by public agricultural extension. Indeed, every retailer is licensed by the state government, and the government encourages them to have some formal education in agriculture. To be successful, retailers thus have to be merchants of knowledge, not only because their advice drives the sales of inputs, but also because farmers are accessing technical advice and innovation through them.

More broadly, the very production of the encounter in which the retailer provides expert technical knowledge to the farmer, sometimes authentic, sometimes erroneous or fraudulent, is enabled by political economic shifts in India, only one trajectory of which has been the scaling back of public agricultural extension as part of liberalization. What I describe in this chapter is another, equally significant trajectory, which has admitted farming castes into higher education and sectors of the economy such as petty retailing, where they were previously absent or underrepresented. Even as this has democratized the purveying of technical expertise to some extent, it has also intensified risk exposure. Agriculture is becoming more and more of a gamble.

The preceding discussion strains credulity in the narrative of farmers pitted against transnational agribusinesses over GM crops. The narrative is not wrong; it is too broad-brush because it is ahistorical. Once we take historical trajectories into account, we are forced to contend with uneven and multiple patterns of capitalist development and differentiation in agriculture and agribusinesses. These patterns sediment in a heterogeneous peasantry on the one hand and, on the other, produce agribusiness capital as neither monolithic nor unified.

We must then relate these patterns with the historical and political sociology of the state, which allows certain classes (and castes) of farmers and certain sections of capitalists access to and influence over political power. As the previous chapter highlights, the politics of Bt cotton in India is being decisively shaped by politically savvy, commercially inclined farmers allied, at least in the short term, with domestic companies refusing to play ball with Monsanto. This cross-sectoral alliance has found enthusiastic support not only from state governments, often beholden to the lobbies of dominant-caste, landowning farmers, but also from the ICAR and the federal government. Ultimately, what this leaves us with are shifting alliances and unexpected antagonisms that drive the politics of GM crops, which are historically and regionally specific.

Finally, this means that GM seeds, like new pesticides or the earlier hybrids, are unlikely to redistribute the risk of commercial agriculture, a point that Buttel (1989) anticipated, as did the late journalist Praful Bidwai (1983c). The gambles of agriculture are too deep to be resolved by a technological package alone. In this context it makes little sense to talk of farmers exercising choice. Whenever Bt eggplant or another GM crop is released, I am certain that it will sell well, but that is hardly the same thing as farmers adopting it autonomously and with sufficient knowledge—"choosing" it in any meaningful sense of the term.

8

Genetically Modified Democracy

Scientific controversies exert unusual pressures on political institutions. Designed to arbitrate among competing interests, institutions of democracy find themselves in uncharted terrain when confronted with disputes over truth. The GM debate is fundamentally one about the workings and limits of democratic politics because it raises the question of how a polity should balance multiple interests, such as those of seed companies, blocs of farmers and consumers, and the state. But before balancing, constituencies need to identify their interests, which are uncertain because facts are disputed. For instance, interests of consumers shift depending on whether food safety concerns are genuine or exaggerated, and interests of domestic seed companies change depending on whether the state is willing to cap royalties and whether the courts will allow it to do so.

I began with the question: How do democracies resolve controversies in which conflicts of interest are intertwined with disputes over truth? Scientific uncertainty destabilizes notions of who is competent to speak truth to matters of concern—precisely because the parameters that frame the problem are themselves up in the air, open to dispute. This is why *uncertainty* is a better concept than *risk* for describing the tumult surrounding GM crops. Uncertainty forestalls any easy discernment of interests and alignment of interest groups. Within the state, such uncertainty muddies established administrative boundaries. The trajectory of the controversy over GM food crops in India suggests that democracies work through politico-scientific controversies by recontouring the decision-making structures within the state, as different authorities conflict and renegotiate their mandates and powers vertically (across the federal structure) and horizontally (across line departments and functional specializations). On the other hand, such controversies remap the terrain of interest groups in society, as new interests emerge and settled interests lose their urgency. This does not mean that structures that sustain unequal relations in society are transcended; rather, they are torqued and rearticulated. Structural inequalities, like those of small and marginal cotton farmers vis-à-vis seed companies, persist, but uncertainty can allow some room for new and marginalized concerns to be voiced. The architecture of democratic politics spanning the state and society and impinging on the boundary between the two gets redrawn. In the process, the forums for participation and debate expand, and the institutional structures and cultural meaning of democracy shift.

This argument may appear to recapitulate strands of reflection in science and technology studies, of which Bruno Latour's *Politics of Nature* (2004) may be taken as paradigmatic. On the face of it, Latour too seems to suggest that the politics of nature redistributes capacity for action and decision making across the polity. Yet, as polities are constituted in history, so must they be reconstituted, and this is what Latour misses. Attention to historical specificity is critical for understanding why and how people come to do what they do, why they rely on certain institutions and resources and not others, why tactical alliances emerge at certain junctures, and what avenues are available to political institutions under pressure. To grasp historical specificity, we have to turn our attention to how actors with unequal access and power mobilize heterogeneous resources like the law, political power, and economic might, in addition to science. In bringing this emphasis to bear on the debate over GM food crops in India, this book draws on other, broader ways of thinking about science and politics, framed through concepts such as state making (Sivaramakrishnan 1999) and coproduction (Jasanoff 2004). There are three ways in which the GM debate has pushed the limits of Indian politics, and these offer broader lessons for democratic functioning globally.

The Challenge to State Science

The last two decades saw a significant expansion in citizens' scrutiny of and dissidence against state science, which has begun to roll back under the Modi regime. The litigations in the Supreme Court over GM crops, running for the last seventeen years, public hearings organized by Environment Minister Jairam Ramesh in January and February 2010 on Bt eggplant, two Parliamentary Standing Committees' reports on GM crops, and vocal activist campaigns spurred more and more people to participate in the GM debate.

This marks a striking contrast to the 1970s and 1980s, when negotiations at the apex of the national science policy-making structure launched biotechnology without any input or scrutiny from the public. Five decades later, if citizens want to weigh in not only on the priorities for agricultural research, but also on the protocols of regulatory testing, this is not a perversion of democracy or sullying of science by politics, as many biotechnologists complain. Who gets to frame a policy issue, who gets to participate in decision making, and what bodies of science feed into policy decisions are fundamental political questions, and keeping citizens out of these processes makes for an impoverished democracy.

Here the Indian case offers a lesson for democratic politics across the world. Where parameters of a problem are themselves up for debate, legislatures and the judiciary can and must get involved. The U.S. tradition of ostensibly leaving questions concerning GM crops to science and the market, which it promotes all over the world, represents a politics of subterfuge. For it allows corporate biotechnological research to masquerade as all of science, and the interests of transnational agribusinesses as all of the market, and it ignores long-term concerns over health and ecology that neither regulatory science nor market mechanisms adequately address—in this respect, it would be important to track how the litigation against glyphosate in the United States plays out.

At the same time, I am not suggesting that the word of an expert agronomist or toxicologist has no role in the GM debate. Rather, more kinds of expert input are required in the debate, and all of these must be ready to open themselves up to scrutiny by citizens and political and legal institutions. In this sense, the case of Bt eggplant in India represents an expansion of democratic oversight, and therefore of citizenship, and this holds irrespective of whether Bt eggplant is ultimately released.

The rising tide of citizens' desire to engage with science owes a debt to the long history of environmental and agrarian struggles in the country. Moreover, the traction that GM-related issues have got from the Parliament, the Environment Ministry under Jairam Ramesh, state governments, and the Supreme Court has created precedents not just for further iterations of the debate, but also for other movements. This reminds us of the importance of science and technology studies connecting the investigation of how scientists make knowledge, which tends to obscure considerations of power and democratic participation, with the study of science policy where these considerations predominate. The call to study science ethnographically must encompass following it to farms, legislatures, protest marches, and social media conversations. These sites are not incidental to the production of science in laboratories; they shape in complex ways the problems that scientists tackle and the context in which their work acquires meaning. This process is, however, not evident exclusively from inside laboratories—no ethnography of agricultural biotechnology laboratories in India, however rich, is likely to reveal the way the field was born, or the power plays surrounding it in recent times.

Remaking the State

Administratively demarcating biotechnology from allied fields of agriculture and environment, among others, ended up framing GM crops as biotechnological products posing a risk to the environment. The second part of this book highlights how this settlement has come under fire since the 1990s. Framing GM crops as seeds, crops, medicines, and food, activists have forged alliances with consumers, scientists within and outside India, and farmers' groups. A singular focus on keeping India "GM-free"—a goal shared by most though by no means all activists—has lent this loose coalition considerable traction with several state governments and political parties, even as numerous technocrats in the government remain unimpressed.

Many advocates complain that GM crops are unfairly targeted. Why should a technology meant for farmers face so many hurdles, when those that consumers favor, such as washing machines and cellular phones, are allowed into the market without comprehensive socioeconomic, ecological, and safety assessments? This is a little disingenuous because, as I report, farmers have a marked preference for GM varieties, whereas companies want to offer only GM hybrids. Nevertheless, it is true that many technologies, even when polluting and labor-displacing, have come into India without much contention. The explanation, however, lies not in activists' unfairness but in the availability of legal, regulatory, and political mechanisms to voice opposition. Further, one can turn the question on its head and demand that other technologies too face critical scrutiny.

There is another long-term implication of the traction that environmental and agrarian struggles, including those over GM crops, have achieved in the states. Agriculture is a state subject, but agricultural research has been directed largely by the Indian Council of Agricultural Research since the Green Revolution, undercutting the capacity of states to shape research agendas recommended by more fine-grained assessments of regional and local needs and ecologies. This may be changing, as states take the lead on transitions to alternative agriculture through programs of organic and zero-budget natural farming, a low-cost method of chemical-free cultivation (see Khadse and Rosset 2019). These transitions are sometimes through direct support from international foundations that bypass the federal government. Setting the priorities for agricultural research is slowly returning to the state governments' agenda, and they might even sidestep the ICAR and work through rural development programs. In the coming years, it will be crucial to critically investigate new research programs and associated support structures led by state governments.

The preceding discussion underscores why ethnographically capturing the different arenas of a scientific controversy is also important for a richer study of democracy. A focus only on claims and contestation between activists and the state often misses the fact that political struggles operate through multiple registers—legal, electoral, bureaucratic, agitational, and so on—with their particular modes of reasoning and operation of power. Each register is hospitable to specific modes of articulation, which can force people's actions to diverge from their stated positions.

Two among several examples illustrate this. Many anti-GM activists advocate for democratizing knowledge and challenge exclusive claims by scientists to technical expertise (for a programmatic statement, see KICS 2009). Yet one of the most important successes of anti-GM campaigns has been the technical challenge to the safety of

Bt eggplant, and it has come from within the esoteric paradigm of regulatory science. This does not mean that anti-GM activists are insincere in their commitment to knowledge *swaraj* (sovereignty) or democracy; rather, the limited institutional windows available for intervening in policy making compel activists to diverge in practice from their commitment. Similarly, many farmers claimed to me that their cropping and inputs decisions were entirely up to them. Only upon spending extended time with them did I learn about their deep dependence on retailers. The study of democracy has to be grounded as much in what people do as in what they say.

Agrarian Change

The narrow focus on keeping GM crops out is crucial because the broader project of farming without relying on synthetic chemical inputs is unlikely to resonate with large sections of Indian farmers. Market-oriented farming dominates agriculture, as farmers seek upward mobility and new habits of consumption. In June 2019 the Shetkari Sanghtana (Farmers' Union), a major farmers' movement in Maharashtra that articulates the interest of large landholders, agitated for the release of Bt eggplant and HT cotton.

The rising demand for corporate seeds, synthetic chemical inputs, and technical know-how has provided an opportunity for insecure employment and entrepreneurship to young men of farming households of the regional dominant castes. In this context insect-resistant and herbicide-tolerant GM crops serve as a bargaining chip in the struggle for advantage among private seed companies and allow seed companies to corner some of the money that farmers might have spent on pesticides or on hiring laborers for weeding.

In this way, this book brings fresh insights to the field of agrarian studies, which rarely interacts with science studies, by exploring how the everyday functioning of science and democracy actually shapes food and agricultural policies and outcomes. The priorities of agricultural research and the scaling back of public extension services are critical ingredients in the rise of merchants of knowledge and the heightened uncertainties of agriculture, as these loop back to shape the market for inputs and seeds.

The courts are yet to pronounce a final verdict on whether the government can regulate royalties and prices, but at this point we have a powerful precedent in place. If Bt eggplant is released at some point, neither Mahyco's competitors nor farm lobbies will perhaps be able to resist demanding similar price caps on the crop, which may place the government in a tight spot. This will probably open another front in the GM debate.

Thus, the interplay of science and politics acquires a different inflection in each site of my study. The vortex of the GM debate in India is fed by historical currents of science and politics as they intersect with contemporary concerns about food, health, and livelihoods, and aspirations for new technologies, food security, and market dominance. These currents rub against and are channeled through structures of uneven capital formation in agriculture and capitalist relations in the wider economy. This foments transient yet powerful alliances that bridge social and political chasms. Some sections of farmers ally with anti-GM activists at times, while other sections play along as domestic seed companies speak on their behalf in their conflict with transnational agribusinesses.

I have taken only an initial step in mapping the controversy over GM crops in India. There is a great deal of work that needs to be done on the history of agricultural research in the public and corporate sectors since independence. The intersection between agrarian and electoral politics at the state level and the politics surrounding GM crops at the national level need much more careful and state-specific research than I have provided. Ethnographic studies of anti-GM campaigns are essential to understand the tensions of holding cross-class, cross-caste coalitions of scientists, urban activists, and farmers' groups together. It is equally important to understand the stakes for groups largely underrepresented even in farmers' groups—marginal farmers from dominant and oppressed castes and, above all, laborers. It cannot be stressed enough how little we know about the rapidly transforming constituency of agricultural laborers.

India is ravaged by multiple, deep crises—economic, social, political, and ecological—and this time, even the middle classes are not spared. In the past few years, vicious draughts have plagued large parts of the country, including parts where water was once abundant. In 2018, on multiple occasions, and again in November 2020, farmers marched hundreds of miles to cities like Mumbai and New Delhi demanding justice, dignity, and a resolution to the agrarian crisis. Beyond stale promises of loan waivers, which are anyway poorly implemented, governments have little to offer. Andhra Pradesh and a few other states implementing a comprehensive transition to alternative models of agriculture may prove to be an exception.

Meteorologists contend that rainfall across India is getting more and more erratic, to adapt to which farmers will have to change their crop mix. These conditions, along with market uncertainties and the dwindling appeal of agrarian life, are leading more and more people out of agriculture into urban and nonagrarian occupations—except there are few jobs on the horizon. The so-called India growth story has unfolded without a commensurate expansion in employment opportunities (Thomas 2014). Meanwhile, it has destroyed ecologies and cultures that could have provided sources of livelihood, creativity, and dignity to people (Shrivastava and Kothari 2012; Padel, Dandekar, and Unni 2013). And the COVID-19 pandemic has blown the lid off India's abysmal public health infrastructure and its environmentally and socially corrosive growth model (Choudhury and Aga 2020a; Vasavi 2020b).

In this context, I am struck by the frequency with which policy makers harp on GM crops as a solution to the deep distress. The fascination with GM crops among policy makers seems to be disproportionate to the actual capacity of the rDNA technology to help matters, a point also buttressed by the up-and-coming field of agro-ecology (Altieri and Rosset 1999). I cannot shake away the feeling that the GM debate, irrespective of which side "wins," is much too narrow to address the pressing problems of sustainable agriculture, nutritious, culturally appropriate food, and dignified lives and livelihoods with some semblance of equal opportunity.

The exaggerated profile of GM crops in agriculture policy was not inevitable, as I have shown. It is an outcome of many contingencies with roots in histories of science, politics, and agriculture.

And because it was not inevitable, critical scrutiny of the gap between the modest capabilities of GM crops and their hype is necessary; it is worth repeating that in the GM debate, we are essentially talking about two traits in a handful of crops. Equally important is exposing how the contingencies have become constraining structures. This can help identify measures to make agricultural policy making more participatory and expand its agenda beyond a focus on production and new technologies. This will certainly bring to the fore many contradictions in the polity, but confronting these is essential to the difficult, necessary work of addressing the deep problems of agriculture.

Specific GM crops introduced under specific conditions may perhaps play a role in resolving some of these problems; but, to be clear, these problems are the target of legitimate agricultural policy making—not GM crops.

In other words, policies must be framed by measures to tackle the agrarian crisis rather than by a technological package. The last decade has seen the development of genome-edited crops, which agribusinesses and their allies are yet again presenting as a solution to the global problem of hunger and farming. The same caveat would apply to them.

Yet despite the criticisms of the GM program in India from within the government and without, neither has the regulatory structure been overhauled, nor has there been any serious attempt at redesigning and implementing participative policy priorities for the development of GM crops. This, too, is as an aspect of democratic functioning and bureaucratic inertia. So far, no government has found it worth its time and resources to fundamentally overhaul the GM program, beyond assembling task forces and plan documents. The second Manmohan Singh–led UPA government (2009–14) proposed a new regulatory authority to replace the twin committee structure, which lapsed in the face of determined opposition from activists, political parties, and some farm lobbies. The same government initiated a crackdown on environmental activists, including Kavitha Kuruganti, Suman Sahai, Vandana Shiva, Aruna Rodrigues, and Greenpeace India, which has intensified under Prime Minister Narendra Modi, who came to power in 2014 and was reelected in 2019.

The authoritarian tendencies in the polity, which were growing for some decades, dramatically accelerated after 2014. Demonization of journalists, activists, and protestors as antinational traitors and violence against them are terrifyingly routine. The Modi government neither brooks any criticism of its policies, nor encourages dialogue and debate. Its spokespersons openly call for assaults on universities and independent-minded people and institutions. The Supreme Court and the High Courts are far more reluctant to take on the federal government than they were in the in the UPA years. In this context, environmental, agrarian, and anti-GM campaigns are fraught with peril and mortal danger for activists. The hard-won gains of environmental and GM-related campaigns for increased public scrutiny and participation in regulation and policy making are being chipped away.

Nevertheless, the opportunities for political parties to build constituencies through GM crops are modest and ambiguous—the domestic seed industry remains small relative to other Indian corporate behemoths. And some of the BJP's grassroots organizations are opposed to GM crops. Consequently, the first Modi government (2014–19) capped the Bt cotton royalty and retail prices, but it did not touch the regulatory process itself. Doing so would certainly amplify the controversy, one way or another, from grassroots nativist (*swadeshi*) organizations close to the BJP and others. In sum, the GEAC and the RCGM are functioning largely as before, which means it is easy for a decisive government—and Prime Minister Modi began his second term in 2019 with an even more comprehensive victory made possible by his strongman appeal—to turn the tide in favor of GM crops, notwithstanding the opposition. The GM issue continues to hang by a whisker, and far more urgent questions of food democracy, agricultural sustainability, health, and justice remain beyond the pale.

Notes

Chapter 1. Introduction

1. I say misplaced because genes are rarely destiny.

2. Bt stands for *Bacillus thuringiensis*, a soil-dwelling bacterium.

3. I do not find this counterargument from proponents very convincing. Crossing plant varieties does lead to shuffling of genes, but the gene order is conserved. In rDNA technology, the novel gene construct coding for the trait of interest gets inserted into the genome at random.

4. How and how much to regulate a particular technology is very much a question for public debate and scrutiny.

5. ISAAA is supported by the U.S. government and transnational agribusinesses like Bayer and BASF, among others.

6. Indian public-sector institutions were going to release Bt eggplant varieties using Mahyco's Bt event (see chap. 5, n. 13).

7. Bangladesh backcrossed Mahyco's Bt event into eggplant varieties popular there.

8. This is the number of operational holdings—that is, land that is used partly or wholly for agricultural production and is operated as one technical unit by one or more persons.

9. The Economic Survey, 2019–20, reports only estimates for subsequent years, and since the Modi government has gone to unprecedented lengths to massage data, the credibility of the estimates is hard to assess. The GVA of agriculture and allied sectors was expected to grow at 2.8 percent in 2019–20.

10. Of course, large parts of India, especially those that did not receive the Green Revolution Package, never really saw substantial investment in agriculture, even in the heydays of independence.

11. Suicide by farmers is actually a worldwide phenomenon, including the United States (Patel 2007).

12. See, for instance, the tone and tenor of the letter by the Nobel laureates mentioned earlier. See also Stone (2002) and Paarlberg (2008). As Sunder Rajan (2006) notes, morally charged messianic claims are integral to the culture of biotechnology ventures in the United States.

13. Food articles include all cereals, pulses, milk, meat and fish products, fruits and vegetables, condiments and spices, and others like tea and coffee.

14. This happened first in the United States, and then elsewhere under the pressure of institutions such as the WTO TRIPS (Trade-Related Aspects of Intellectual Property, a World Trade Organization agareement). In India, however, as in many other parts of the world, the extension of property regimes to seeds remains an unfinished and fiercely contested endeavor (see Chandra 2013).

15. One unhelpful strand in this vein traces the roots of opposition to GM crops in terms of ignorance and irrational beliefs. For a review and critique, see Wynne (2001).

16. This translation of historical contingencies of the West to the rest is not unique to debates over biotechnology. Sivaramakrishnan and Agrawal (2003) and Kaviraj (2005) notice the same tendency in the theories of modernity outside the West.

17. More powerful are the critiques of mainstream science and technology that trace their exclusions to the pervasive casteism of Indian society (Ilaiah 2009).

18. In the last few years, however, serious questions have emerged again about the independence of India's higher judiciary.

19. In April 2012 a Brazilian court affirmed farmers' right to save and replant seeds without paying a royalty. This was overturned in October 2019 on an appeal decided in favor of Monsanto.

Chapter 2. Revolution of the Chemists

1. On August 15, 2015, the Modi government changed its name to the Ministry of Agriculture and Farmers' Welfare.

2. There were also state agricultural universities, which combined teaching with limited research work under the aegis of state governments and the ICAR.

3. Planning Commission was the institution that drafted India's five-year plans, chaired by the prime minister.

4. There were some specialized institutes for subfields of biology, such as the National Botanic Gardens in Lucknow. These institutes were set up in colonial times and not by the government of independent India.

5. I spoke on the phone with Maheshwari in December 2014.

6. Interview with Professor Tushar Chakraborty, New Delhi, February 2014. Chakraborty did his doctoral research under B. B. Biswas's supervision at the Bose Institute.

7. The applied-basic distinction recapitulates the tension between field and laboratory that, as Robert Kohler (2002, 1) notes, "demarcates differences of standing and credibility, physical location, and modes of scientific practice."

8. It is worth noting that the basic-applied distinction breaks down very quickly in practice. For a recent investigation of these categories, see Hoffman (2015).

9. The quote and the section below draw on interviews with Bhargava in July 2014 in Hyderabad and May 2013 in New Delhi.

10. At Calcutta University, there were B. C. Guha and his students. Homi J. Bhabha set up a group working on molecular biology at the Tata Institute of Fundamental Research in Bombay, which bloomed around the figure of Obaid Siddiqi. The newly established All India Institute of Medical Sciences inaugurated a group around Pran Talwar.

11. See de Chadarevian (1996) and Gooday (1991) for how this bias animated scientific disputes in biology.

12. The mission mode became very popular in the 1980s, especially with Prime Minister Rajeev Gandhi (1984–89), who ran government programs this way.

13. I have masked identifying details, upon request.

14. This and subsequent quotes are from an interview I conducted in January 2014 in New Delhi.

15. For a history of the emergence of rDNA technology in the San Francisco Bay Area and the wider political economic currents set in motion as a consequence, see Wright (1994) and Hughes (2001).

16. The other laboratory was Joseph Padayatty's, at the Indian Institute of Science Bangalore.

17. In the 1970s, creating plants that could fix their own nitrogen was the holy grail of a section of new biologists and agricultural scientists (Simmonds 2007).

18. This is the partnership of Ford and other foundations, governments, and UN organizations that set up institutes like the International Maize and Wheat Improvement Center, and which drove the Green Revolution.

19. For histories of material transfers and exchanges that contributed to the development of botany, see Arnold (2005) and Raj (2007), among others.

Chapter 3. The Bureaucratic Consolidation of Biotechnology

1. The following section draws on the letter DO No. 6(17)/61-STP-II, dated December 23, 1981, written by D. R. Ram of the DST to Pushpa Bhargava, and its annexures.

2. The CSIR and ICMR, along with the ICAR, formulate policies for the promotion and administration of state-led scientific research.

3. The SACC was set up by a government resolution on March 12, 1981, as the principal advisory body to the federal government in the field of science and technology. Its stature can be gauged from the fact that a special Committee of Secretaries under the chairmanship of the secretary of the DST was simultaneously constituted for expeditious execution.

4. This is a quote from page 13 of the Demand for Grants No. 73 for 1985–86 by the DST.

5. The summary below is based on the annual reports of the DST from 1982 to 1987 and the annual report of the Biotechnology Department in 1986–87.

6. See starred question 634, titled "Genetic Research in the Country," of the Lok Sabha Budget Session, April 29, 1985. The question was directed to the Ministry of Food and Agriculture.

7. Interview with Dr. R. Srinivasan, project director, NRCPB, February 2014, New Delhi.

8. The committee tasked with preparing the guidelines was named the Recombinant DNA Advisory Committee, copying the name of the committee created by the National Institutes of Health in the United States after the Asilomar Conference of 1975 (Jasanoff 2005, 47–48).

9. Letter Bio/Conf/PMB/GEC, February 4, 1985, by Pushpa Bhargava to M. G. K. Menon, member (science), Planning Commission.

10. In 1987, under Prime Minister Rajeev Gandhi, such transient structures evolved into National Technology Missions, steered by Sam Pitroda.

11. The Committee of Secretaries is a body of all secretaries to the Government of India, chaired by the Cabinet secretary.

12. Interview with Dr. P. K. Ghosh, February 2013, New Delhi.

13. Notification no. CD-172/86, February 27, 1986, and Notification no. CD-87/87, January 31, 1987.

14. Interview with Dr. P. K. Ghosh, February 2013, New Delhi.

15. Some entry points into the vast literature on Bt cotton in India are provided by Herring (2007b), Shah (2005), Kumbamu (2006), Scoones (2006), Tripp (2009), Ramamurthy (2010), and Flachs (2019). There are also many reports by activists and journalists working in different parts of India, as well as reports released by the biotechnology industry and different state governments. For an excellent historical account of cotton and its politics, including an analysis of the Bt cotton debate, see Menon and Uzramma (2017).

16. Interview in early 2013 with a retired senior officer of the Biotechnology Department who preferred to remain anonymous.

17. Interviews conducted in July 2012 and February 2013.

18. Figures taken from the Minutes of the Fifth Meeting of the Scientific Advisory Committee to the Department of Biotechnology, held in May 1994. No details were available for 344 cases (39 percent).

19. The Department of Rural Development within the Ministry of Food and Agriculture was elevated to an independent Ministry of Rural Reconstruction in 1979. In 1985 it was brought back within the Ministry of Agriculture, and then elevated again as the Ministry of Rural Development in 1991.

20. In an early study, Avramovic (1996) concluded that for countries like India without venture capital, vaccines and other pharmaceutical applications of biotechnology were a better bet for state investment.

21. The symposium was organized in the honor of Dr. Y. Nayudamma in the wake of his tragic and untimely death. Arnold was the last director of the Namulonge Research Station in Uganda.

22. Starred question 343, answered in the Rajya Sabha on August 20, 1987.

23. In particular, the national Congress government struggled to reconcile the demands of industrial capitalists, the dominant castes of landholding farmers in Green Revolution areas, and the vast majority of dry-land farmers, land-poor and tenant farmers, and landless laborers.

Chapter 4. Regulating GM Crops

1. As Latour (1998, 425) notes, scientific documents maintain "constant features through shifts in representations." This ability to maintain constant features through shifts in representations is what allows scientific documents to be immutably mobile.

2. These were the Water (Prevention and Control of Pollution) Act of 1974, the Water (Prevention and Control of Pollution) Cess [tax] Act of 1977, and the Air (Prevention and Control of Pollution) Act of 1981.

3. Annual report of the Department of Science and Technology, 1981–82, p. 16.

4. See Wright (1994) for an overview of regulatory developments for rDNA research in the United States and United Kingdom.

5. The Manufacture, Storage and Import of Hazardous Chemical Rules, 1989, issued under the EPA 1986.

6. Minutes of the Meeting of Committee of Secretaries, July 26, 1989. I accessed these and other documents through the Right to Information Act, 2005.

7. The quote is from D.O. no. J-18029/3/97-IC/HSMD, September 7, 1989, archived in the Ministry of Environment, Forest and Climate Change

8. Mathur's (2015) study of another federal act implemented by the districts bears this out as well. Though it is set in the mid-2000s, even in the late 1980s and 1990s the collector was heading multiple committees.

9. Some chief secretaries in recent years have started appointing their nominees to chair the state-level committees. Maharashtra's committee serves as one example.

10. D.O. no. J-18029/3/87-IC/HSMD, November 28, 1990.

11. Recent writings on Indian bureaucracies somewhat uncritically observe that acts and rules are framed by elite bureaucrats and activists with barely a thought for the "subaltern" bureaucrats at the district and village levels who have to implement them (Mathur 2015; Gupta 2012). It is equally true, however, that very often states fail to provide feedback on draft rules when explicitly and repeatedly asked by senior bureaucrats to do so. Further, senior bureaucrats do have experience working at the district level as collectors.

12. The RCGM for several years appointed a Monitoring and Evaluation Committee, which conducted inspections of field trials in order to verify that RCGM and GEAC directions were being observed (Scoones 2006, chap. 7).

13. Since 2012, the GEAC has met infrequently. First Jayanthi Natarjan, as the minister of Environment and Forests (July 2011—December 2013), informally blocked the meetings, even though the GEAC is a statutory body. Since the Modi government came to power, in May 2014, the GEAC has again met irregularly because of grassroots right-wing groups' opposition to GM crops.

14. All the managers representing private seed companies that I encountered during my fieldwork were men.

15. In 2013 the Manmohan Singh–led UPA government introduced the Biotechnology Regulatory Authority of India Bill in the Parliament. Framed by the Biotechnology Department, this bill sought to replace the committee structure of regulation with an independent, single-window office. The bill was opposed by a range of groups and lapsed in 2014.

16. Only recently has the Biotechnology Department initiated steps to appoint some technical staff full-time to support regulation.

17. Minutes of the 85th meeting of the GEAC, Ministry of Environment and Forests, May 28, 2008.

18. Minutes of the 86th meeting of the GEAC, Ministry of Environment and Forests, June 25, 2008.

19. Minutes of the 88th meeting of the GEAC, Ministry of Environment and Forests, August 13, 2008.

20. Jai Krishna, who was coordinating Greenpeace India's GM food–related campaign in 2008, told me in April 2018 that he had provided a copy of the receipt to the

GEAC. When I examined the relevant files with the Food Safety Authority and the GEAC through Right to Information requests, I did not find records of the receipt.

21. Interview with Neha Saigal, Greenpeace India, January 2014. Saigal also kindly made some documents related to this incident available to me.

22. Letter no. F.3(2)Agri-3/2011, September 19, 2011, from Anil Gupta, deputy secretary, Agriculture Department, Government of Rajasthan, to Deepak Pental, Delhi University.

23. Letter no. 02/02/11–11/568, November 11, 2011, available from the Government of Rajasthan.

24. The GEAC recommends that farmers plant rows of non-GM seeds of the same crop (refugium) in order to delay development of resistance among pests. This recommendation is rarely followed because it is unfeasible for the vast majority of farmers with small and marginal landholdings.

25. The original letter is in Hindi. The translation provided is my own.

26. Pental probably got the NOC because his was the only application from the public sector.

27. Note in file F8(5)/ATC/GM Seeds/2011–12, 20. I accessed this file through the Right to Information Act, 2005.

28. Letter no. F. 3(6)/Agri.-3./2012, March 9, 2012, from Anil Gupta to Deepak Pental.

29. The more familiar dispute over unauthorized Bt cotton crop in Gujarat in 2002 among the Environment Ministry, on the one hand, and the Textiles Ministry and the Gujarat government, on the other, was straightforwardly about jurisdiction and not about biosafety. It was a legal-administrative matter, but cases where legal-administrative and scientific modes intersect illuminate my argument better.

30. These get articulated in other ways—through popular protests, social movements, and electoral politics.

31. This partition was the signature move of the Subaltern Studies Project. It follows, then, that this approach suffers from some of the same infirmities as the project (Sivaramakrishnan 1995).

32. In 2017, only for already approved Bt cotton, the GEAC authorized the ICAR to oversee the evaluation and monitoring of the agronomic performance of different hybrids.

Chapter 5. Emergence and Deepening of Activism against GM Crops

1. Interview with Vandana Shiva, December 2013, New Delhi.

2. Writ Petition (Civil) 71 of 1999 in the matter of RSFTE v. Union of India.

3. There had, however, been litigation relating to nonagricultural GMOs earlier; see Jasanoff (2005).

4. LMO refers to living GMOs such as plants, rather than nonliving products such as food additives.

5. Order dated October 8, 2003, vis-à-vis Appeal no. 2/2002 by the appellate authority.

6. Writ Petition (Civil) no. 115 of 2004, in the matter of Gene Campaign & Anr. v. Union of India & Ors.

7. The Sangha had physically destroyed the field trials, incorrectly claiming that Monsanto's Bt cotton contained Gene Use Restriction Technology, also called the "terminator gene."

8. I am grateful to Suman Sahai and her colleagues at the Gene Campaign, Ranjan Mishra and Richa Srivastava, for their help and generosity with accessing these materials.

9. For a review of the historical evolution and current state of environmental jurisprudence in India, and the importance of the expansive definition of life that the Supreme Court has read into the Right to Life, see Dias (1994), Ramanathan (2004), and Sivaramakrishnan (2011).

10. This assumes significance under Article 14 (Right to Equality) of the Constitution.

11. Writ Petition (Civil) no. 260 of 2005, in the matter of Aruna Rodrigues & Ors. v. Union of India & Ors. before the Supreme Court.

12. The other individuals were the food and agricultural policy commentator Devinder Sharma, P. V. Satheesh, who cofounded the NGO Deccan Development Society and was on the Board of Directors of GRAIN, and Rajeev Baruah, a management specialist based in Mhow.

13. A GM event is a particular gene introduced into a particular host plant genome at a specific location. Since an event indexes the combination of gene X insertion location on the genome, it can differentiate among GM variants of the same crop.

14. Interviews conducted with Suman Sahai in December 2013 and January 2014.

15. Gilles-Éric Séralini is a molecular biologist at the University of Caen in France and has published many articles and peer-reviewed studies challenging the consensus on the safety and substantial equivalence of some commercialized GM crops. His recent, explosive study on the adverse effect of Monsanto's HT maize NK603 and the herbicide glyphosate was first published in the peer-reviewed journal *Food and Chemical Toxicology*; it was retracted without prejudice when the article drew flak from some scientists and agribusiness corporations. It was subsequently published by an-

other peer-reviewed journal, *Environmental Sciences Europe* (Fagan, Traavik and Bøhn 2015). Judy Carman is a nutrition biologist who is considered an anti-GM activist by scientists advocating GM crops. Jack Heinemann is a lecturer in genetics at the University of Canterbury, New Zealand. Doug Gurian-Sherman holds a doctorate in plant pathology and did further research on rice and wheat molecular biology at a U.S. Department of Agriculture laboratory. He then worked with the Environmental Protection Agency on safety assessment of GM crops, and he later became associated with the Union of Concerned Scientists and the Center for Science in the Public Interest, all in the United States.

16. According to documents submitted by Mahyco, the protein coded was 99.4 percent identical to the Bt cry1Ac protein.

17. In the late 1990s, Pusztai reported adverse health effects on rats fed with GM potatoes. The research, published in the prestigious journal *Lancet*, remains controversial.

18. I accessed these and other documents under the Right to Information Act, 2005.

19. The letter was dated November 14, 2008, and was endorsed by Greenpeace India, Thanal, and other organizations and individuals.

20. The six doctors included Dr. G. P. I. Singh of the Environmental Health Action Group and Dr. Mira Shiva, Initiative for Health, Equity and Society, who happens to be Vandana Shiva's sister.

21. D.O. no. P.15025/72/2008-PH (Food)/SFC, January 13, 2009, from Debashish Panda, joint secretary, Ministry of Health and Family Welfare, to A. K. Goyal, joint secretary, Ministry of Environment and Forests.

22. The Swadeshi Jagran Manch is another organization affiliated with the BJP that emphasizes national self-sufficiency and is opposed to foreign presences in the Indian economy.

23. After sustained pressure from activists, the Indian government disallowed GURTs in 2001. Seeds with GURTs have not been commercially released anywhere in the world.

24. The Save Narmada Campaign was protesting a mega-dam on the Narmada River that displaced a large number of people (Oza et al. 2017).

25. Admittedly, these are neither perfectly representative nor neutral to structural inequalities, but nothing in practical democratic politics is.

Chapter 6. Profiting from Seeds

1. I say *expert farmers* deliberately to highlight the skills, insights, and knowledge that go into saving seeds and conserving biodiversity.

2. Rallis India (belonging to the Tata group of companies) and SPIC are two domestic companies present in both the seeds and the agrochemicals sector.

3. Earlier research focused on a few crops important for the colonial and post-independence cash-crop economy, as in the case of cotton (Guha 1985), soy (Kumar 2016), and the field crops that propelled the Green Revolution (Anderson et al. 1982).

4. The public sector produced only breeder and foundation seeds and contracted the private sector for certified seeds.

5. I am grateful to Usha Barwale Zehr, chief technology officer at Mahyco, for this insight.

6. For this account of Barwale's life, I have drawn on his autobiography (Barwale 2008) and Joshi (2013, chap. 1). I have also drawn on his biographical note published by the World Food Prize, which he received in 1998, along with media articles and an interview with Barwale's daughter, Usha Barwale Zehr, chief technology officer at Mahyco, in September 2014, in Jalna.

7. *Marwari* is an umbrella term for mercantile castes spread all over India, but hailing originally from present-day Rajasthan.

8. *Ryotwari* was a colonial taxation regime that directly assessed the cultivator (*ryot*).

9. In this aspect Barwale is similar to the horticulturalists in the nineteenth-century United States who popularized their fruits through pictures and pamphlets (Kevles 2011).

10. Pray and Ramaswami (2001) found thirty-eight firms engaged in R&D in 1995. Most of these were involved in breeding work without much investment in expensive biotechnological work.

11. In addition, MMBL demanded a onetime royalty payment of 5 million rupees from each licensee (Jishnu 2010).

12. Using an average conversion rate of 44.27 rupees to a dollar for 2005–6.

13. In effect, Monsanto captured half the value earned by MMBL, the remaining going to Mahyco, of which a certain share would have accrued back to Monsanto on account of its investment in the latter.

14. The objectives of the MRTP are similar to those of antitrust laws in the United States.

15. In 2008 Gujarat enacted its own legislation to regulate the market for Bt cottonseeds. In 2011, however, on a petition by the industry association National Seed Association of India (NSAI), the Gujarat High Court invalidated the act on the grounds that cottonseeds came within the purview of the federal Essential Commodities Act, 1955 (amended 2009), and hence the state government was not empow-

ered to legislate on the issue. The Gujarat government has appealed the decision before the Supreme Court. The seed industry has filed similar petitions before the High Courts of other states as well, and there are appeals and counterappeals in different courts, including the Supreme Court.

16. Section 11 of the Andhra Pradesh Act and Section 10(1) of the Maharashtra Act both read: "The Government, after taking into consideration the costs of production, etc., including trait value, wherever necessary, obtained from various agencies concerned, may fix, from time to time, the maximum sale price of all types of cotton seeds."

17. MMBL licenses Bt events to seed companies, which incorporate those in their proprietary lines through backcrossing.

18. The investigation and associated litigation are ongoing in the Delhi High Court and the Supreme Court. In September 2019 Bayer CropScience completed the acquisition of Monsanto India.

19. Different scholars lend differing levels of importance to this lacuna either to express skepticism about the success of Bt cotton or to defend it; see, for instance, Kuruganti (2009); Lalitha, Ramaswami, and Viswanathan (2009); Herring and Rao (2012); Stone (2012). Some agricultural economists are of the view that Bt cotton has improved yields, lowered pesticide use, and enhanced net returns to farmers, though studies by activists and a recent review article by Kranthi and Stone (2020) challenge this narrative. A detailed analysis of the case for and against Bt cotton is beyond the scope of this book.

20. For this reason, fine-grained, season-by-season, class-, caste-, and landholding-sensitive studies, dissected by specific Bt cotton hybrids, are urgently required to determine whether farmers spent more on seeds and less on pesticide purchases and the labor to spray them, or whether they spent more on seeds and then some more on pesticides. In the absence of such studies, it is hard to settle the debate over efficacy of Bt cotton.

21. Of course, Mahyco too is a domestic company. It has, however, thrown its lot in with the transnationals in their conflict with Nuziveedu and the NSAI. Moreover, Monsanto owns a stake in Mahyco.

22. This has been one of the main findings of a review conducted jointly by the German Federal Agency for Nature Conservation (BfN), the Swiss Federal Office for the Environment (FOEN), and the Environment Agency Austria (EAA) (Tappeser, Reichenbecher, and Teichmann 2014).

23. Field note, March 2014, New Delhi.

24. Interview with Dr. Jagdish Pandit, November 2014, Maharashtra. Though his remarks may be incorrect in their specific details, the overall thrust of his argument is hardly misplaced.

25. Field note, October 2013, Nashik.

26. Even after price caps, Bt hybrids were more expensive than non–GM hybrids and cotton varieties.

27. The University of Agricultural Sciences Bengaluru is one center where there has been much work on drought tolerance; Deepak Pental has developed mustard hybrids through the genetically engineered male sterility and herbicide tolerance traits.

28. It is worth noting that the survey of Bt and non–Bt cotton farmers reported by Narayananmoorthy and Kalamkar (2006) includes only farmers with access to irrigation.

29. See the quote from Dr. Keshav Kranthi, then the director of the Central Institute of Cotton Research, in Bhattacharya (2012).

Chapter 7. Merchants of Knowledge

1. See, for instance, Herring (2007a, 136), Khadi (2007), and Choudhary and Gaur (2010).

2. In order to protect their identity, I have disguised the names of people and villages.

3. All the retailers I encountered in my research were men. Their customers, too, were exclusively men.

4. Beyond Nashik city, petty retailers diffused to smaller market towns like Pimpalgaon. Such shops have only recently begun to open in villages like Khedgaon, and many villages remain without a single retailer.

5. It was difficult to estimate retailers' costs for a number of reasons. Material costs constituted the largest expense in a year, and these were also the hardest to pin down. Retailers place orders several times a year, and they store stock over years, until it expires (and sometimes thereafter, too), and receive discounts and cash back through company schemes at the end of the fiscal year. Other costs included transportation, fertilizer, seeds, and insecticide licenses that have to be renewed every two to three years, monthly electricity bills, interest on loans, and "gifts" to the district agricultural bureaucracy to renew licenses on time and during festivals. A few retailers also hired helpers to assist with storage, transport, and running the shop; their monthly pay averaged 7,000–9,000 rupees.

6. *Open category* comprises the (forward) castes that are not eligible for reservations or affirmative action benefits. In the context of a declining number of government jobs, and increasingly insecure private-sector jobs, the Marathas, like some other dominant, landowning castes in India, have been agitating for reservations for several years.

7. The classification of farmers in terms of landholding is as follows: marginal, less than 2.5 acres (1 hectare); small, between 2.5 and 5 acres (1 and 2 hectares); semi-

medium, between 5 and 10 acres (2 and 4 hectares); medium, between 10 and 25 acres (4 and 10 hectares); large, beyond 25 acres (10 hectares). This is according to the Agricultural Census, 2010–11, commissioned by the federal Ministry of Agriculture.

8. Petty commodity production is "a more or less independent productive activity for the market, reproduced through relationships mediated by the exchange of commodities . . . almost all of which is in the informal domain" (Shah and Harriss-White 2011, 17).

9. These are two of the most important and geographically widespread caste groups powering trade and commerce in India. For a historical account of the peasant-*baniya* relations in western India, see Hardiman (1996).

10. In the past, rains generally ceased by early October in this region.

11. A farmer is free to go to any retailer while purchasing in cash. The issue is that cash is scarce, especially around Diwali, and the need for credit binds farmers to specific retailers. At the same time, these are not crop-tying credit extensions.

12. In this respect, agri-inputs retailers can be usefully compared to those running pharmacies in India.

13. Dance bars offer alcohol, food, and adult entertainment in the form of dances by women for male patrons.

14. Marketing teams of transnational companies make extra efforts to seek out and cultivate large landholding farmers.

15. According to the Maharashtra Agricultural Produce Marketing (Regulation) Act 1963, the state government set up agricultural produce marketing committees (APMCs) at all the market yards in the state. These committees licensed commission agents to auction farmers' produce to buyers in order to protect farmers from exploitative middlemen, at least in theory.

16. In September 2020 the Modi government passed new laws to allow farmers to sell directly to traders, outside the oversight of APMCs, an arrangement that was already quite common in my field site. The passage of these laws, however, triggered large-scale protests by farmers, demanding their rollback.

17. Even critical accounts that emphasize the sociohistorical context that embeds technology do not pay adequate heed to retailers, instead zooming out to agri-businesses (Visvanathan and Parmar 2002; Shah 2005) or focusing exclusively on farmers (e.g. Roy, Herring, and Geisler 2007; Stone 2007).

18. Since merchants' capital is fused with productive and finance capital (Harriss-White 1990), and since retailers are in a position to appropriate some of the surplus of their cultivator-clients, we can think of retailers as potentially being able to stabilize as a class.

References

Abraham, Itty. 1998. *The Making of the Indian Atomic Bomb: Science, Secrecy, and the Postcolonial State*. London: Zed.

Aga, Aniket. 2016. "Golden Rice Isn't Ready Yet." *Hindu*, August 5. https://www.thehindu.com/opinion/columns/Golden-rice-isn%E2%80%99t-ready-yet/article14556873.ece.

———. 2018. "Merchants of Knowledge: Petty Retail and Differentiation without Consolidation among Farmers in Maharashtra, India." *Journal of Agrarian Change* 18 (3): 658–76.

———. 2019. "The Marketing of Corporate Agrichemicals in Western India: Theorizing Graded Informality." *Journal of Peasant Studies* 46 (7): 1458–76.

Aga, Aniket, and Chitrangada Choudhury. 2018. "A Dappled Sun: Bureaucratic Encounters in the Working of the Right to Information Act in India." *Comparative Studies of South Asia, Africa and the Middle East* 38 (3): 540–56.

———. 2019. "Cotton Has Now Become a Headache." *People's Archive of Rural India*, October 7. https://ruralindiaonline.org/articles/cotton-has-now-become-a-headache/.

Agarwal, Anil, and Sunita Narain. 1985. *The State of India's Environment, 1984–85: The Second Citizens' Report*. New Delhi: Centre for Science and Environment.

Aiyar, Swaminathan S. Anklesaria. 2002. "Green Killers and Pseudo-Science." *Times of India*, September 22.

Albert, Victor. 2016. *The Limits to Citizen Power: Participatory Democracy and the Entanglements of the State*. London: Pluto.

Altieri, Miguel A. 1998. "Ecological Impacts of Industrial Agriculture and the Possibilities for Truly Sustainable Farming." *Monthly Review* 50 (1): 60–71.

Altieri, Miguel A., and Clara I. Nicholls. 2005. *Agroecology and the Search for a Truly Sustainable Agriculture*. Colonia Lomas de Virreyes, Mexico: United Nations Environment Programme.

Altieri, Miguel A., and Peter Rosset. 1999. "Ten Reasons Why Biotechnology Will Not Help the Developing World." *AgBioForum* 2 (3–4): 155–62.

Alvares, Claude. 1992. *Science, Development and Violence: The Revolt against Modernity*. New Delhi: Oxford University Press.

Amrith, Sunil S. 2006. *Decolonizing International Health: India and Southeast Asia, 1930–1965*. New York: Palgrave Macmillan.

Anderson, Robert S. 2010. *Nucleus and Nation: Scientists, International Networks, and Power in India*. Chicago: University of Chicago Press.

Anderson, Robert S., Paul R. Brass, Edwin Levy, and Barrie M. Morrison, eds. 1982. *Science, Politics, and the Agricultural Revolution in Asia*. AAAS Selected Symposium 70. Boulder, Colo.: Westview.

Arnold, David. 2005. *The Tropics and the Traveling Gaze: India, Landscape, and Science, 1800–1856*. New Delhi: Orient Blackswan.

———. 2013. "Nehruvian Science and Postcolonial India." *Isis* 104 (2): 360–70.

Arnold, M. H. 1987. "The Application of Molecular Biology to Plant Breeding." In *Agricultural Applications of Biotechnology: Proceedings of the Nayudamma Memorial Symposium, 15–17 December 1986*, edited by A. N. Rao and H. Y. Mohan Ram, 4–16. Madras: COSTED.

Arora, R. S. 1995. "Considerations Leading Towards Formulation and Introduction of Plant Variety Protection in India." Paper presented at Asian Seed '95, New Delhi, September 27–29.

Avramovic, Mila. 1996. *An Affordable Development? Biotechnology, Economics and the Implications for the Third World*. London: Zed.

Bajpai, Vikas. 2015. "India's Second Green Revolution: Portends for Future and Possible Alternatives." *Agrarian South: Journal of Political Economy* 4 (3): 289–326.

Balagopal, K. 1985. "Indira Gandhi—An Attempt at a Political Appraisal." *Economic & Political Weekly* 20 (12): 496–503.

———. 1986. "'Agrarian Struggles.' Review of Agrarian Struggles in India after Independence, Edited by A. R. Desai." *Economic & Political Weekly* 21 (32): 1401–5.

———. 1987. "An Ideology for the Provincial Propertied Class." *Economic and Political Weekly* 22 (50): 1544–46.

———. 1992. "Economic Liberalism and Decline of Democracy—Case of Andhra Pradesh." *Economic & Political Weekly* 27 (37): 1958–62.

Banerjee, Mukulika. 2007. "Sacred Elections." *Economic and Political Weekly* 42 (17): 1556–62.

Baru, Sanjaya. 2014. *The Accidental Prime Minister: The Making and Unmaking of Manmohan Singh*. New Delhi: Penguin.

Barwale, Badrinarayan R. 1987. "Seed Industry: Problems and Prospects." In *Seed Programme Review: Problems and Prospects of Indian Seed Industry*, 55–70. New Delhi: Seed Association of India.

———. 2008. *My Journey with Seeds and the Development of the Indian Seed Industry*. Hyderabad: Barwale Foundation.

Baviskar, Amita. 2004. *In the Belly of the River: Tribal Conflicts over Development in the Narmada Valley*. New Delhi: Oxford University Press.

Baviskar, B. S. 1980. *The Politics of Development: Sugar Co-Operatives in Rural Maharashtra*. Delhi: Oxford University Press.

Bera, Sayantan. 2014. "Modi Says Farmers' Income Should Rise with Increasing Output." *Mint*, July 30.

Berman, Elizabeth Popp. 2008. "The Politics of Patent Law and Its Material Effects: The Changing Relationship between Universities and the Marketplace." In *Living in a Material World: Economic Sociology Meets Science and Technology Studies*, edited by Trevor Pinch and Richard Swedberg, 191–216. Cambridge: MIT Press.

Bhardwaj, Mayank, Rupam Jain, and Tom Lasseter. 2017. "Seed Giant Monsanto Meets Its Match as Hindu Nationalists Assert Power in Modi's India." *Reuters*, March 28.

Bhargava, Pushpa M. 2002. "Foreword." In *CCMB 25 Years: 1977–2002*, xi–xxv. Hyderabad: Centre for Cellular and Molecular Biology.

Bhargava, Pushpa M., and Chandana Chakrabarti. 2003. *The Saga of Indian Science since Independence: In a Nutshell*. Hyderabad: Universities Press.

Bhargava, Pushpa M., and G. Shanmugam. 1971. "Uptake of Nonviral Nucleic Acids by Mammalian Cells." *Progress in Nucleic Acid Research and Molecular Biology* 11: 103–92.

Bhargava, Pushpa M., and S. Husain Zaheer. 1953. "A New Synthesis of Some Derivatives of 4,4'-Stilbenediol." *Nature* 171: 746–47.

Bhatnagar, Shanti S. 1950. "The NPL, Its Genesis, Origin, Scope and Function." *Current Science* 19 (2): 35–38.

Bhattacharya, Pramit. 2012. "Vidarbha's Tryst with Bt Cotton." *Mint*, October 3. https://www.livemint.com/Politics/ldOqQmHGPlK2asIyoSQY4I/Vidarbhas-tryst-with-Bt-Cotton.html.

Bhushan, Chandra, Amit Khurana, Sonam Taneja, and Bhavya Khullar. 2018. *Genetically Modified Processed Foods in India: Need to Curb Illegal Sales in the Indian Market*. New Delhi: Centre for Science and Environment.

Bidwai, Praful. 1983a. "II—Biotechnology's Brave New World." *Times of India*, November 19, 8.

———. 1983b. "III—The Seamy Side of the Gene Business." *Times of India*, November 21, 8.

———. 1983c. "The Biotechnology Challenge: Where Do India's Options Lie?" *Times of India*, December 27, 8.

Blackett, P. M. S. 1963. "Report on the National Physical Laboratory." Delhi: CSIR.

Bowring, Finn. 2003. *Science, Seeds and Cyborgs: Biotechnology and the Appropriation of Life*. New York: Verso.

Brass, Tom, ed. 1995. *New Farmers' Movements in India*. London: Frank Cass.

Breman, Jan. 2007. *The Poverty Regime in Village India: Half a Century of Work and Life at the Bottom of the Rural Economy in South Gujarat*. New York: Oxford University Press.

British Medical Journal. 1975. "Safe Manipulation of Microbial Genes." 1 (5952): 234.

Bud, Robert. 1993. *The Uses of Life: A History of Biotechnology*. New York: Cambridge University Press.

Busch, Lawrence, William B. Lacy, Jeffrey Burkhardt, and Laura R. Lacy. 1991. *Plants, Power, and Profit: Social, Economic, and Ethical Consequences of the New Biotechnologies*. Cambridge, Mass.: Blackwell.

Business Standard. 2005. "Andhra Govt to Challenge Bt Cotton Pricing." December 29.

———. 2015. "Double-Digit Growth for Indian Seed Industry: ICRA." August 17.

Buttel, Frederick H. 1989. "How Epoch Making Are High Technologies? The Case of Biotechnology." *Sociological Forum* 4 (2): 247–61.

———. 2003. "The Global Politics of GEOs: The Achilles' Heel of the Globalization Regime?" In *Engineering Trouble: Biotechnology and Its Discontents*, edited by Rachel A. Schurman and Dennis D. T. Kelso, 152–73. Berkeley: University of California Press.

Byatnal, Amruta. 2012. "Study Questions Sustainability of Bt Cotton in Water-Starved Vidarbha." *Hindu*, June 24. https://www.thehindu.com/news/national/study-questions-sustainability-of-bt-cotton-in-water-starved-vidarbha/article3563411.ece.

Callon, Michel, Pierre Lascoumes, and Yannick Barthe. 2011. *Acting in an Uncertain World: An Essay on Technical Democracy*. Translated by Graham Burchell. Cambridge: MIT Press.

Chaba, Anju A., and Raakhi Jagga. 2016. "Farm Suicides in Punjab Now Claim Six Middlemen in Six Months." *Indian Express*, March 25.

Chakrabarti, Samrat. 2009. "Uber Gene." *Tehelka*, November 7.

Chand, Ramesh. 2009. "Capital Formation in Indian Agriculture." In *Agrarian Crisis in India*, edited by D. Narasimha Reddy and Srijit Mishra, 44–60. New Delhi: Oxford University Press.

Chandra, Rajshree. 2013. *Knowledge as Property: Issues in the Moral Grounding of Intellectual Property Rights*. New Delhi: Oxford University Press.

Chandrashekhar, G. 2006. "Monsanto Anxious over Pricing of Bt Cottonseed." *Hindu Business Line*, August 23. https://www.thehindubusinessline.com/todays-paper/tp-corporate/Monsanto-anxious-over-pricing-of-Bt-cottonseed/article20218571.ece.

Chatterjee, B., and D. P. Burma. 2004. "Bires Chandra Guha—Father of Modern Biochemistry in India." *Current Science* 87 (6): 823–30.

Chatterjee, Partha. 2006. *The Politics of the Governed: Reflections on Popular Politics in Most of the World*. New York: Columbia University Press.

Chibber, Vivek. 2003. *Locked in Place: State-Building and Late Industrialization in India*. Princeton: Princeton University Press.

Choudhary, Bhagirath, and Kadambini Gaur. 2010. "Bt Cotton in India: A Country Profile." Ithaca, N.Y.: ISAAA.

Choudhury, Chitrangada. 2017. "Guardians of the Grain." *Hindu*, September 23. https://www.thehindu.com/sci-tech/agriculture/guardians-of-the-grain/article19735976.ece.

———. 2019. "A 56,000-Crore Rupee 'Afforestation' Fund Threatens India's Indigenous Communities." Pulitzer Center on Crisis Reporting, June 25. https://pulitzercenter.shorthandstories.com/india_compensatory_fund_indigenous_communities/index.html.

Choudhury, Chitrangada, and Aniket Aga. 2019. "Sowing the Seeds of Climate Crisis in Odisha." *People's Archive of Rural India*, October 4. https://ruralindiaonline.org/articles/sowing-the-seeds-of-climate-crisis-in-odisha/.

———. 2020a. "India's Pandemic Response Is a Caste Atrocity." *NDTV*, May 27. https://www.ndtv.com/opinion/india-s-pandemic-response-is-a-caste-atrocity-2236094.

———. 2020b. "Manufacturing Consent: Mining, Bureaucratic Sabotage and the Forest Rights Act in India." *Capitalism Nature Socialism* 31 (2): 70–90.

Coalition for a GM-Free India. 2006. *"Uttaranchal Will Not Give Permission for GM Seeds": Chief Minister.* June 19. Dehradun: Coalition for a GM-Free India.

———. 2013. *Adverse Impacts of Transgenic Foods/Crops: A Compilation of Scientific Abstracts*. New Delhi: Coalition for a GM-Free India.

Cohen, Seymour. 1984. "The Biochemical Origins of Molecular Biology: Introduction." *Trends in Biochemical Sciences* 9: 334–36.

Cohn, Bernard S. 1996. *Colonialism and Its Forms of Knowledge: The British in India*. Princeton: Princeton University Press.

Committee on Agriculture. 2012. "Cultivation of Genetically Modified Food Crops—Prospects and Effects." 37th Report, August 9. New Delhi: Lok Sabha Secretariat.

Creager, Angela N. H. 2002. *The Life of a Virus: Tobacco Mosaic Virus as an Experimental Model, 1930–1965*. Chicago: University of Chicago Press.

CSDS (Centre for the Study of Developing Societies). 2014. "Reaping Uncertainty: Report on the State of the Indian Farmer." *Farmers' Forum*.

Damodaran, Harish. 2008. *India's New Capitalists: Caste, Business, and Industry in a Modern Nation*. New York: Palgrave Macmillan.

———. 2015. "For Agricultural Sector, It Is Going Back to Control Raj Days." *Indian Express*, December 24.

———. 2017. "B R Barwale, 1931–2017: The Engine Oil Dealer Who Fathered India's Seed Industry." *Indian Express*, August 3. https://indianexpress.com/article/india/b-r-barwale-1931-2017-the-engine-oil-dealer-who-fathered-indias-seed-industry-4779620/.

———. 2018. "The Age of Surplus." *Indian Express*, June 12.

Deb, Debal. 2009. *Beyond Developmentality: Constructing Inclusive Freedom and Sustainability*. New Delhi: Daanish Books.

———. 2017. "We Have More Hardy, Nutritious Grains Than GM Can Offer." *Ecologise*. April 26. https://www.ecologise.in/2017/04/26/debal-deb-hardy-nutritious-grains-gm-can-offer/.

de Chadarevian, Soraya. 1996. "Laboratory Science versus Country-House Experiments: The Controversy between Julius Sachs and Charles Darwin." *British Journal for the History of Science* 29: 17–41.

Delborne, Jason A. 2008. "Transgenes and Transgressions: Scientific Dissent as Heterogeneous Practice." *Social Studies of Science* 38 (4): 509–41.

Dewey, John. 1927. *The Public and Its Problems*. New York: Henry Holt.

Dhanagare, D. N. 1987. "Green Revolution and Social Inequalities in Rural India." *Economic & Political Weekly* 22 (19–21): AN137–44.

Dias, Ayesha. 1994. "Judicial Activism in the Development and Enforcement of Environmental Law: Some Comparative Insights from the Indian Experience." *Journal of Environmental Law* 6 (2): 243–62.

DNA. 2014. "I Did Not Give Consent for GM Field Trials: Veerappa Moily to Farmers." *DNA*, March 19.

Dowd-Uribe, Brian, and Matthew A. Schnurr. 2016. "Briefing: Burkina Faso's Reversal on Genetically Modified Cotton and the Implications for Africa." *African Affairs* 115 (458): 161–72.

Dronamraju, Krishna. 2010. "J. B. S. Haldane's Last Years: His Life and Work in India (1957–1964)." *Genetics* 185: 5–10.

Dungdung, Gladson. 2015. *Mission Saranda: A War for Natural Resources in India*. Ranchi: Deshaj Prakashan.

Economic Times. 2012. "India's Seed Industry to Grow by 53% by 2015: Assocham." December 9.

Etzkowitz, Henry. 2002. *MIT and the Rise of Entrepreneurial Science*. New York: Routledge.

Evenson, R. E., and D. Gollin. 2003. "Assessing the Impact of the Green Revolution, 1960 to 2000." *Science* 300 (5620): 758–62.

Fagan, John, Terje Traavik, and Thomas Bøhn. 2015. "The Seralini Affair: Degeneration of Science to Re-Science?" *Environmental Sciences Europe* 27 (19): 1–9.

Federoff, Nina V. 2003. "Prehistoric GM Corn." *Science* 302 (5648): 1158–59.

Ferguson, James. 1990. *The Anti-Politics Machine: "Development," Depoliticization, and Bureaucratic Power in Lesotho*. Minneapolis: University of Minnesota Press.

Fernandes, Leela, and Patrick Heller. 2006. "Hegemonic Aspirations: New Middle Class Politics and India's Democracy in Comparative Perspective." *Critical Asian Studies* 38 (4): 495–522.

Fitting, Elizabeth. 2011. *The Struggle for Maize: Campesinos, Workers, and Transgenic Corn in the Mexican Countryside*. Durham: Duke University Press.

Flachs, Andrew. 2017. "Transgenic Cotton: High Hopes and Farming Reality." *Nature Plants* 3: 1–2.

———. 2019. *Cultivating Knowledge: Biotechnology, Sustainability, and the Human Cost of Cotton Capitalism in India*. Tucson: University of Arizona Press.

Foucault, Michel. 1980. *Power/Knowledge: Selected Interviews and Other Writings, 1972–1977*. Edited by Colin Gordon. New York: Pantheon.

Frankel, Francine R. 1971. *India's Green Revolution: Economic Gains and Political Costs*. Princeton: Princeton University Press.

———. 2005. *India's Political Economy, 1947–2004: The Gradual Revolution*. 2nd ed. New Delhi: Oxford University Press.

Ghosh, J. C. 1943. "A National Research Council in India." *Science & Culture* 9 (7): 255–58.

Ghosh, P. K. 1997. "Genetically Engineered Plants in Indian Agriculture." *Journal of National Botanical Society* 51: 11–32.

Gliessman, Stephen R. 2015. *Agroecology: The Ecology of Sustainable Food Systems*. Boca Raton: CRC.

Glover, Dominic. 2010. "The Corporate Shaping of GM Crops as a Technology for the Poor." *Journal of Peasant Studies* 37 (1): 67–90.

Gooday, Graeme. 1991. "'Nature in the Laboratory': Domestication and Discipline with the Microscope in Victorian Life Science." *British Journal for the History of Science* 24: 307–41.

Guha, Ramachandra. 2007. *India after Gandhi: The History of the World's Largest Democracy*. London: Picador.

Guha, Sipra, and Satish C. Maheshwari. 1964. "*In vitro* Production of Embryos from Anthers of *Datura*." *Nature* 204 (4957): 497.

———. 1966. "Cell Division and Differentiation of Embryos in the Pollen Grains of *Datura* in Vitro." *Nature* 212 (5057): 97–98.

Guha, Sumit. 1985. *The Agrarian Economy of the Bombay Deccan, 1818–1941*. Delhi: Oxford University Press.

Gupta, Akhil. 1998. *Postcolonial Developments: Agriculture in the Making of Modern India*. Durham: Duke University Press.

———. 2012. *Red Tape: Bureaucracy, Structural Violence, and Poverty in India*. Durham: Duke University Press.

Gupta, Pushpendra Kumar, Bhagirath Choudhary, and Godelieve Gheysen. 2015. "Removing Bt Eggplant from the Face of Indian Regulators." *Nature Biotechnology* 33 (9): 904–7.

Haldule, Saee. 2012. "Seeds of Disenchantment: Seed Networks in the Indian State of Maharashtra." Master's thesis, Central European University, Budapest.

Hardikar, Jaideep. 2016. "Suicides by Debt-Ridden Farmers' Children in Marathwada, Vidarbha Remain Unnoticed." *Wire*, May 9. https://thewire.in/agriculture/suicides-by-debt-ridden-farmers-children-in-marathwada-vidarbha-remain-unnoticed.

———. 2018a. "Lethal Pests, Deadly Sprays." *People's Archive of Rural India*, March 2. https://ruralindiaonline.org/articles/lethal-pests-deadly-sprays/.

———. 2018b. "SIT Report: Pest Attack Unprecedented, Ferocious." *People's Archive of Rural India*, March 16. https://ruralindiaonline.org/articles/sit-report-pest-attack-unprecedented-ferocious/.

Hardiman, David. 1996. *Feeding the Baniya: Peasants and Usurers in Western India*. Delhi: Oxford University Press.

Harriss-White, Barbara. 1990. "Another Awkward Class: Merchants and Agrarian Change in India." In *The Food Question*, edited by H. Bernstein, B. Crow, M. Mackintosh, and C. Martin, 91–103. London: Routledge.

———. 2012. "Capitalism and the Common Man: Peasants and Petty Production in Africa and South Asia." *Agrarian South: Journal of Political Economy* 1 (2): 109–60.

Heap, Brian. 2013. "Europe Should Rethink Its Stance on GM Crops." *Nature* 498: 409.

Heller, Chaia. 2001. "McDonald's, MTV and Monsanto: Resisting Biotechnology in the Age of Informational Capital." In *Redesigning Life? The Worldwide Challenge to Genetic Engineering*, edited by Brian Tokar, 405–19. New York: Zed.

———. 2002. "From Scientific Risk to Paysan Savoir-Faire: Peasant Expertise in the French and Global Debate over GM Crops." *Science as Culture* 11 (1): 5–37.

———. 2013. *Food, Farms, and Solidarity: French Farmers Challenge Industrial Agriculture and Genetically Modified Crops*. Durham: Duke University Press.

Herring, Ronald J. 2007a. "Stealth Seeds: Bioproperty, Biosafety, Biopolitics." *Journal of Development Studies* 43 (1): 130–57.

———. 2007b. "The Genomics Revolution and Development Studies: Science, Poverty and Politics." In *Transgenics and the Poor: Biotechnology in Development Studies*, edited by Ronald J. Herring, 1–30. New York: Routledge.

———. 2008. "Opposition to Transgenic Technologies: Ideology, Interests and Collective Action Frames." *Nature Reviews Genetics* 9 (6): 458–63.

———. 2010. "Framing the GMO: Epistemic Brokers, Authoritative Knowledge, and Diffusion of Opposition to Biotechnology." In *The*

Diffusion of Social Movements: Actors, Mechanisms and Political Effects, edited by Rebecca K. Givan, Sarah A. Soule, and Kenneth M. Roberts, 78–98. New York: Cambridge University Press.

———. 2013. "Reconstructing Facts in Bt Cotton: Why Skepticism Fails." *Economic & Political Weekly* 48 (33): 63–66.

———. 2015. "State Science, Risk and Agricultural Biotechnology: Bt Cotton to Bt Brinjal in India." *Journal of Peasant Studies* 42 (1): 159–86.

Herring, Ronald J., and N. Chandrasekhara Rao. 2012. "On the 'Failure of Bt Cotton': Analysing a Decade of Experience." *Economic & Political Weekly* 47 (18): 45–54.

Hindu. 2007. "PMK Opposes Cultivation of GM Crops in Tamil Nadu." March 3.

———. 2008. "Anbumani to Oppose Entry of Genetically Modified Seeds." December 10.

Hoffman, Steve G. 2015. "Thinking Science with Thinking Machines: The Multiple Realities of Basic and Applied Knowledge in a Research Border Zone." *Social Studies of Science* 45 (2): 242–69.

Hughes, Sally S. 2001. "Making Dollars Out of DNA: The First Major Patent in Biotechnology and the Commercialization of Molecular Biology, 1974–1980." *Isis* 92: 541–75.

Hull, Matthew S. 2012. *Government of Paper: The Materiality of Bureaucracy in Urban Pakistan*. Berkeley: University of California Press.

Ilaiah, Kancha. 2009. *Post-Hindu India: A Discourse on Dalit-Bahujan, Socio-Spiritual and Scientific Revolution*. New Delhi: Sage.

Indiastat. 2017. "State-Wise Consumption of Pesticides (Technical Grade) in India (2000–2001 to 2009–2010)." https://www.indiastat.com/table/agriculture/2/consumptionofpesticides/206872/425463/data.aspx.

———. 2019. "State-Wise Consumption of Pesticides (Technical Grade) in India (2010–11 to 2018–19)." https://www.indiastat.com/table/agriculture-data/2/consumption-of-pesticides/206872/1135962/data.aspx.

ISAAA (International Service for the Acquisition of Agri-Biotech Applications). 2017. *Global Status of Commercialized Biotech/GM Crops in 2017*. ISAAA Brief 53. Ithaca, N.Y.: ISAAA.

Jain, H. K. 1985. "Agriculture of Tomorrow—Greater Productivity, Efficiency, and Diversity." In *Biotechnology in International Agricultural Research*, 327–40. Manila: International Rice Research Institute.

Jain, Sonu. 2008. "Trouble on the Plate for Bt Brinjal." *Indian Express*, May 8.

Jansen, Kees, and Aarti Gupta. 2009. "Anticipating the Future: 'Biotechnology for the Poor' as Unrealized Promise?" *Futures* 41: 436–45.

Jasanoff, Sheila. 1995. *Science at the Bar: Law, Science, and Technology in America*. Cambridge: Harvard University Press.

———, ed. 2004. *States of Knowledge: The Co-Production of Science and the Social Order*. New York: Routledge.

———. 2005. *Designs on Nature: Science and Democracy in Europe and the United States*. Princeton: Princeton University Press.

———. 2007. "Bhopal's Trials of Knowledge and Ignorance." *Isis* 98 (2): 344–50.

———. 2012. "Genealogies of STS." *Social Studies of Science* 42 (3): 435–41.

Jha, Praveen, and Nilachala Acharya. 2011. "Expenditure on the Rural Economy in India's Budgets since the 1950s: An Assessment." *Review of Agrarian Studies* 1 (2): 134–56.

Jishnu, Latha. 2010. "Not a Nice Trait to Have." *Business Standard*, April 1. https://www.business-standard.com/article/opinion/latha-jishnu-not-a-nice-trait-to-have-110040100057_1.html.

Jodhka, Surinder S. 2006. "Beyond 'Crises': Rethinking Contemporary Punjab Agriculture." *Economic & Political Weekly* 41 (16): 1530–37.

———. 2012. "Agrarian Change in the Times of (Neo-Liberal) 'Crises': Revisiting Attached Labour in Haryana." *Economic & Political Weekly* 47 (26–27): 5–13.

Joseph, Jacquleen, and S. Mohammed Irshad. 2015. "An Invisible Disaster: Endosulfan Tragedy of Kerala." *Economic & Political Weekly* 50 (11): 61–65.

Joshi, Datta. 2013. *Jalna Icons*. Translated by Vikram Ghate. Dawalwadi: Vinodrai Engineers.

Kasturi, Kannan. 2014. "Have Farmers Benefited from High Vegetable Prices in 2013?" *Economic and Political Weekly* 49 (5): 14–17.

Kathage, Jonas, and Matin Qaim. 2012. "Economic Impacts and Impact Dynamics of Bt (*Bacillus thuringiensis*) Cotton in India." *Proceedings of the National Academy of Sciences* 109 (29): 11652–56.

Kaviraj, Sudipta. 1986. "Indira Gandhi and Indian Politics." *Economic & Political Weekly* 21 (38–39): 1697–1708.

———. 1988. "A Critique of the Passive Revolution." *Economic & Political Weekly* 23 (45–46–47): 2429–44.

———. 2005. "An Outline of a Revisionist Theory of Modernity." *European Journal of Sociology* 46 (3): 497–526.

Kay, Lily E. 1993. *The Molecular Vision of Life: Caltech, the Rockefeller Foundation, and the Rise of the New Biology*. New York: Oxford University Press.

Kendrew, J. C. 1970. "Some Remarks on the History of Molecular Biology." *Biochemical Society Symposium* 30: 5–10.

Kenney, Martin. 1986. *Biotechnology: The University-Industrial Complex*. New Haven: Yale University Press.

Kevles, Daniel J. 1994. "Ananda Chakrabarty Wins a Patent: Biotechnology, Law, and Society, 1972–1980." *Historical Studies in the Physical and Biological Sciences* 25 (1): 111–35.

———. 1997. "Big Science and Big Politics in the United States: Reflections on the Death of the SSC and the Life of the Human Genome Project." *Historical Studies in the Physical and Biological Sciences* 27 (2): 269–97.

———. 2011. "Cultivating Art." *Smithsonian* (July–August): 76–82.

Khadi, B. M. n.d. "Present Status of Bt Cotton in India." https://www.icac.org/tis/regional_networks/asian . . . /PapKhadiB1.pdf.

———. 2007. "Success Story of Bt Cotton in India." https://www.icac.org/meetings/biotech_2007/documents/english/additional_contributions/e_khadi.pdf.

Khadse, Ashlesha, and Peter M. Rosset. 2019. "Zero Budget Natural Farming in India—From Inception to Institutionalization." *Agroecology and Sustainable Food Systems* 43 (7–8): 848–71.

KICS (Knowledge in Civil Society). 2009. *Knowledge Swaraj: An Indian Manifesto on Science and Technology*. Secunderabad: Centre for World Solidarity.

Kinchy, Abby. 2012. *Seeds, Science, and Struggle: The Global Politics of Transgenic Crops*. Cambridge: MIT Press.

Kinchy, Abby J., Daniel Lee Kleinman, and Robyn Autry. 2008. "Against Free Markets, against Science? Regulating the Socio-Economic Effects of Biotechnology." *Rural Sociology* 73 (2): 147–79.

Kloppenburg, Jack Ralph, Jr. 2004. *First the Seed: The Political Economy of Plant Biotechnology, 1492–2000*. Madison: University of Wisconsin Press.

Knorr Cetina, Karin. 1992. "The Couch, the Cathedral, and the Laboratory: On the Relationship between Experiment and Laboratory in Science." In *Science as Practice and Culture*, edited by Andrew Pickering, 113–38. Chicago: University of Chicago Press.

———. 1999. *Epistemic Cultures: How the Sciences Make Knowledge*. Cambridge: Harvard University Press.

Kohler, Robert E. 1991. *Partners in Science: Foundations and Natural Scientists, 1900–1945*. Chicago: University of Chicago Press.

———. 2002. *Landscapes and Labscapes: Exploring the Lab-Field Border in Biology*. Chicago: University of Chicago Press.

Kolady, Deepthi, David J. Spielman, and Anthony J. Cavalieri. 2010. "Intellectual Property Rights, Private Investment in Research, and Productivity Growth in Indian Agriculture: A Review of Evidence and Options." International Food Policy Research Institute.

Kothari, Rajni, ed. 1970. *Caste in Indian Politics*. New York: Gordon and Breach.

Koundal, K. R., and P. K. Lawrence. 2000. "Transgenics—At Crossroads." *Current Science* 79 (5): 548.

Kranthi, Keshav R. 2011. "Part II: 10 Years of Bt in India." https://www.cottongrower.com/cotton-news/part-ii-10-years-of-bt-in-india/.

———. 2012. *Bt Cotton: Q&A*. Mumbai: Indian Society for Cotton Improvement.

Kranthi, Keshav R., S. Naidu, C. S. Dhawad, A. Tatwawadi, K. Mate, E. Patil, A. A. Bharose, G. T. Behere, R. M. Wadaskar, and S. Kranthi. 2005. "Temporal and Intra-plant Variability of Cry1Ac Expression in Bt-Cotton and Its Influence on the Survival of the Cotton Bollworm, *Helicoverpa armigera* (Hübner) (Noctuidae: Lepidoptera)." *Current Science* 89 (2): 291–98.

Kranthi, Keshav R., and Glenn D. Stone. 2020. "Long-Term Impacts of Bt Cotton in India." *Nature Plants* 6: 188–96.

Krige, John, and Helke Rausch, eds. 2012. *American Foundations and the Coproduction of World Order in the Twentieth Century*. Göttingen: Vandenhoeck and Ruprecht.

Krishna, V. V. 1987. "Scientists in Laboratories: A Comparative Study on the Organisation of Science and Goal Orientations of Scientists in CSIRO (Australia) and CSIR (India) Institutions." PhD thesis, University of Wollongong.

———. 2011. "Organization of Industrial Research: The Early History of CSIR, 1934–47." In *Science and Modern India: An Institutional History, c. 1784–1947*, edited by Uma Das Gupta, 157–84. Delhi: Pearson Longman.

Krishna, Vijesh, and Matin Qaim. 2012. "Bt Cotton and Sustainability of Pesticide Reductions in India." *Agricultural Systems* 107 (C): 47–55.

Kumar, Deepak. 2006. *Science and the Raj: A Study of British India*. 2nd ed. New Delhi: Oxford University Press.

Kumar, Richa. 2016. *Rethinking Revolutions: Soyabean, Choupals, and the Changing Countryside in Central India*. New Delhi: Oxford University Press.

———. 2019. "India's Green Revolution and Beyond: Visioning Agrarian Futures on Selective Reading of Agrarian Pasts." *Economic & Political Weekly* 54 (34): 41–48.

Kumar, Sant, P. A. Lakshmi Prasanna, and Shwetal Wankhade. 2010. "Economic Benefits of Bt Brinjal—An Ex-Ante Assessment." Policy Brief 34. New Delhi: National Centre for Agricultural Economics and Policy Research.

Kumbamu, Ashok. 2006. "Ecological Modernization and the 'Gene Revolution': The Case Study of Bt Cotton in India." *Capitalism Nature Socialism* 17 (4): 7–31.

Kuruganti, Kavitha. 2006. "Biosafety and Beyond." *Economic & Political Weekly* 41 (40): 4245–47.

———. 2009. "Bt Cotton and the Myth of Enhanced Yields." *Economic & Political Weekly* 44 (22): 29–33.

Lalitha, N., Bharat Ramaswami, and P. K. Viswanathan. 2009. "India's Experience with Bt Cotton: Case Studies from Gujarat and Maharashtra." In *Biotechnology and Agricultural Development: Transgenic Cotton, Rural Institutions and Resource-Poor Farmers*, edited by Robert Tripp, 135–65. New York: Routledge.

Lapegna, Pablo. 2016. *Soybeans and Power: Genetically Modified Crops, Environmental Politics, and Social Movements in Argentina*. New York: Oxford University Press.

Latour, Bruno. 1998. "How to Be Iconophilic in Art, Science, and Religion?" In *Picturing Science, Producing Art*, edited by Caroline A. Jones and Peter Galison, 418–40. New York: Routledge.

———. 1999. *Pandora's Hope: Essays on the Reality of Science Studies*. Cambridge: Harvard University Press.

———. 2004. *Politics of Nature: How to Bring the Sciences into Democracy*. Cambridge: Harvard University Press.

Laureates Letter Supporting Precision Agriculture (GMOs). 2016, June 29. https://supportprecisionagriculture.org/nobel-laureate-gmo-letter_rjr.html.

Levidow, Les. 2001. "Precautionary Uncertainty Regulating GM Crops in Europe." *Social Studies of Science* 31 (6): 842–74.

Lewontin, Richard C. 1998. "The Maturing of Capitalist Agriculture: Farmer as Proletarian." *Monthly Review* 50 (3): 72–84.

Macnaghten, Phil, and Susana Carro-Ripalda, eds. 2015. *Governing Agricultural Sustainability: Global Lessons from GM Crops*. New York: Routledge.

Madsen, Stig Toft. 2001. "The View from Vevey." *Economic & Political Weekly* 36 (39): 3733–42.

Maheshwari, Satish C. 1990. "Tissue Culture, Molecular Biology and Plant Biotechnology—A Historical Overview." In *The Impact of Biotechnology in Agriculture*, edited by R. S. Sangwan and B. S. Sangwan-Norreel, 1–12. Boston: Kluwer Academic.

Mathur, Nayanika. 2015. *Paper Tiger: Law, Bureaucracy, and the Developmental State in Himalayan India*. New York: Cambridge University Press.

McMichael, Philip. 2013. *Food Regimes and Agrarian Questions*. Halifax, N.S.: Fernwood.

Menon, Meena, and Uzramma. 2017. *A Frayed History: The Journey of Cotton in India*. New Delhi: Oxford University Press.

Michelutti, Lucia. 2008. *The Vernacularisation of Democracy: Politics, Caste and Religion in India*. New Delhi: Routledge.

Ministry of Finance. 2020. *Economic Survey, 2019–20*. Vol. 2. New Delhi: Government of India.

Ministry of Industry. 1991. *Statement on Industrial Policy*. July 24. New Delhi: Government of India

Mishra, S. N., and Ramesh Chand. 1995. "Public and Private Capital Formation in Indian Agriculture—Comments on Complementarity Hypothesis and Others." *Economic & Political Weekly* 30 (25): A64–A79.

Mitchell, Timothy. 2002. *Rule of Experts: Egypt, Techno-Politics, Modernity*. Berkeley: University of California Press.

Mohan Ram, H. Y. 2003. "Brij Mohan Johri." *Current Science* 85 (1): 100–102.

———. 2004. "Remembering My Guru P. Maheshwari." *Current Science* 87 (12): 1760–64.

Mohanty, B. B. 2005. "'We Are Like the Living Dead': Farmer Suicides in Maharashtra, Western India." *Journal of Peasant Studies* 32 (2): 243–76.

Morange, Michel. 1998. *A History of Molecular Biology*. Cambridge: Harvard University Press.

Mosse, David. 2005. *Cultivating Development: An Ethnography of Aid Policy and Practice*. London: Pluto.

Mukherjee, Sanjeeb. 2013. "Seed Companies Reap Rich Harvest on Bt Cotton Wave." *Business Standard*, January 20.

Mukherji, Rahul. 2014. *Globalization and Deregulation: Ideas, Interests, and Institutional Change in India*. New Delhi: Oxford University Press.

Murugkar, Milind, Bharat Ramaswami, and Mahesh Shelar. 2007. "Competition and Monopoly in Indian Cotton Seed Market." *Economic and Political Weekly* 42 (37): 3781–89.

Nair, Sthanu R., and Leena M. Eapen. 2012. "Food Price Inflation in India (2008 to 2010)—A Commodity-Wise Analysis of the Causal Factors." *Economic & Political Weekly* 47 (20): 46–54.

Nanda, Meera. 2004. *Prophets Facing Backward: Postmodernism, Science, and Hindu Nationalism*. Delhi: Permanent Black.

Nandi, Jayashree. 2013. "Scientists Write to PM against Open Field Trials of GM Crops." *Times of India*, November 22. http://timesofindia.indiatimes.com/india/Scientists-write-to-PM-against-open-field-trials-of-GM-crops/articleshow/26167566.cms.

Nandy, Ashis, ed. 1988. *Science, Hegemony and Violence: A Requiem for Modernity*. Delhi: Oxford University Press.

Narain, Sunita, Chandra Bhushan, Richard Mahapatra, Vibha Varshney, Archana Yadav, Kaushik Das Gupta, and Aruna P. Sharma, eds. 2017. *Bhopal Gas Tragedy after 30 years.* New Delhi: Centre for Science and Environment.

Narayanamoorthy, A., and S. S. Kalamkar. 2006. "Is Bt Cotton Cultivation Economically Viable for Indian Farmers? An Empirical Analysis." *Economic & Political Weekly* 41 (26): 2716–24.

National Commission on Farmers. 2004. *Serving Farmers and Saving Farming*. First Report. New Delhi: Government of India.

Nayudamma, Y., and Baldev Singh. 1976. "Towards the Evolution of a Technology Policy." In *Science and Development: Essays on Various Aspects of Science and Development Dedicated to the Hon'ble Shri C. Subramaniam on the Occasion of His Sixty-fifth Birthday*, edited by B. K. Nayar, 42–56. Bombay: Orient Longman.

Nehru, Jawaharlal. 1946. *The Discovery of India*. Delhi: Oxford University Press.

Nestle, Marion. 2002. *Food Politics*. Berkeley: University of California Press.

Newell, Peter. 2009. "Bio-Hegemony: The Political Economy of Agricultural Biotechnology in Argentina." *Journal of Latin American Studies* 41 (1): 27–57.

NSAI (National Seed Association of India). 2015. "NSAI for Full Regulation of Cotton Seed Price; To Move Court." December 29.

NSSO (National Sample Survey Office). 2014. *Key Indicators of Situation of Agricultural Households in India*. 70th round. New Delhi.

Omvedt, Gail. 2005. "Farmers' Movements and the Debate on Poverty and Economic Reforms in India." In *Social Movements in India: Poverty, Power, and Politics*, edited by Raka Ray and Mary Fainsod Katzenstein, 179–202. Lanham, Md.: Rowman & Littlefield.

Otero, Gerardo, ed. 2008. *Food for the Few: Neoliberal Globalism and Biotechnology in Latin America*. Austin: University of Texas Press.

Oza, Nandini, Kesava Vasave, Kevalasinga B. Vasave, and Narmada Bachao Andolan. 2017. *Ladha Narmadecha: Narmada bacava andolanaca maukhika itihasa: Dona pramukha adivasi netyasi savada*. Pune: Rajhans Prakashan.

Paarlberg, Robert. 2001. *The Politics of Precaution: Genetically Modified Crops in Developing Countries*. Baltimore: Johns Hopkins University Press.

———. 2008. *Starved for Science: How Biotechnology Is Being Kept Out of Africa*. Cambridge: Harvard University Press.

Padel, Felix, Ajay Dandekar, and Jeemol Unni. 2013. *Ecology, Economy: Quest for a Socially Informed Connection*. New Delhi: Orient Blackswan.

Paley, Julia. 2002. "Toward an Anthropology of Democracy." *Annual Review of Anthropology* 31: 469–96.

Parsai, Gargi. 2011. "Withdraw Nod for Field Trials of Bt Maize in Bihar, GEAC Told." *Hindu*, March 9.

———. 2013. "Global Scientists Back 10-Year Moratorium on Field Trials of Bt Food Crops." *Hindu*, April 27.

Patel, Raj. 2007. *Stuffed and Starved*. London: Portobello.

———. 2009. "Food Sovereignty." *Journal of Peasant Studies* 36 (3): 663–706.

———. 2013. "The Long Green Revolution." *Journal of Peasant Studies* 40 (1): 1–63.

Paul, Cuckoo. 2014. "5 Unlisted Marwari Enterprises Worth Noting." *Forbes India*, March 24.

Pearson, Thomas W. 2012. "Transgenic-Free Territories in Costa Rica: Networks, Place, and the Politics of Life." *American Ethnologist* 39 (1): 90–105.

Pechlaner, Gabriela. 2012. *Corporate Crops: Biotechnology, Agriculture, and the Struggle for Control*. Austin: University of Texas Press.

Pelaez, Victor, and Letícia Rodrigues da Silva. 2008. "Social Resistance to Biotechnology: Attempts to Create a Genetically Modified–Free Territory in Brazil." *International Journal of Technology and Globalisation* 4 (3): 207–22.

Pental, Deepak. 2003. "Transgenics for Productive and Sustainable Agriculture: Some Considerations for the Development of a Policy Framework." *Current Science* 84 (3): 413–24.

Peschard, Karine E. 2019. "Monsanto Wins $7.7b Lawsuit in Brazil—But Farmers' Fight to Stop Its 'Amoral' Royalty System Will Continue." *Conversation*, October 31. https://theconversation.com/monsanto-wins-7-7b-lawsuit-in-brazil-but-farmers-fight-to-stop-its-amoral-royalty-system-will-continue-125471.

Peschard, Karine, and Shalini Randeria. 2020. "Taking Monsanto to Court: Legal Activism around Intellectual Property in Brazil and India." *Journal of Peasant Studies* 47 (4): 792–819.

Phalkey, Jahnavi. 2013. *The Atomic State: Big Science in Twentieth-Century India*. Ranikhet: Permanent Black.

Pickering, Andrew. 1995. *The Mangle of Practice: Time, Agency, and Science*. Chicago: University of Chicago Press.

Planning Commission. 2007. *Recommendations of the Task Force on Biodiversity and Genetically Modified Organisms for the Environment & Forests: Eleventh Five Year Plan (2007–12)*. New Delhi: Government of India.

Prabu, M. J. 2010. "Improved Agronomic Practices Drive India's Bt Cotton Revolution." *Hindu*, September 23.

Prakash, C. S., Gurdev S. Khush, G. Padmanaban, M. Mahadevappa, Hanu R. Pappu, and C. Kameswara Rao. 2014. "Please Allow Scientific Field Testing of GM Crops in India." Change.org, August 6. https://www.change.org/p/mr-narendra-modi-hon-prime-minister-of-india-please-allow-scientific-field-testing-of-gm-crops-in-india.

Pray, Carl E., and Bharat Ramaswami. 2001. "Liberalization's Impact on the Indian Seed Industry: Competition, Research, and Impact on Farmers." *International Food and Agribusiness Management Review* 2 (3–4): 407–20.

Pray, Carl E., Bharat Ramaswami, and Timothy Kelley. 2001. "The Impact of Economic Reforms on R&D by the Indian Seed Industry." *Food Policy* 26 (6): 587–98.

Pulla, Priyanka. 2018. "A Perfect Storm in the Cotton Field." *Hindu*, March 27.

Purkayastha, Prabir, and Satyajit Rath. 2010. "Bt Brinjal: Need to Refocus the Debate." *Economic and Political Weekly* 45 (20): 42–48.

Qaim, Matin. 2009. "The Economics of Genetically Modified Crops." *Annual Review of Resource Economics* 1 (1): 665–94.

Raghunandan, T. R. 2013. "The Mysterious Dealings of a Government File." *Accountability Initiative India*, October 11. http://demo.accountability-india.in/raghubytes/mysterious-dealings-government-file.

Raina, Rajeswari S. 2011. "Institutional Strangleholds: Agricultural Science and the State in India." In *Shaping India: Economic Change in Historical Perspective*, edited by D. Narayana and Raman Mahadevan, 99–128. New Delhi: Routledge.

Raj, Kapil. 2007. *Relocating Modern Science: Circulation and the Construction of Knowledge in South Asia and Europe, 1650–1900*. New York: Palgrave Macmillan.

Rajagopal, Balakrishnan. 2003. *International Law from Below: Development, Social Movements, and Third World Resistance*. New York: Cambridge University Press.

Rajeswari, S. 1995. "Agricultural Research Effort: Conceptual Clarity and Measurement." *World Development* 23 (4): 617–35.

Ramachandran, V. K., Vikas Rawal, and Madhura Swaminathan, eds. 2010. *Socioeconomic Surveys in Three Villages in Andhra Pradesh: A Study of Agrarian Relations*. New Delhi: Tulika.

Ramakumar, R., and Pallavi Chavan. 2014. "Bank Credit to Agriculture in India in the 2000s: Dissecting the Revival." *Review of Agrarian Studies* 4 (1). http://www.ras.org.in/bank_credit_to_agriculture_in_india_in_the_2000s.

Ramamurthy, Priti. 2010. "Why Are Men Doing Floral Sex Work? Gender, Cultural Reproduction, and the Feminization of Agriculture." *Signs: Journal of Women in Culture and Society* 53 (2): 397–424.

Ramanathan, Usha. 2004. "Communities at Risk: Industrial Risk in Indian Law." *Economic & Political Weekly* 39 (41): 4521–27.

Ramasundaram, P., and S. Vennila. 2013. "A Decade of Bt Cotton Experience in India: Pointers for Transgenics in Pipeline." *Current Science* 104 (6): 697–98.

Ramesh, Jairam. 2010. "Decision on Commercialisation of Bt-Brinjal." February 9. New Delhi: Ministry of Environment and Forests.

———. 2014. "The Humble Brinjal's Bt Moment?" *Hindu*, August 1. https://www.thehindu.com/opinion/op-ed/the-humble-brinjals-bt-moment/article6268758.ece.

Ranganathan, Thiagu, Sarthak Gaurav, and Imdadul I. Halder. 2018. "Pesticide Usage by Cotton Farmers in India: Changes over a Decade." *Economic & Political Weekly* 53 (19): 43–51.

Rangarajan, Mahesh. 2009. "Striving for a Balance: Nature, Power, Science and India's Indira Gandhi, 1917–1984." *Conservation and Society* 7 (4): 299–312.

Rao, C. Niranjan. 2004. "Indian Seed System and Plant Variety Protection." *Economic & Political Weekly* 39 (8): 845–52.

Rao, N. Chandrasekhara. 2013. "Bt Cotton Yields and Performance: Data and Methodological Issues." *Economic & Political Weekly* 48 (33): 66–69.

Reddy, D. Narasimha, and Srijit Mishra, eds. 2009. *Agrarian Crisis in India*. New Delhi: Oxford University Press.

Reddy, V. Ratna, and S. Galab. 2006. "Agrarian Crisis: Looking beyond the Debt Trap." *Economic & Political Weekly* 41 (19): 1838–41.

Rheinberger, Hans-Jorg. 1997. *Toward a History of Epistemic Things: Synthesizing Proteins in the Test Tube*. Stanford: Stanford University Press.

Robbins-Roth, Cynthia. 2000. *From Alchemy to IPO: The Business of Biotechnology*. Cambridge, Mass.: Perseus.

Roy, Devparna, Ronald J. Herring, and Charles C. Geisler. 2007. "Naturalising Transgenics: Official Seeds, Loose Seeds and Risk in the Decision Matrix of Gujarati Cotton Farmers." *Journal of Development Studies* 43 (1): 158–76.

Saha, Madhumita. 2013. "The State, Scientists, and Staple Crops: Agricultural 'Modernization' in Pre–Green Revolution India." *Agricultural History* 87 (2): 201–23.

Sahai, Suman. 1993. "Dunkel Draft Is Bad for Agriculture." *Economic & Political Weekly* 28 (25): 1280–81.

———. 1997. "The Bogus Debate on Bioethics." *Biotechnology and Development Monitor* 30: 24.

———. 1998. "Target Monsanto for the Right Not the Wrong Reasons." *Suman Sahai Blog*, December 16. http://sumansahai-blog.blogspot.com/1998/12/target-monsanto-for-right-not-wrong.html.

———. 2003. "Does India Have a Policy for GM Crops?" *Suman Sahai Blog*, June 15. http://sumansahai-blog.blogspot.com/2003/06/does-india-have-policy-for-gm-crops.html.

———. 2006. "Biotech Policy: Secretive and Hasty." *India Together*, April 29. http://indiatogether.org/btpolicy-agriculture.

Sally, Madhvi, and Karunjit Singh. 2019. "Monsanto Abused Dominant Position in India: CCI Probe." *Economic Times*, May 22.

Schurman, Rachel, and William A. Munro. 2010. *Fighting for the Future of Food: Activists versus Agribusiness in the Struggle over Biotechnology*. Minneapolis: University of Minnesota Press.

Scoones, Ian. 2006. *Science, Agriculture and the Politics of Policy: The Case of Biotechnology in India*. New Delhi: Orient Longman.

———. 2008. "Mobilizing against GM Crops in India, South Africa and Brazil." *Journal of Agrarian Change* 8 (2–3): 315–44.

Scott, James C. 1998. *Seeing Like a State: How Certain Schemes to Improve the Human Condition Have Failed*. New Haven: Yale University Press.

Sekhsaria, Pankaj. 2019. *Instrumental Lives: An Intimate Biography of an Indian Laboratory*. New York: Routledge.

Sen, Debarati. 2017. *Everyday Sustainability: Gender Justice and Fair Trade Tea in Darjeeling*. Albany: State University of New York Press.

SenGupta, Anuradha. 2019. "Agrarian Crisis Can Even Be Described as Civilizational Crisis, Says P. Sainath." *News18*, April 8.

Sethi, Nitin. 2011. "MP Protests against Trials of GM Maize." *Times of India*, April 28. https://timesofindia.indiatimes.com/india/MP-protests-against-trials-of-GM-Maize/articleshow/8103855.cms.

Shah, Alpa, and Barbara Harriss-White. 2011. "Resurrecting Scholarship on Agrarian Transformations." *Economic and Political Weekly* 46 (39): 13–18.

Shah, Esha. 2005. "Local and Global Elites Join Hands." *Economic & Political Weekly* 40 (43): 4629–39.

———. 2011. "'Science' in the Risk Politics of Bt Brinjal." *Economic and Political Weekly* 46 (31): 31–38.

———. 2012. "'A Life Wasted Making Dust': Affective Histories of Dearth, Death, Debt and Farmers' Suicides in India." *Journal of Peasant Studies* 39 (5): 1159–79.

Shapiro, Ian. 2003. *The State of Democratic Theory*. Princeton: Princeton University Press.

Sharma, Aradhana, and Akhil Gupta, eds. 2006. *The Anthropology of the State: A Reader*. Malden, Mass.: Blackwell.

Sharma, Devinder. 1994. *GATT and India: The Politics of Agriculture*. Delhi: Konark.

Shetty, S. L. 2009. "Agricultural Credit and Indebtedness: Ground Realities and Policy Perspectives." In *Agrarian Crisis in India*, edited by D. Narasimha Reddy and Srijit Mishra, 61–86. New Delhi: Oxford University Press.

Shiva, Vandana. 1991. *The Violence of the Green Revolution: Third World Agriculture, Ecology, and Politics*. London: Zed.

———. 2013. "Seeds of Suicide and Slavery versus Seeds of Life and Freedom." *Al Jazeera*, March 31. https://www.aljazeera.com/indepth/opinion/2013/03/201332813553729250.html.

Shrivastava, Aseem, and Ashish Kothari. 2012. *Churning the Earth: The Making of Global India*. New Delhi: Penguin.

Siegel, Benjamin R. 2018. *Hungry Nation: Food, Famine, and the Making of Modern India*. New York: Cambridge University Press.

Simmonds, Jeanette. 2007. "Community Matters: A History of Biological Nitrogen Fixation and Nodulation Research, 1965 to 1995." PhD dissertation, Rensselaer Polytechnic Institute.

Simmonds, Norman W. 1983 "Conference Review: Genetic Engineering of Plants." *Tropical Agriculture* 60 (1): 66–69.

Singh, Phundan, and M. S. Kairon. n.d. "Cotton Varieties and Hybrids." Nagpur: Central Institute for Cotton Research.

Singh, Sukhpal. 2002. "Contracting Out Solutions: Political Economy of Contract Farming in the Indian Punjab." *World Development* 30 (9): 1621–38.

Sivaramakrishnan, K. 1995. "Situating the Subaltern: History and Anthropology in the Subaltern Studies Project." *Journal of Historical Sociology* 8 (4): 395–429.

———. 1999. *Modern Forests: Statemaking and Environmental Change in Colonial Eastern India.* Stanford: Stanford University Press.

———. 2011. "Environment, Law, and Democracy in India." *Journal of Asian Studies* 70 (4): 905–28.

Sivaramakrishnan, K., and Arun Agrawal, eds. 2003. *Regional Modernities: The Cultural Politics of Development in India.* Stanford: Stanford University Press.

Sopory, Sudhir K., and Satish C. Maheshwari. 2001. "Plant Molecular Biology in India—The Beginnings." *Current Science* 80 (2): 270–79.

Specter, Michael. 2014. "Seeds of Doubt: An Activist's Controversial Crusade against Genetically Modified Crops." *New Yorker*, August 25.

Steward, F. C. 1967. "Panchanan Maheshwari, 1904–1966." *Biographical Memoirs of Fellows of the Royal Society* 13: 256–66.

Stone, Glenn Davis. 2002. "Both Sides Now: Fallacies in the Genetic-Modi fication Wars, Implications for Developing Countries, and Anthropological Perspectives." *Current Anthropology* 43 (4): 611–30.

———. 2007. "Agricultural Deskilling and the Spread of Genetically Modified Cotton in Warangal." *Current Anthropology* 48: 67–103.

———. 2010. "The Anthropology of Genetically Modified Crops." *Annual Review of Anthropology* 39 (1): 381–400.

———. 2012. "Constructing Facts: Bt Cotton Narratives in India." *Economic & Political Weekly* 47 (38): 62–70.

Stone, Glenn D., and Dominic Glover. 2017. "Disembedding Grain: Golden Rice, the Green Revolution, and Heirloom Seeds in the Philippines." *Agriculture and Human Values* 34 (1): 87–102.

Strathern, Marilyn. 2000. "Introduction: New Accountabilities." In *Audit Cultures: Anthropological Studies in Accountability, Ethics, and the Academy*, edited by Marilyn Strathern, 1–18. New York: Routledge.

Subramani, M. R. 2013. "Seeds of Fortune." *Frontline*, June 28. https://frontline.thehindu.com/other/data-card/seeds-of-fortune/article4803870.ece.

Subramanian, Kapil. 2015. "Revisiting the Green Revolution: Irrigation and Food Production in Twentieth-Century India." PhD dissertation, King's College London.

Subramanian, T. S. R. 2013. "High Time India Wakes Up to the Dangers of Field Trials of GM Crops." *New Indian Express*, June 23. http://www.newindianexpress.com/magazine/voices/High-time-India-wakes-up-to-the-dangers-of-field-trials-of-GM-crops/2013/06/23/article1644577.ece.

Sunder Rajan, Kaushik. 2006. *Biocapital: The Constitution of Postgenomic Life*. Durham: Duke University Press.

Suresh, A., P. Ramasundaram, and Ramesh Chand. 2011. "Manipulating Technology for Surplus Extraction: The Case of Bt Cotton in India." *Economic & Political Weekly* 46 (43): 23–26.

Sushma, Meenakshi. 2019. "Damning Allegations: India's Fields Still Have Bt Brinjal." *Down to Earth*, April 25. https://www.downtoearth.org.in/news/agriculture/damning-allegations-india-s-fields-still-have-bt-brinjal-64187.

Swaminathan, M. S. 2010. *From Green to Evergreen Revolution*. New Delhi: Academic Foundation.

Tappeser, B., W. Reichenbecher, and H. Teichmann, eds. 2014. "Agronomic and Environmental Aspects of the Cultivation of Genetically Modified Herbicide-Resistant Plants." BfN-Skripten 362. Bonn: BfN.

Tarlo, Emma. 2001. *Unsettling Memories: Narratives of the Emergency in Delhi*. Berkeley: University of California Press.

Tembhekar, Chittaranjan. 2013. "Over 4 Lakh Citizens Demand Withdrawal of Biotech Bill." *Times of India*, August 26.

Thackray, Arnold. 1998. *Private Science: Biotechnology and the Rise of the Molecular Sciences*. Philadelphia: University of Pennsylvania Press.

Thomas, Jayan Jose. 2014. "The Demographic Challenge and Employment Growth in India." *Economic & Political Weekly* 49 (6): 15–17.

Thompson, Carol B. 2012. "Alliance for a Green Revolution in Africa (AGRA): Advancing the Theft of African Genetic Wealth." *Review of African Political Economy* 39 (132): 345–50.

Times of India. 1983. "PM Warns against Genetic Misuse." December 13, 9.

Tripp, Robert, ed. 2009. *Biotechnology and Agricultural Development: Transgenic Cotton, Rural Institutions and Resource-Poor Farmers*. New York: Routledge.

Tsing, Anna. 2009. "Supply Chain and the Human Condition." *Rethinking Marxism* 21 (2): 148–76.

Uberoi, J. P. S. 2002. *The European Modernity: Science, Truth, and Method.* New Delhi: Oxford University Press.

Vaidyanathan, A. 2006. "Farmers' Suicides and the Agrarian Crisis." *Economic & Political Weekly* 41 (38): 4009–13.

Vandermeer, John, Aniket Aga, Jake Allgeier, Catherine Badgley, Regina Baucom, Jennifer Blesh, Lilly F. Shapiro, et al. 2018. "Feeding Prometheus: An Interdisciplinary Approach for Solving the Global Food Crisis." *Frontiers in Sustainable Food Systems* 2 (39). https://doi.org/10.3389/fsufs.2018.00039.

Vasavi, A. R. 1999. *Harbingers of Rain: Land and Life in South India.* New Delhi: Oxford University Press.

———. 2012. *Shadow Space: Suicides and the Predicament of Rural India.* Gurgaon: Three Essays Collective.

———. 2020a. "The Tiger and the Tube Well: Malevolence in Rural India." *Critical Asian Studies.* https://doi.org/10.1080/14672715.2020.1764855.

———. 2020b. "India's Lockdown Tragedy: Bleeding along the Fault Lines of a Nation." *Corona Times*, June 23. https://www.coronatimes.net/india-lockdown-tragedy-fault-lines-nation/.

Venkata, Rekhadevi P., M. F. Rahman, M. Mahboob, S. Indu Kumari, Srinivas Chinde, Bhanuramya M., Naresh Dumala, and Paramjit Grover. 2016. "Assessment of Genotoxicity in Female Agricultural Workers Exposed to Pesticides." *Biomarkers* 22 (5): 446–54.

Visvanathan, Shiv. 1985. *Organizing for Science: The Making of an Industrial Research Laboratory.* Delhi: Oxford University Press.

———. 2014. "Harvest of Controversy." *Hindu*, July 29. https://www.thehindu.com/opinion/lead/harvest-of-controversy/article6258680.ece.

Visvanathan, Shiv, and Chandrika Parmar. 2002. "A Biotechnology Story: Notes from India." *Economic and Political Weekly* 37 (27): 2714–24.

Vyas, V. S., and V. Ratna Reddy. 1998. "Assessment of Environmental Policies and Policy Implementation in India." *Economic & Political Weekly* 33 (1–2): 48–54.

Weis, Tony. 2007. *The Global Food Economy: The Battle for the Future of Farming.* New York: Zed.

Witsoe, Jeffrey. 2013. *Democracy against Development: Lower-Caste Politics and Political Modernity in Postcolonial India*. Chicago: University of Chicago Press.

Witt, H., Raj Patel, and M. Schnurr. 2006. "Can the Poor Help GM Crops? Technology, Representation & Cotton in the Makhathini Flats, South Africa." *Review of African Political Economy* 33 (109): 497–513.

Wright, Susan. 1994. *Molecular Politics: Developing American and British Regulatory Policy for Genetic Engineering, 1972–1982*. Chicago: University of Chicago Press.

Wynne, Brian. 2001. "Creating Public Alienation: Expert Cultures of Risk and Ethics on GMOs." *Science as Culture* 10 (4): 445–81.

———. 2007. "Risky Delusions: Misunderstanding Science and Misperforming Publics in the GE Crops Issue." In *Genetically Engineered Crops: Interim Policies, Uncertain Legislation*, edited by Iain E. P. Taylor, 341–72. New York: Haworth Food & Agricultural Products Press.

Yi, Doogab. 2015. *The Recombinant University: Genetic Engineering and the Emergence of Stanford Biotechnology*. Chicago: University of Chicago Press.

Index